TAB Guide 2020 to
Money, Pensions and Tax
Jill Kerby, Sandra Gannon, Neil Brooks

34 Fitzwilliam Place, Dublin 2.

Telephone: (01) 6768633   Fax: (01) 6766576

email: info@tab.ie

www.tab.ie

 www.facebook.com/tabtaxation

 @TABGroupIE

This book has been prepared as a general guide for use in the Republic of Ireland and is based on our understanding of present law and practice. While every effort has been made to ensure accuracy, neither the publisher nor editor are liable for any errors or omissions.

© Copyright

SANDRA GANNON 2019

Published by

TAB TAXATION SERVICES LTD.

34 Fitzwilliam Place, Dublin 2, D02 P60.

Telephone: (01) 6768633

E-mail: catherine@tab.ie

Web Site: www.tab.ie

www.facebook.com/tabtaxation

@TABGroupIE

ISSN No: 0790 9632

ISBN No 978-1-9999370-2-7

Produced by Catherine McGuirk / TAB Taxation Services Ltd.

Printed by Typeform, Dublin.

Jill Kerby is one of Ireland's best know personal finance journalists. Jill is also a co-author of TAB Guide to Money, Pensions & Tax.

Sandra Gannon is a director of TAB Taxation Services Ltd. providing advice to individuals on personal tax issues. Sandra is also a co-author of TAB Guide to Money, Pensions & Tax.

Neil Brooks is a director of TAB Financial Services Ltd., an independent financial services company. Neil is also a co-author of TAB Guide to Money, Pensions & Tax.

Table of Contents

Diversify and Rebalance Investments and Pensions with

Physical Gold

- Physical gold is a Revenue Commissioners approved asset in self-administered, occupational and group pension schemes

- Physical gold is a proven hedging instrument, safe haven asset and an important diversification in investment and pension portfolios

- During times of financial uncertainty and the resulting 'flight to quality', gold acts as a store of value

- Protect and grow your pensions and investments with gold

Call GoldCore on 01 632 5010
Visit www.GoldCore.com

Gold is not regulated by the Central Bank of Ireland

GOLDCORE

Goldcore Limited
Block D, Ground Floor, Iveagh Court
Harcourt Road, Dublin, D02 VH94

ROYAL LONDON

2020
OUR CLEAR VISION

Building on our proud 190 year heritage in Ireland, in 2020, we will continue to provide market-leading financial protection with our life, income and serious illness products, including our unique Multi Claim Protection Cover.

Our products are only available from authorised Financial Brokers, who can offer you personalised financial advice **to help you meet your needs.**

Contact your Financial Broker to find out more about Royal London's award-winning products. They'll be delighted to hear from you!

1 Risk and rewards

Your personal finances involve more than putting a little money aside every week, or buying a life insurance policy to ensure a decent burial. Irish people are increasingly aware of not just how their money is earned and spent, but how it is taxed, saved and invested. Not all the purchases and investments we made during the boom years - in property, pensions, stocks, shares, and consumer goods were prudent or wise and the last several years have involved reducing debt and rebuilding personal balance sheets, as well as the nation's. There is a greater awareness that wealth creation is not a quick event, but requires a combination of earnings, savings, sound investments, and time.

The Irish economy is still recovering, even if the benefits, like higher employment, fewer people on the jobless registers and modest wage growth isn't being felt evenly.

The recovering economy means that plans have been resumed. Couples are starting families, moving house and taking on all kinds of new responsibilities and good personal financial planning is as important as ever, if only to ensure that our personal balance sheets are as solid as possible and better able to sustain the ups and downs of both our own economy and the global economy on which Ireland is so dependent.

Proper financial planning doesn't take place in a vacuum: someone starting their first job may not be thinking about the cost of retirement, but may still need to find the best finance package for a first car or for the longer term goal of a home of their own, especially since the cost of renting is so high. They should also be asking, what is the most tax-efficient way to save for a pension? How can you protect your savings from higher taxation and the potential threat of price inflation?

Whether in good times or bad, the future beckons and young couples may be planning a family, moving house, taking on all kinds of responsibilities. They need to make their Wills, get the best finance deal for their new home, make sure they have insured each other's lives (especially when a baby arrives) and they need to set up a viable family budget.

Children bring enormous joy - and bills! If a parent does not stay at home with the baby, someone else may have to be hired to provide childcare. Either way a significant cost is going to be incurred.

Since your child is going to have to be fed, dressed, educated and amused for the next two decades, the sooner you start planning for all these costs the better. Difficult as it may be, it is always advisable to start putting aside even a modest amount of money each week or month. Beginning to save or invest regularly two or three years before secondary or third level school fees fall due is really about 10 years too late.

"Children bring enormous joy - and bills!"

If you don't have an occupational pension scheme at your workplace to join, you should also be considering ways to invest for your retirement, perhaps in a Personal Retirement Savings Account (PRSA) or Additional Voluntary Contribution (AVC) if you are unlikely to have full-service years as a member of an occupational scheme. You also need to review your life and health insurance policies. Debt management should continue to be a high priority.

The financial needs of someone middle aged are very different from those of a single person or a young parent. Though your monthly outlay may be high, there is light at the end of the child-rearing tunnel; ideally you are earning more and will have built up some equity in your home and in some kind of savings or investment funds. You may still have 15 or 20 years before retirement, but do you have a pension plan? How has it fared? Is your occupational scheme meeting its legal funding standard requirements?

For the over 60's, retirement can be a blessing or a burden. Without an adequate pension or other assets, day to day spending may have to be curtailed and outstanding debts may provoke a serious financial crisis. For the financially secure, retirement can provide exciting new opportunities to enjoy life at your own pace. Whether you work for someone else or have your own business, you certainly need to take stock of your financial position, including your assets and debts, your short and long term health care provisions.

Aside from matters like budgeting, home ownership, saving and investing, and social welfare entitlements, this book also takes you through a number of financial issues that must be dealt with when somebody dies: Wills, Inheritance Tax, Probate, Intestacy and the tax adjustments that come with widowhood.

Financial planning is best done with a trusted advisor and independent, objective advice is by far the best option; the fee you pay such a person may well be one of the best investments you will ever make.

Risk and rewards

Everyone takes chances at some time in their lives. One of the ingredients of success, aside from talent and luck, is the ability to take a few risks to achieve a difficult task or goal.

Unfortunately, reckless lending and borrowing by institutions and individuals resulted in reckless investing and the global financial crisis that has taken its toll not just on the wealth of the profligate, but the prudent as well. A decade later, the appetite of many for risk-taking has been tempered by the big losses people suffered on property, pensions and the stock market. Nevertheless, higher risk investment strategies produce potentially higher rewards. The challenge is to take educated risks.

"The challenge is to take educated risks."

Financial institutions recognise this reluctance on the part of many people to take chances with their income or savings and offer both deposit accounts and a range of capital guaranteed savings certificate and bond products with little or no risk. But because interest rates are still so low they also offer low to negative returns once you factor in tax and inflation.

Low growth/low risk

Deposit-based bank, building society and post office accounts that operate in this State come under the government Deposit Guarantee Schemes, including the 100% deposit guarantee for Irish institutions, see page 18 for more details. Interest rates have ebbed and waned since the financial crisis began in 2007 but deposit rates are still at historic low levels and deposit interest retention tax (DIRT) is 33% in 2020. Where the deposit holder, even a PAYE earner, has total unearned income of more than €5,000 per annum they are liable to PRSI at 4% on such income. (Unearned income includes returns from savings and investments, rental income and deposit returns subject to DIRT. Individuals aged over 66 are exempt from PRSI.)

At the end of 2018 the European Central Bank rate remained at 0% as the ECB continued its effort to encourage economic growth and stave off the kind of deflationary crisis that has stalked Japan. The danger remains that any reversal of this low interest rate policy could have a catastrophic impact on the ability of indebted mortgage borrowers here to meet their monthly repayments.

A clear winner of the loose monetary and interest rate policies of central banks has been the stock markets though there are signs that the decade long bull run may be coming to an end. Share owners who have kept their nerve have had their patience rewarded, but should be reviewing their portfolios or investment funds to ensure they are well diversified and as shock proof as possible.

Unfortunately, the manipulation of interest rates and high taxation means that there are no obvious, low risk places anymore for surplus savings. You need to carefully consider your circumstances and ability to deal with risk taking.

For example, an elderly widow relying on a State pension for her income is not a suitable candidate to invest her modest savings in the stock market no matter how buoyant the performance of shares. A younger person with a steady rising income, or a professional with existing assets and excellent earning potential is a much better candidate because of their capacity to make up any losses.

Living with risk

To establish your own level of risk, you need to ask yourself the following questions:

- Can I afford to lose my money? Will I be able to meet all my regular, day-to-day obligations if it disappears?

- Am I prepared to accept a negative deposit return due to the impact of high DIRT and the corrosive effect of price inflation on the spending power of my savings?

- Am I prepared for the fact that investment markets are cyclical and values are likely to go down as well as up?

- Can I wait for investment markets to recover if they go down?

If you answer No to any of these questions, then you probably have a relatively low risk threshold. Investing directly in the stock market, or even in unitised funds or property - which all require relatively long term investment period - may not be for you.

Risk also needs to be related to age. A young person taking out a pension plan which will mature in 40 years should take some risk with the underlying investments in the fund in the early years while someone in their 50's investing in a pension needs to be more cautious, especially if retirement is coming up in just five or ten years time. Parents of young children who want to save for their education costs in just a few years will also want to take fewer risks than a long term pension investor.

Matching the risk

Tax-free State Savings Certificates, Bonds and Instalment Savings Plans have always been considered good options for low risk savers (like pensioners) or people with short term funding needs. Aside from the credit and solvency risk that has not completely disappeared, the biggest danger associated with deposit type investments is that they are no longer inflation proof and your capital is eroded by the rise in the price of everyday goods (and higher tax). Today, unfortunately, savers must also consider that sovereign default risks and devaluation in the wider global economy can also impact on the value of your savings.

Unitised investment products, especially those that are well diversified, either geographically or by industrial sector but more often by asset classes that include the likes of property, bonds, cash and commodities as well as equities (stocks and shares), have been designed for people with medium risk personal profiles who could save on a regular or lump sum basis for up to 10 years or more. With a unitised investment product your contributions are used to buy units in your chosen investment funds.

For people willing to take more investment risk, there are opportunities to move into more specialised equity asset funds spread between investment sectors, such as all financial, industrial or retail shares; companies in 'developed' geographic locations like Europe, America or Japan, and increasingly into 'emerging markets' like Brazil, Russia, India and China (the BRIC nations). Commodities like steel, coal, oil, precious metals and grains can also be purchased as pooled 'funds', either through an investment firm or increasingly as a direct investment in the form of low cost Exchange Traded Funds (ETFs) that trade on stock markets in the form of a single share. Bought in this form, you need to be willing to do your own research and of course, to take full personal responsibility for all your buying decisions. You also need to take the tax implications of any kind of pooled investment into account before you commit your money: high exit taxes will not be refundable, even if you are outside the high rate tax net.

Independent financial advice

Volatility has never gone away in spite of the huge sums that governments and central banks have pumped into the system to keep it afloat since 2008.

Unless you are a financial expert yourself, the variety and types of savings and investment products on the market make it very difficult for you to know which one is suitable to your particular needs and circumstances. An independent financial adviser could be of great assistance in helping you choose which deposit account to open and which savings policy, pension or stocks and shares to buy.

"An independent financial adviser could be of great assistance ...."

Independent financial advice is not available from the Post Office, banks or building societies, stockbrokers or life assurance companies since they all want you to buy their individual products. A bank official is not going to recommend that you take out a State Savings Instalment plan, even if it happens to pay more interest than the bank's equivalent scheme. The credit union will not recommend that you borrow from the building society, even if the society's interest rate is lower. A life assurance company wants you to buy into their managed equity fund, not go directly to the stock market.

Commissions are paid by financial institutions as a sales reward to the broker or sales agent when you opt to buy one of their products. The size of the commission will vary in size from institution to institution and also depends on whether you are contributing a lump sum or are making regular monthly or even weekly payments.

Many people advertise themselves as 'independent' financial advisers on mortgages, general and life assurance policies, pensions, deposit accounts and investment funds. Yet nearly all of them accept commission payments from the institution. Those institutions which do not pay broker commissions - the Post Office, some banks and building societies (depending on the product), are unlikely to be recommended by a broker or salesperson who relies solely on commission for their own income.

From January 2018, under the new EU markets in Financial Instruments Directive (Mifid II) only someone who charges a fee for their services is able to call themselves an independent financial adviser. Those who accept sales commission for their financial products must call themselves financial brokers.

Avoid misselling

The best way to reduce the danger of being missold an expensive financial service or product is to seek advice from a genuinely independent financial adviser, who charges you a fee. Knowing that their time and expertise is being rewarded, regardless of whether you buy a product, your wider financial situation will more likely be taken into account and the risk of you being sold an unsuitable product should be lessened.

Such advisers may be specialist life and pensions brokers, mortgage brokers and/or investment brokers, accountants and management consultants who deal with the personal finances of their private clients.

If you prefer to deal with a commission-based adviser rather than pay a fee, make sure they explain why they are recommending one product or policy over another, and satisfy yourself that they are not being influenced by the size of the commission they are being paid.

2 Make the most of your savings

Deposit yields are now at historic lows, and savers are increasingly frustrated in their quest for a positive return especially older people who rely on such returns to supplement modest pensions. Meanwhile, because the banking sector remains fragile in Europe, larger deposit holders need to be aware that along with shareholders and bondholders, they too could be drawn into a 'bail-in' of a failed bank under new EU banking rules.

So before you commit your savings to any financial institution, you should always be asking yourself the following questions:

- Why you are saving?

- How accessible do you want your money to be?

- What is the interest rate on offer?

  and

- How secure is this institution? In the event of a failure, will I get my money returned?

At the height of the global banking and stock market crisis, the Irish government moved to guarantee bank deposits.

Today, all Irish deposits up to €100,000 are covered by the Deposit Guarantee Scheme which protects your money in the event that the bank, building society or credit union is declared insolvent or a liquidator declares they cannot repay its deposits.

Deposit guarantee and compensation schemes

Deposit Guarantee Scheme

The Deposit Guarantee Scheme is a permanent scheme set up to provide compensation to depositors if a regulated firm covered by the scheme goes out of business. The maximum each individual can claim for under the scheme is €100,000 for each bank, building society or credit union regulated by the Financial Regulator. This means that even if you have an amount greater than €100,000 in deposits with an institution, you will only be entitled to a maximum of €100,000. The Deposit Guarantee Scheme does not have an end date. The following institutions are covered by the deposit guarantee scheme.

Name of Institution
Allied Irish Bank plc (AIB)
Bank of Ireland
Credit unions
EBS Building Society
Irish Life and Permanent
KBC Bank Ireland Plc
Ulster Bank

Some banks that operate in Ireland are regulated in their home country and operate here under the EU rules. If you have a deposit account with a bank which operates in Ireland but is regulated in its home country, you would usually make a claim under a compensation scheme, equal to €100,000 in the country where the institution is regulated.

Type of deposit accounts

Fixed term accounts

These accounts require you to leave your money with the deposit institution for an agreed period of time - usually from 1 to 12 months. Normally, the interest paid on these type of accounts is higher than on normal demand deposit accounts. The downside of these accounts is that you cannot access your funds until the maturity date. If you do you will be liable to an interest penalty.

Regular savings accounts

These accounts reward the regular saver with a slightly higher interest rate than is paid by a demand deposit account. For this, you must save an agreed amount over a set period of months. The account may include a number of withdrawal terms and penalties for not adhering to conditions regarding the size of your deposit.

Regular income accounts

These are ideal for someone who needs a regular income, though they usually require a minimum initial deposit. Interest rates can be quite low, however some banks/building societies offer a high rate if you agree to certain restrictions on the amounts you can withdraw at any one time. The income may vary if interest rates go up or down.

Fixed interest accounts

A sort of savings bond, these accounts are extremely popular and involve the bank or building society guaranteeing to pay a fixed amount of interest for a minimum sum over a specific period.

State Savings™ (sold through An Post and the Prize Bond company)

State Savings™ is the brand name used by the National Treasury Management Agency (NTMA) to describe the range of savings products offered by the State to personal savers. State Savings™ are sold through the NTMA's agents An Post and the Prize Bond Company. When you place your money in State Savings™ you are placing your money directly with the Irish government, there is no upper limit on the amount of your money that the government protects and the government's obligation to repay you does not have any expiry date.

The returns on State Savings have been cut more than a dozen times since 2008 and are no longer the good value they once were. However, the return earned on Saving Certificates, Savings Bonds, the Instalment Savings Scheme and the National Solidarity Bond are not liable to DIRT, which is 35% from 1 January 2019.

Savings bonds

Savings Bonds last for three years and require a minimum investment of €100. At the end of the three years you will earn a return of 1% tax-free or AER of 0.33%. Since the interest is cumulative, and increases towards the latter part of the savings period, you should avoid encashing savings bonds early. Withdrawals are subject to seven days notice.

Savings certificates

With a minimum purchase of €50, Savings Certificates pay 5% interest tax-free over a five year period. This is equivalent to AER of 0.98% per annum.

National Solidarity Bond

The 10 year National Solidarity Bond Issue 6 gives a tax-free fixed rate total return of 16% or AER of just 1.5%. The minimum purchase is €50 and the maximum is €120,000 per individual per issue.

The 4 year National Solidarity Bond Issue 6 gives a tax free fixed rate total return of 2% or an AER of 0.50%. The minimum purchase is €50 and the maximum is €120,000 per individual per issue.

Instalment savings scheme

To join State Savings'™ Instalment Savings Scheme, the saver - who must be at least age seven - must make regular monthly payments for a minimum of one year, of between €25 and €1,000. Left for another five years, the accumulated savings will then earn 5.5% tax free, or AER of 0.98%, including the first 12 month contribution period, when no interest is paid.

Instalment Savings have been a popular - and tax free way - to watch savings grow over the medium to longer term, say for a child's education and other domestic goals. Many parents take advantage of the automatic facility on offer which deposits the monthly child benefit allowance (worth €140 a month per child) directly into the Instalment Savings Scheme as well as into Savings Certificates and other An Post accounts.

Deposit accounts

State Savings™ offer a number of deposit accounts comparable to bank and building society demand accounts, but these are not tax-free.

Prize Bonds

Prize Bonds are another product in the State Savings™ suite of products. They pay no interest and are therefore vulnerable to the ravages of inflation if you hold them for a long time. The National Treasury Management Agency (NTMA) sets the variable percentage rate used to calculate the prize fund. From August 2017 the rates is set at 0.5% of the total prize bonds outstanding. Each eligible Prize Bond is entered into every weekly Prize Bonds draw, with a €1 million prize awarded on the last weekly draw of June and December. In the weekly draws other than the Prize Bonds €1 million prize draw, the top prize is €50,000. Other weekly cash prizes include 10 prizes of €1,000, 10 prizes of €500 and all other prizes of €50.

"Savings Certificates are another very tax-efficient way to save money."

Credit union

The credit union movement has more than 3.6 million members in the 32 counties and total assets of approximately €16 billion. Credit unions are essentially financial co-ops in the community or at the saver's place of work. Members come together to save on a regular basis and to provide loans to each other at fair rates of interest from the collective savings fund.

Members can save in two ways in a credit union:

- Shares which pay a dividend, the amount of which is determined at the end of the credit union financial year

- Deposits which pay interest that may be determined in advance. Not all credit unions operate deposit accounts.

Most, but not all credit unions offer all eligible members certain insurance services. Some insurances are paid directly by the credit union. Examples of such insurance covers are Loan Protection Insurance, Life Savings Insurance and Death Benefit Insurance (though not all credit unions directly pay for Death Benefit Insurance). The 'member pay' insurance services are Repayment Protection Insurance (RPI), Home Insurance, Car Insurance, Travel Insurance and Private Health Insurance schemes. Terms and conditions of cover apply to these insurance products and you should check with local credit union for details.

Loan protection insurance

Loan Protection Insurance is designed to clear the loans outstanding in the unfortunate event of the death of a member. In a credit union the loan balances of all eligible members are automatically covered (up to certain limits) at no direct cost to the member. This means that eligible members can borrow in the confidence that their dependents will not be obliged to repay the outstanding loan balance in the event of their death. Should an eligible member with an outstanding loan balance die, the balance is repaid in full. Cover ceases on the member's 70th birthday, though individual credit unions can extend the cover to the 80th or 85th birthday.

Life savings cover

- Life Savings Cover pays a benefit on the death of an eligible member. It benefits members who have saved regularly and maintained their savings with their credit union over the lifetime of their membership.

The Life Savings Benefit accrues based on amount of savings and the age of the member when the savings were lodged. The benefit payable is also limited to the maximum cover limit held by each credit union. Terms and conditions apply and you should check with your credit union for more information. Amounts saved after a member's 70th birthday are not insured and withdrawals of savings may reduce any benefit payable.

- Some credit unions extend life savings cover to include the "Accidental, Death and Dismemberment" rider. Under this extension in some eligible cases the amount of the Life Savings claim can be doubled. Also if the member loses a limb or sight as the result of an accident then a benefit may be paid to that member. The amount of the benefit is based on the savings that the member makes during the term of membership and the age that lodgements are made.

Death benefit insurance

Death Benefit Insurance is designed to pay a fixed benefit in the event of the death of a member to help with bereavement costs at a difficult time. The cover limit is set by the credit union, which is the policyholder. The size of death benefit will vary from one credit union to the other but the minimum benefit offered is €1,000 in the Republic of Ireland and the maximum is €3,250. If you are a member of a participating credit union, you are eligible for this insurance provided a premium has been paid and:

- You are over 16 years of age (some credit unions also cover members under 16 years)

- Have joined the credit union before age 70 years.

- Remained a fully paid up member of the credit union until your death

- Were in good health or working when you joined your credit union and were eligible for cover under the Life Savings Policy.

You should check annually with your credit union that you are covered by their insurance policy and terms and conditions of cover apply. The cover limit is set by the credit union and can be subject to change.

Tax

All returns from credit union accounts are subject to DIRT at 33% in 2020 (35% in 2019), unless the member is exempt from income tax and therefore not liable for DIRT (see page 113 for income tax exemption limits).

Summing up

Deposit accounts are not particularly good value savings options anymore. However, cash deposits do offer safety and ready access to your money. So it makes sense to use them:

- To provide cash reserves for emergencies.

- When you know you will need money for a particular purpose soon (deposit for a house, a new car, wedding etc.).

- When you think other types of investments are particularly risky and you want to play safe.

Tax

Irish Interest

DIRT at 33% (35% in 2019) is deducted at source from interest earned on deposit accounts. While no further income tax is payable, interest earned should be included on your tax return as it may be liable to PRSI. Deposit interest is not liable to the universal social charge (USC).

PRSI at a rate of 4% is now payable on all unearned income in excess of €5,000. Unearned income includes deposit interest, rental income, and dividends. Individuals over the age of 66 are not liable to pay PRSI on their income.

This PRSI charge will not give rise to any social insurance benefits.

UK interest

Where UK tax has been deducted at source on savings you may have in a UK deposit account, the tax will be repaid in full from the UK tax authorities on completion of the appropriate form IRL/Individual/Int. You can obtain this form from the UK Inland Revenue website at www.hmrc.co.uk If you are resident in Ireland you will only be liable to tax in Ireland on deposit interest earned in the UK.

Other deposit interest

If you receive interest from an account in another EU Member State, you must pay the current rate of DIRT on the interest income. You must include the details of this on your annual tax return. The income will be subject to a higher rate of 40% tax if it is not returned on time. Deposit interest from non-EU countries will be taxed at the current DIRT rate if you are a standard rate taxpayer and have made a timely return. However, a rate of 40% will apply if you are a higher rate taxpayer or if you have not made a return of this income on time.

Any tax paid abroad will generally be available as a credit against tax payable here.

DIRT free deposit accounts for those aged 65 and over

These accounts allow you to receive any interest earned on money on deposit, paid to you without deduction of DIRT, where you satisfy certain conditions.

If you meet these conditions, you can apply directly to your financial institution to have the interest paid without deduction of DIRT.

In order to claim this exemption from DIRT you must complete a declaration form stating that you or your spouse/partner (if you are married or in a civil partnership) meet the following conditions:

- Are aged 65 or over when making the declaration.

- If married or in a civil partnership the total annual income for you and your spouse/partner will be below the relevant annual exemption limit. The current annual exemption limits are listed on page 113.

Saving for your children

Sometimes it seems as if there is no end to the financial sacrifices that parents will make for their children. For many young parents it begins with the high cost of pre-school childcare, which can be the equivalent of a second mortgage. On top of all the other family expenses will come the price of schoolbooks and uniforms, music and drama lessons, sports club membership, etc.

Tax relief, allowances and social welfare benefits make a very small contribution to the total cost of raising a child in Ireland today, estimated by some financial institutions to be as much as €200,000 from cradle to college.

Spread over 20 years or so, this annual outgoing will be diluted, but prudent parents will make provision for this huge outlay by reassessing their own spending habits, their earning capacity and their ability to save and invest on a regular basis.

A good place to start is with the monthly child benefit payment from the Department of Social Protection, which is €140 a month for each child.

Many new parents take advantage of the opportunity given to them at the maternity hospital to choose a deposit account from a list of financial institutions (including the tax free State Savings™) to which their monthly child benefit payment can be automatically transferred.

Over the course of 18 years, a monthly child benefit payment of €140 can grow to €34,691 gross assuming an annual growth rate of 1.5%. But unless you are exempt from DIRT or invest in a longer term, tax-free State Savings, or Solidarity Bond the 33% DIRT (35% in 2019) deduction on your interest will considerably lower that final value. The spending power of a deposit account is also vulnerable to the impact of price inflation over that period.

Investing your child benefit for such a long period should, based on historic past performance of stock and shares, produce even higher returns that will ideally offset both taxation and inflation. Given the huge volatility in stock markets however, you need to choose the fund or asset even more carefully for its growth potential, relative to the level of risk you are prepared to take.

Traditional unitised managed funds widely sold by life assurance companies, into which you invest on a monthly basis, are a popular but expensive choice because of high set-up and on-going charges and commissions unless you arrange the investment with a fee-based adviser who strips out the commission.

Lower cost indexed and sectoral funds should also be considered. The lowest cost of all are ETFs (Exchange Traded Funds) which trade on stock markets like a single share and can be purchased directly through a stockbroker, who will charge a commission, or directly via your own on-line share-dealing account, where commission costs are lower. Online trading accounts are execution only, that is, without any advice from the stockbroker.

The attraction of buying investment funds on a regular, monthly basis is that you buy both on dips and rises and do not expose a lump sum from the start to sudden downward movements in asset markets. The downside is that investment growth is subject to exit tax at 41%.

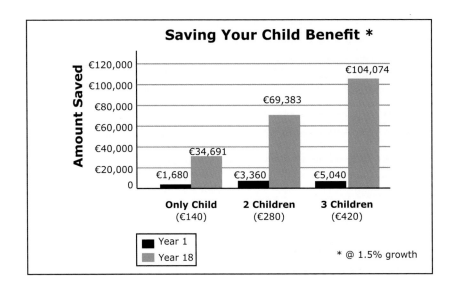

Money knowledge doesn't grow on trees

Most parents try to do their best for their children, providing more than just a roof over their heads, food on the table and an education. Finding the money these days - what with incomes under pressure, higher taxation and unemployment - for holidays, entertainment and even braces on their teeth is a huge balancing act.

But what about also passing on a good financial education to your children, something they are unlikely to find on their everyday school curriculum? You might want to start by creating a proper family budget and getting your own personal finances in order. (see page 65).

First, open a joint savings account for each child in the Post Office, the credit union or bank; do it on-line if this is more convenient. Then come up with a consistent pocket-money plan that is both practical and flexible.

For example, it's not a very good idea to give your young children a few cent or euro every week if you think all they are going to spend it on are sweets and you are dead set against them rotting their teeth. Together you might want to set some junk food parameters.

Next, decide whether pocket money is awarded automatically, or on receipt of chores. Some parents prefer the compromise that promises a weekly sum that is then supplemented by the offer of extra pay for more time-consuming or 'difficult' jobs outside the usual household chores.

How much do you give? This too depends on the size of the family budget, number of children, their ages and the amount of peer pressure you get sucked into. It also depends on how much you spend on ice-creams, phone credit, the odd book or comic and clothes: kids don't 'need' to buy themselves anything when they have such willing parents.

A healthy respect and understanding of money is an invaluable gift you can pass on to them, especially in difficult economic times.

It's never easy to know how much young children understand about money, but using your own judgement, the following are issues that you and your children should talk about on an on-going basis:

"A healthy respect and under-standing of money is an invaluable gift you can pass onto your children."

1   "Debt is the pits" or, "totally uncool".

Explain how not paying your bills on time is like not doing your homework - it can get you into a lot of trouble. Explain how banks and credit card companies are in business to make money from personal loans and credit cards.

2   Teach them about the importance of having savings.

Explain how savings leave them free to make choices about what to spend their money on. Debt, on the other hand is a form of slavery that gives that control to other people. (Any child "in debt" to an older sibling knows what that means).

3   Explain to them how money can make money.

The credit union, State Savings ™ (in the post office) or bank that accepts minimum €1 deposits - as opposed to their piggy bank - offers the best interest rate for small sums and reinforces the importance of a regular savings routine.

4   A little self-denial goes a long way.

Children like the idea of watching their savings grow (they always prefer to spend your money than their own). But you need to convince them that this will only happen if they forego that extra toy, the really expensive item of clothing or disco night (for older kids) in favour of putting that regular tenner into a savings fund which over a long time could actually make them rich. Just €10 a week into an indexed fund growing at 5% over 10 years will be worth over €6,700 gross over 10 years and nearly €18,000 gross over 20 years.

5   Take any opportunity to talk about the cost of running the family - but not in a hectoring way.

Older children should be told - approximately - how much income the family earns, and how much is spent on overheads: mortgage, food, utilities, holidays, etc.

6   Encourage children to create their own budget - to decide how much they want to save and how much to spend, and on what.

It will show them that splurging on a large, single item means going without something else. Older children who earn from babysitting, stacking shelves or other part-time work should be compelled to save a portion of their money for school expenses and to make an appropriate contribution to mam and dad for their personal upkeep.

7   Tell them not to fully trust anyone with their money except themselves.

As we have all found out to our peril, the world is full of people with get-rich schemes to share, or who want you to buy something from them (or for them). They need to learn to take responsibility for their own money and how it is spent, saved or wasted.

8   Encourage any entrepreneurial shoots you may see.

Explain how some of the best business people started selling surplus comic books (or computer games) to their friends.

9   Money doesn't buy happiness.

Having money does make it easier, however, to cope with some of life's hardships, such as poor health, especially in old age. It can also bring the greatest joy - when it's shared with others less fortunate.

3 Investing wisely

With practically no safe returns left for the cautious investor, an understanding of the concept of risk and reward has never been so urgent. The direct aftermath of the 2008 financial crisis meant that cash became king for anyone who had lost heavily in the property or stock markets. Now, the relentless fall in bank interest rates and the negative return on bond yields from several years of quantitative easing by central banks means that even people trying to save and invest for their retirement, and even pension fund managers, are forced to take more risk than ever before.

Near zero returns from deposits and the bond market look like they could be with us for a while longer.

Risk opportunities

There is a long held, contrarian view that fortunes can always be made when the fear factor is greatest. Experienced investors with a sharp understanding of risk – including sovereign risk – still see opportunities even in the most volatile markets. Here in Ireland these opportunities even included the beaten-down bank loans that have been the responsibility of the National Asset Management Agency to sell. Sharp investors understand how to accurately price a share, and their strategy varies depending on whether they are using their own money - from accumulated capital or capital gains, retirement or redundancy lump sums or even inheritances – or borrowed funds.

Investment options for individual investors mainly come in three basic forms:

- Bonds
- Stocks & Shares
- Property

Historically, high quality shares – those that represent successful companies with solid capital bases, low amounts of debt, strong management and recession-proof products or services, have, on average tended to give greater long term returns than any other class of investment, beating property, bonds and deposits.

Bonds

Capital security was once the appealing cornerstone of bank and building society deposits and fixed rate assets like bonds. In recent years these cautious investment vehicles have been put to the test by the zero interest rate policies of central banks. Nevertheless, the investment value of fixed income assets like bonds continue to be dependent on fluctuations in national and world economies for their day-to-day values.

Bonds are long-term fixed-interest debt issued by companies and governments - particularly by governments. Historically the 'safer' the government (or sovereign), as determined by the international debt ratings agencies, usually the more costly the bond and the lower the annual yield and capital. (You are paying for the security of knowing that the yield will be paid.) When you buy a bond, the government or corporation takes your money now, and promises to repay you your money at an agreed date in the future. Unfortunately, with so many sovereign bonds now producing negative yields, you may find yourself paying your debtor to take your money in 2020!

Nominal value

This is the value guaranteed to be repaid to you by a government or company at maturity where there is a positive bond yield. The price of a particular bond is normally quoted in terms of €100 nominal value of the stock. For example, a price of €116.31 for the 3.40% Treasury Bond 2024, means that €100 of the nominal value of the stock could be bought today for €116.31.

Maturity date

Most bonds have a maturity date, i.e. the date at which the nominal value of the stock is guaranteed to be repaid to you by a government or company. Remember that the guaranteed payment at maturity is not the original sum you invested, but the nominal value of the stock you hold.

There is a wide choice of bonds available - with maturity dates that may only be a few months away or as much as 20 or more years away.

Gilts

Because they have always been regarded as being extremely safe, government bonds are often called 'gilt-edged' securities, or simply 'gilts'.

However, it is important to note that unlike bank or building society deposits, bonds are only completely safe if you are willing to hold them until they mature and the country that issues them is credit worthy. If you need to get at your money earlier you can sell your holding in the 'gilts market'. Gilts are traded in much the same way as shares and, as in the case with shares, prices fluctuate daily.

Coupon

The "coupon" is the term used to describe the rate of interest payable on a gilt. It is expressed as a percentage of the nominal value of stock. In the case of the 3.40% Treasury Bond 2024, the coupon is 3.4%. So, if you buy €100 nominal value of this stock, the annual payment guaranteed by the government is €3.40

Stock types

Gilts are generally categorised by reference to their maturity dates:

Short term gilts:	The maturity date of the stock is within the next five years.
Medium term gilts:	The maturity date of the stock is more than five and less than 15 years away.
Long term gilts:	The maturity date of the stock is more than 15 years away.

Ex div/cum div

In general, interest payments are made on gilts at six monthly intervals. To facilitate these payments, the Register of Gilt Owners is closed 31 days before a dividend is due to be paid and each registered owner on this closing date is paid the upcoming dividend.

If you buy stock before this closing date you are said to buy it "cum div" and you will be entitled to receive all of the next dividend payment when it becomes due. If you buy a stock after this closing date, you are said to buy it "ex div" and you will not receive the upcoming dividend.

Tax

If you sell a gilt "cum div", the price you receive will reflect an interest element which the purchaser will receive. This interest element is liable to income tax at your marginal rate of tax.

"In general, interest payments are made on gilts at six monthly intervals"

Example

You invested €20,000 in 3.4% Treasury Bond 2024 on 20 March 2014 and resold the stock on 20 January 2020 for €24,000. The details are as follows;

Last dividend date   20/03/2019

Ex dividend date   17/02/2020

Next dividend date   20/03/2020

You held the stock for 145 days and received no interest payment. However the following interest will be deemed to have accrued and may be taxable,

$$€20,000 \quad \times \quad 3.4\% \quad \times \quad \frac{306}{365} \quad = €570.08$$

No tax may be payable on this amount if:

- The stock transfer was between you and your spouse.

    or

- The stock has been held by you for a continuous period of two or more years.

If you are deemed to be trading in "gilts", the full gain will be taxed as income.

Other interest received from gilts will be taxed in the normal way under Schedule D Case III. If you made a capital gain on a gilt, no tax is payable unless you are deemed to be trading in gilts.

UK gilts

Where UK tax has been deducted at source, the tax will be repaid in full from the UK tax authorities on completion of the appropriate form IRL/Individual/Int which is available for the UK Inland Revenue at www.hmrc.co.uk. The gross interest is taxed in Ireland.

Stocks and shares

Ten years after the great economic crisis, the markets mostly continue to produce positive performances. Economic growth in the European Union and in the United States is reflected in higher employment and less personal debt, but the purchase of both sovereign and corporate bonds by the EU Central Bank is still providing fiscal stimulus to the financial sector and existing shareholders. Corporate entities continue to use their access to this artificially cheap credit to buy back their own shares, boosting share prices though not necessarily adding economic growth to the dismay of Central Banks.

No one can reliably predict how the artificially stimulated markets will keep evolving because true price discovery is so difficult today. The circumstances that fed previous growth from the middle of the last century – post war rebuilding, the great baby boom, huge growth in technology and globalization - is waning and Western economies, with their ageing populations have shifted to consuming rather than growing their personal wealth.

That said, up to the beginning of this century, the historic potential of stock market returns over other asset classes was undisputed.

For example, suppose that at the end of 1919, one of your relatives had invested €1,000 on the London Stock Exchange and reinvested the annual dividends, this portfolio would have been worth nearly €6.7 million in early 2007, before markets nose-dived.

Of course, €1,000, even in the heady early days of 2007, didn't buy what it used to in 1919 - in real terms the purchasing power of the €1,000 then would have turned into something like €222,003 in 2007 due to the ravages of inflation. Nevertheless, it represented a more than 30-fold increase in the wealth of the lucky shareholder by 2007. Meanwhile, anyone who sold their holdings that year would have avoided the huge losses that most stockholders experienced by 2009. Since then the losses recorded by diversified investment portfolios, as opposed to those experienced by Irish bank shares, have mostly recovered their 2007-8 prices, proof that holding your nerve and not panic selling after dramatic falls in financial markets is a better long term investment strategy than trying to time the markets.

Dividend payments

When you buy stocks and shares, you become a part owner of the company and are usually entitled to a percentage of its profits by way of a dividend. Dividends are normally paid twice a year. Unlike the income from a bank or building society, share dividends are not directly related to the money you invest but, instead, are linked to the growth in the company's profits and its dividend policy. When you invest money in shares, you may be more interested in capital growth or the increase in the relevant stock market valuation.

However, if you are going to need your money next month or next year, shares are not for you - whether you are buying in a 'bear' or 'bull' market - you would be better off putting your money in a more secure place. On the other hand, conventional wisdom up to now has suggested that if you can wait for five, ten or even twenty years for your investment to "mature" and you can cope with periodic 'crashes' along the way, then well chosen shares could still have the best potential to give you a very good return.

Buying shares is, as we all know now, a risky business and there is always the possibility of a bad investment and of losing some, if not all of your money. This risk of loss usually diminishes over time, provided you spread your risk by choosing a widely diversified pool of assets.

If you decide to invest in shares, you may want to keep an eye on their performance by reading the financial pages of your daily newspaper (or by subscribing to a recommended financial newsletter or web-site). Take a good investing course that can help teach you about the markets and how they work. It's certainly useful to know how to read the markets columns on the financial pages of your newspaper, which looks like this.

High	Low	Company	Share Price	+ -	Div. yld	P/E	Times cover
14.05	8.70	ABC Ltd.	10.73	-0.47	3.10	10.60	2.80
20.40	11.22	XYZ Ltd.	14.70xd	0.00	1.91	9.70	5.14
11.15	6.26	Z Ltd.	7.23	+0.05	2.20	9.40	3.22

High and low

The first column usually gives the highest price paid for that individual share in the current year and the second column gives the lowest price. The idea is to buy as close as possible to the lowest price and sell as close as possible to the highest price.

Company

The next section gives the relevant company or stock name.

Share price

The share price in column four is usually the previous day's closing price.

Ex-dividend

As we said earlier, companies usually pay dividends twice a year. About six to eight weeks before a dividend is paid, the company announce what the next dividend will be. A week or two after this announcement, the company's share register is temporarily closed. Upcoming dividends will be paid to the registered shareholders on this date. The company's shares will then go ex-dividend and are marked "xd" in the paper. So, if you buy shares marked xd you will not get the upcoming dividend.

Rise or fall

Column five gives the difference between the opening and closing prices of each share in the previous day's trading.

Dividend yield

The dividend yield is the ratio of a share's annual dividend to the share price. Column six gives the gross dividend yield i.e. the dividend yield before tax.

Price earnings ratio (p/e)

Traditionally, many people related a share price to a company's net asset value. Another way of valuing a share is to relate the share price to the company's flow of profits. The price earnings ratio in column seven is calculated by dividing the company's share price by the after-tax earnings due to each share over the company's most recent financial year. This ratio can also be calculated using expected rather than historical earnings. A high P/E ratio shows that investors have a lot of confidence in that company's future prosperity. A low P/E ratio can mean an investor is getting earnings "cheap" or can imply a lack of confidence in that company's future prosperity.

Times cover

The times cover is the ratio of last year's profits to the dividends paid. In the case of XYZ Ltd., it is 5.14. In other words, if XYZ Ltd. had paid out all of its profits to shareholders, the dividend would have been 5.14 times higher.

Tax

Buying and selling shares can give rise to two taxes:

- Income tax on dividends you receive.

- Capital Gains Tax (CGT) on investment gains.

Dividend income

You are liable to income tax on dividend income at your marginal rate of tax. When you receive a dividend from an Irish resident company, withholding tax at the 20% standard rate tax is deducted by the company. If the amount of tax withheld exceeds your total tax liability you can claim a refund. However, if you are a higher rate taxpayer you will have to pay the difference between the standard rate and the higher rate.

Example

You receive a dividend of €1,000 in January 2020. Dividend withholding tax of €200 (20%) is withheld by the company. Assuming you have already used up your standard rate cut off point your tax liability will work out as follows:

		2020 €
	Irish dividend gross	€1,000
	Tax @ 40%	€400
Less:	Withholding tax	€200
	Additional tax payable	€200

PRSI and the universal social charge (USC) may also apply.

UK dividends

When you obtain a dividend from a UK company it will normally show:

(a) The net dividend; and

(b) A tax credit which is equivalent to 1/9th of the net dividend.

Only the net dividend is taxable in Ireland, i.e. the cash amount received exclusive of any tax credit.

Example

You get a net dividend from UK Ltd. of €1,800, your dividend voucher will also show a tax credit of €200 (1/9th). You pay Irish income tax as follows, assuming that your marginal rate of tax is 40% in 2020 (ignoring rates of exchange).

The UK tax credit of £200 is non-refundable even if you are a non-taxpayer.

	2020 €
UK dividend (€1,800 net)	€1,800
Tax @ 40%	€720

PRSI and the universal social charge (USC) may also apply.

Capital gains tax

All realised gains in excess of your annual exemption limit (€1,270) will be liable to Capital Gains Tax at 33%.

Exchange Traded Funds (ETFs)

Exchange Traded Funds (EFTs) are a low cost alternative to buying stocks and shares or indexed funds directly. An ETF represents a company whose only asset is a collection of shares (or even commodities).

The early ETF market was dominated by index-based ones that represented all or a selection of shares on a well-known stock market, such as the FTSE-100, the Dow Jones index, or even our own ISEQ 20, Ireland's top 20 capitalised private companies. This single share trades just like any other share on the Irish exchange.

The attraction of ETFs are manifold: your risk is diversified between a number of companies, yet you only pay the transaction costs associated with a single share. The transaction and management costs are very low compared to actively managed funds. Typically, there are no entry charges other than a stockbroking commission and annual management charges will often be 0.5% or less.

"Typically, there are no entry charges other than stock-broking commissions."

An ETF, like a stock market indexed fund, is considered a good long-term option for investors who prefer to hold their shares rather than actively trade them, on the grounds that 90% of fund managers never consistently beat the performance of a stock market.

Priced daily, you also always know the value of your ETF and can buy into and exit your position at the daily price quickly, something that is not possible with a unitised investment fund.

There are thousands of ETFs available, ranging from large stock market indices, geographical funds (such as a country ETF), to obscure industrial sectors. There are commodity ETFs that track the daily price of gold or silver, for example, or commodity-based ones that bundle together companies in local or global mining industries.

The energy sector is well represented with companies that explore for oil or water, as well as the firms that supply the rigs, pipes, drilling equipment, etc. and ETF investors can also buy 'soft' agri-commodities - wheat, corn, sugar, coffee, cotton, etc which are in increasing demand in developing economies.

The value risks associated with ETFs are no different than any other fund, and global ETFs take the same beating from stock market volatility that shares and funds experience. You need to research your ETF and its underlying companies and assets carefully. Commodities are particularly volatile: a bad harvest can push up the price of wheat or corn, but a bumper harvest can push it down just as easily, which can not only affect the actual price of your ETF commodity, but also impact all they way up the line from the farmer to the combine harvesting company to the trucking and shipping lines that transport the wheat or corn halfway around the world.

Tax on ETFs

In general, income and gains included in payments made from an Irish-domiciled investment fund to investors are subject to deduction of tax at source by the fund at the rate of 41%, which is a final liability tax and is commonly referred to as "exit tax". However, in the case of an ETF investment, because unit/shares in the underlying fund are bought and sold between investors on the stock market, tax cannot be deducted at source by the fund. The onus is on the investor to make a self-assessment tax return of the income and gains, and to account for income tax at the rate of 41% on all such Irish-domiciled ETF-related income and gains. This 41% rate is applicable to income (dividends) and gains on disposals arising on or after 1 January 2014.

Such income and gains do not attract Pay Related Social Insurance (PRSI) or Universal Social Charge (USC) liabilities.

Irish Stamp duty does not apply to the transfer of shares in Irish domiciled ETFs.

ETFs domiciled in EU Countries other than Ireland

In the case of ETFs that are domiciled in EU countries other than Ireland, it seems to be the case that the majority of such funds are structured and regulated as UCITS under the UCITS Directive (as are the vast majority of Irish domiciled ETFs.

The tax treatment of such investments mirrors the tax treatment applicable to Irish ETFs. In other words, income payments (dividends) and gains on disposals are liable to income tax at the rate of 41% for payments arising on or after 1 January 2014. The investor is obliged to make a self-assessment tax return of the relevant income or gains, and to account for any tax liability arising.

Such income and gains do not attract PRSI or USC liabilities.

Offshore policies

Most Irish investment managers are as competent, professional and lucky (or unlucky) as their counterparts in the UK, America or Japan. Some concentrate solely on the Irish market. Others buy and sell equities and other assets in far flung parts of the world. Certainly all the larger investment companies here offer a selection of domestic and international equity funds (such as UK, American, Japanese, European, developing economies and sectoral funds) to their clients as well as fixed asset funds such as Government gilts or currency funds.

One of the perceived advantages of buying an investment from a larger player is that it will usually have considerably greater access to research and analytical resources, often directly on the ground in the country where the investments originate. This in-depth knowledge has produced mixed results for many of the big international players familiar to Irish investors, such as Fidelity, Gartmore, HKSB, Invesco and others, but the financial crisis has shown that few fund managers - or funds - have been able to escape unscathed.

Tax

The tax payable on offshore funds depends on where the fund is domiciled and whether it is a regulated fund. Every person acquiring an offshore policy or fund is obliged to make a tax return to the Revenue Commissioners no later than 31 October following the end of the relevant tax year. This return will detail:

●   When and how the policy or investment was acquired.

●   The description of the product including premiums payable.

●   Name and address of the person through whom the offshore product was acquired e.g. an intermediary.

Property

Booms and busts are an all too-common feature of the Irish property market. The tradition has been that Irish families will always want a home of their own in which to raise their children and to see out their retirement. The collapse in property values from 2008 shook that convention to its core, but house prices have been rising steadily, nearly fully recovering their pre-2008 levels, especially in the greater Dublin area.

The intervention of the Central Bank at the end of 2014 which imposed strict borrowing conditions dampened down the price overheating in the capital, but the severe shortage in affordable family-sized properties continues, fuelled by economic recovery, continues to spill over into the rental sector. Supply is simply not keeping up with demand.

The Central Bank's lending rules mean that first time buyers must find 10% of the downpayment, second time buyers, 20% and 30% for buy to let property buyers. Loan to income limits remain three and half times the borrowers' annual income. There is only a small discretionary lending window over these limits, specifically no more than 20% of the banks lending book for first time buyer loans and now only 10% over the lending limit for second time and subsequent buyers.

Mortgage lending is still a fraction of what it was at the peak of the property boom. Nevertheless, buying a property remains a popular aspiration for many, both to own a valuable asset and to provide themselves and their families with a homestead.

The ups and downs of property prices

Property prices rose steadily over 30 years to 2007, but the increases, as the figures below show, were not always consistent. The property bubble that blew up from 2001 well and truly burst, both here in Ireland and around the world.

Property prices rose steadily over 30 years to 2007, but the increases, as the figures below show, were not always consistent. The property bubble that blew up from 2001 well and truly burst, both here in Ireland and around the world and only stared recovering in 2013.

Average price of house nationwide

Q1 in year	New	Second hand
1987	€48,350	€46,622
1997	€91,947	€89,971
2007	€313,087	€375,577
2017	€322,680	€284,348

The table below illustrates how an average three bed semi-detached house in Dublin has increased in price over the past 30 years.

Figure 1.1: Residential Property Price Index

Source: CSO Ireland

Recovery

Propertyprices nationally have increased by 85.3% from their trough in early 2013. Dublin residential property prices have risen 94.7% from their February 2012 low, whilst residential property prices in the Rest of Ireland are 84.0% higher than at the trough, which was in May 2013.

Commercial property

The value of commercial property is normally directly related to the rental income it can generate. In the table below, we highlight how rental income from commercial properties has been increasing at different speeds over the years. This illustration outlines the average cost per square foot of commercial properties in the Dublin area over the past 30 years.

Year	Average office rental cost per sq. ft.	Average retail rental cost per sq. ft. (shopping centres)	Average industrial rental cost per sq. ft.
1989	€8.50	n/a	€3.00
1999	€22.50	€52.00	€4.75
2009	€48.00	€390.00	€10.50
2019	€65.00	€470.00	€9.50

(The above figures relating to property were provided by CBRE Research)

"Undertaking any property investment without a sound rental stream is not recommended"

Rental Properties

The profit made from renting a property is liable to income tax at your marginal rate of tax - USC and PRSI are also payable on the profit made. Landlords who purchase rental properties normally have substantial incomes so in 2020 the rate of tax on rental income could be as high as 52% when marginal rate income tax, USC and PRSI is taken into account.

Profit from a rental property owned by a company is liable to corporation tax at a rate of 25%. Rental income in a company which is not distributed is liable to a surcharge of 20% and the effective corporation tax rate can be as high as 40%.

Tax on disposal

When a property is sold the chargeable gain will normally be subject to CGT at 33%. So, if you own the property personally you retain the proceeds, less 33% CGT. If the property is owned by a company it also pays CGT at 33%. However, there will be a further personal tax liability if you wish to gain access to the cash within the company. If you access the cash by way of salary or dividend, the rate could be nearly 52% (income tax, PRSI and USC). The other option is to liquidate the company, which will give rise to a further 33% CGT liability.

Example

You set up "A" Limited ten years ago with ordinary share capital of €2. "A" Limited bought a property for letting for €130,000. "A" Limited sells the building now for €500,000. Assuming the company has no other assets or liabilities below we illustrate the tax position if the property is purchased through a company or by you personally.

	Personal purchase €	"A" Limited €
Sale proceeds	€500,000	€500,000
Less: Cost of property plus indexation	€130,000	€130,000
Taxable amount	€370,000	€370,000
CGT on €370,000 @ 33%	€122,100	€122,100
Available for distribution		€377,900
CGT on liquidation of A Limited €377,900 @ 33%		€124,707
Net personal proceeds	€377,900	€253,193
Total tax payable	**€122,100**	**€246,807**

Stamp Duty

The rate of Stamp duty on residential property for instruments executed on or after 8 December 2010 are as follows;

Aggregate consideration	Rate of duty
First €1,000,000	1%
Excess over €1,000,000	2%

The stamp duty rate for non-residential properties is a flat 6% rate in respect of instruments executed after 11 October 2017.

Where VAT is included in the cost of the property, it should be deducted before calculating the charge or rate of stamp duty.

Income tax

Rents are taxed under Schedule D Case V on the basis of the actual year's income - e.g. rents arising in the year ending 31 December 2020 are assessed to tax in the income tax year 2020. The following expenses can normally be deducted from the gross rents for tax purposes.

- Interest paid on money borrowed to purchase residential property. From 7 April 2009 only 75% of mortgage interest paid on a residential property was allowable as a tax deduction against rental income. This increased to 80% for the 2017 tax year, 85% in the 2018 tax year and 100% in the 2019 tax year.

- From 1 January 2016 landlords who rent to tenants receiving certain social housing supports can claim 100% of mortgage interest paid as an expense. The landlord must also be registered with the PRTB.

- Rent payable on the property.

- Rates payable on the property.

- Goods provided and services rendered in connection with the letting of the property.

- Repairs, insurance, maintenance and management fees.

- Capital allowance of 12.5% per annum on the value of the fixtures and fittings.

- Mortgage protection premiums.

Be sure to keep all receipts, especially for repairs and maintenance, as your Inspector of Taxes may wish to examine these.

Pre-letting expenses

The 2017 Finance Act introduced a new tax deduction for pre-letting expenses to encourage owners of vacant residential property, bring vacant properties into the rental market for a minimum period of 4 years. The property must have been vacant for at least 12 months to qualify. A cap on allowable expenses of €5,000 per property will apply. This relief will be available for qualifying expenses incurred up to the end of 2021. It will be subject to clawback if the property is withdrawn from the rental market within four years.

The Local property tax charge is not an allowable expense and cannot be offset against your gross rental income.

"VAT should be deducted before calculating the charge or rate of stamp duty."

In order to claim mortgage interest as an expense it is necessary to be registered with the RTB (Residential Tenancy Board).

A typical rental income and expenditure account is shown on page 48.

Rent-a-room scheme

Where a room or rooms in a person's private principal residence is let as residential accommodation, gross annual rent received of up to €14,000 will be exempt from income tax. You do not have to be a home owner to avail of the scheme.

The Rent-a-Room Scheme is the single most generous tax free earning opportunity but it is not available where the rent received was from a child who in turn is claiming rent relief.

Airbnb / Income from providing short term guest accommodation

Airbnb lettings have soared in recent years, but owner hosts must declare this income on their annual tax return. You are not obliged to register with the Residential Tenancies Board, but from June, 2019 under the new 'One Host One Home' model introduced by the government to prevent entire properties being rented to tourists in areas of high demand, Air BnB hosts are now required to register with their local authority and seek special planning permission.

Homeowners of a second property will no longer be able to rent out the property on a short-term basis.

A room or rooms in the owner's own principal private residence can be rented out for short term use without restriction, but the owner will only be able to sub-let their entire house without planning permission for up to 14 days or less at a time and an annual cap of 90 days will apply.

Income from providing short term guest accommodation such as Air BnB or any other similar accommodation is taxable as;

- Other income (Case IV) where the income is occasional in nature
- Trading income (Case I) where you are trading as an ongoing business, such as bed and breakfast or a guesthouse.

Expenses incurred in the letting of the property may be claimed as an expense against the income received.

Residential Property Rental Income and Expenditure Account Y/E 31st December 2020 Name: _____ PPS No. _____ Y/E: _____		
		€
Rent received		€15,000
Less **Allowable expenses**		
Rates / ground rents payable	€100	
Insurance on premises	€500	
Repairs & renewals	€900	
Light, heat and telephone	€400	
Cleaning & maintenance	€1,000	
Agency & advertising	€700	
RTB registration	€70	
Interest on borrowed money (100%)	€6,800	
Mortgage protection premiums	€300	
Sundry expenses	€300	
Total expenses		€11,070
Net rental income		**€3,930**
Less Capital allowances on fixtures & fittings		(€875)
Taxable rental income after capital allowances		€3,055
Income tax & levies – assuming a 40% rate of tax, 4% PRSI & 8% USC		€1,588.60

Residential tenancy board (RTB)

The Residential Tenancy Board (RTB) was established to operate a national tenancy registration system and to resolve disputes between landlords and tenants. It also provides policy advice to the Government on the private rental sector. Entitlement to a deduction for interest paid on borrowed money used to purchase, improve or repair a rental residential property is conditional on compliance with the registration requirements of the Residential Tenancies Act 2004.

Persons who are required to register

The Act applies to the vast majority of private rented dwellings situated in Ireland but does not apply to;

- Business premises.

- Former rent controlled dwellings occupied by the original tenant or by their spouse.

- A dwelling let by a local authority or a voluntary housing body.

- A dwelling occupied under a shared ownership lease.

- A dwelling in which the landlord also resides (this would include the 'rent-a-room' scheme).

- A dwelling in which the spouse, parent or child of the landlord is resident and where there is no written lease or tenancy agreement.

- Holiday lettings.

A dwelling let by, or to, a public authority is also excluded. A "public authority" includes a recognised educational institution. Therefore, owners of student accommodation dwellings let to third level college for onward letting to students are excluded from the requirement to register. However, tenancies in dwellings that are let directly to students must be registered.

Registration requirements

Landlords are required to register details of all their tenancies - now including student specific accommodation - within one month of the commencement of those tenancies. The cost of registration is €90 per tenancy provided the completed application to register is received within one month from the tenancy commencement date. The registration fee increases to €180 where an application to register a tenancy is received more than one month from the commencement of the tenancy. Once it is registered it remains a registered tenancy for as long as the tenancy remains in existence. Once it is terminated, any new tenancy created in respect of the dwelling must be registered with the RTB. If the tenancy has not previously been terminated it will be deemed to have terminated when it has lasted four years and a new tenancy will then be deemed to commence. This new tenancy must be registered with the RTB and the appropriate fee paid.

The registration application form RTB1 is available from the Residential Tenancies Board (RTB) www.rtb.ie. The registration can also be completed online.

Local property tax (LPT)

Private residential property owners became liable for full rate local property tax (LPT) from 1 January 2014. Those rates have been extended to 2020.

Property values are grouped into value bands. A rate of 0.18% applies to the midpoint of the value band up to €1m. To calculate how much you will have to pay select the value band appropriate to the market value of your property and read across in the table shown on page 51. For properties values at over €1m the LPT liability will be calculated as follows: 0.18% on the first €1m and 0.25% on the portion over €1m.

Exemptions

Certain properties are exempt from LPT. An exemption applies to all owners of new and previously unused properties purchased from a builder or developer between 1 January 2013 and 31 October 2016 and will be exempt until the end of 2019. The exemption also applies to new owners of second-hand properties purchased in 2013 provided the house is the persons sole or main residence.

Certain owners living on so-called 'ghost estates' or receiving mortgage interest supplement are also exempt from LPT.

Local Property Tax charges for 2020

Valuation band	Standard Rate	Local authority reduced LPT rate by				
		1.5%	3%	7.5%	10%	15%
€	€	€	€	€	€	€
€0 to €100,000	€90	€88	€87	€83	€81	€76
€100,001 to €150,000	€225	€221	€218	€208	€202	€191
€150,001 to €200,000	€315	€310	€305	€291	€283	€267
€200,001 to €250,000	€405	€398	€392	€374	€364	€344
€250,001 to €300,000	€495	€487	€480	€457	€445	€420
€300,001 to €350,000	€585	€576	€567	€541	€526	€497
€350,001 to €400,000	€675	€664	€654	€624	€607	€573
€400,001 to €450,000	€765	€753	€742	€ 707	€668	€650
€450,001 to €500,000	€855	€842	€829	€790	€769	€726
€500,001 to €550,000	€945	€930	€916	€874	€850	€803
€550,001 to €600,000	€1,035	€1,019	€1,003	€957	€931	€879
€600,001 to €650,000	€1,125	€1,108	€1,091	€1,040	€1,012	€956
€650,001 to €700,000	€1,215	€1,196	€1,178	€1,123	€1,093	€1,032
€700,001 to €750,000	€1,305	€1,285	€1,265	€1,207	€1,174	€1,109
€750,001 to €800,000	€1,395	€1,374	€1,353	€1,290	€1,255	€1,185
€800,001 to €850,000	€1,485	€1,462	€1,440	€1,373	€1,336	€1,262
€850,001 to €900,000	€1,575	€1,551	€1,527	€1,456	€1,417	€1,338
€900,001 to €950,000	€1,665	€1,640	€1,615	€1,540	€1,498	€1,415
€950,001 to €1,000,000	€1,755	€1,728	€1,702	€1,623	€1,579	€1,491
Property valued at €1.2m	€2,300	€2,265	€2,231	€2,127	€2,070	€1,955
Property valued at €1.5m	€3,050	€3,004	€2,958	€2,821	€2,745	€2,592

Deferring payment of LPT

A system of deferral arrangements for owner-occupiers applies under specified conditions to address cases where there is an inability to pay the LPT. In order to qualify for a deferral the gross income must not exceed €15,000 for a single person and €25,000 for a couple. Some owner-occupiers may be eligible to apply for marginal relief, which allows them to defer up to 50% of their LPT liability. Deferral is not an exemption of the tax, it is deferred and the tax becomes payable at a later date and is liable to interest at 4% per annum. The deferred tax remains a charge on the property and will have to be paid to the Revenue Commissioners when the property is sold or transferred to another person.

Managed funds

As the name implies, "Managed Funds" are funds where investors pool their resources to create a common investment fund which is controlled by professional managers. The two main benefits of this collective approach are, more efficient and economical investment management, plus greater security to investors, as the risk is spread over a diverse range of investments.

Life assurance products

With-profit investment plans also invest your money in various assets over a fixed number of years. However, instead of your money being subject to the daily movement of the investment markets, the company sets out future minimum guaranteed values, as profits are earned and annual bonuses are declared, and this will increase your overall guaranteed values. Once declared, these bonuses cannot be taken away. The aim is to pay a bonus that relates to market growth but one that can also be sustained if the market falls. Some companies pay a higher proportion of performance growth in the form of a final bonus than others. This can penalise policyholders who encash their policies early and reward those who stay the course of the contract.

The smoothing-out effect of the bonus system protects with-profit funds from the volatility that is part and parcel of the market place. However, with-profits policies cannot buck the market: The values that are paid out at maturity will reflect the overall growth achieved by these stocks, property, gilts and cash investments that have underpinned them.

Investment bonds

Aimed at the lump sum investor, bonds come in different guises, such as

- Unit-linked and with-profit bonds.
- Tracker bonds.
- Special Investment bonds.

Life assurance bonds are among the most widely sold. Nearly all require a minimum investment of €5,000 and at least a five year investment time frame. Ideally, these should be regarded as medium to long-term investments to allow a good maturity value to build-up. Entry costs are usually between 3%-5% and annual management charges are usually 0.75%-1%.

Tracker bonds were considered a relatively safe, if expensive way of participating in international stock markets, such as the FTSE-100, the Dow and Japanese Nikkei, without many of the associated risks. Most tracker bonds have an investment term of three to six years and normally require minimum investments of €5,000. However, tracker bond fund managers are not buying actual stocks and shares, just the options on the performance of shares represented by a particular stock market index. In order to guarantee the safety of the investor's capital - a strong selling point for tracker bonds - a large portion of your investment must be put on deposit.

A number of years ago many tracker funds guaranteed the return of virtually the entire capital so long as the investors left their money untouched. With interest rates so low, the cost of this guarantee has risen, and recent tracker bonds are poor performers compared to the returns once achieved.

Absolute return funds

Most conventional investment funds only reward investors when markets go up and penalise them when they fall. Absolute return funds seek to deliver positive returns whether markets are rising or falling. They use a wide variety of assets, such as equities, bonds, property and cash. They can also use advanced instruments, such as derivatives, to gain additional returns or guard against market falls.

Most fund managers work on the basis of benchmarking against a stock market index or average fund in its sector – relative return. Objectives can be achieved even in a "negative" market.

Absolute return basically attempts to produce a "positive" investment return over a specific term, irrespective of whether markets are positive or negative.

Most absolute return funds work towards a specific target return, e.g. 'X'% above Euribor over 'Y' period.

Tax

The returns from life assurance product funds commenced before 1 January 2001 are paid tax-free. All taxes due on profits earned will have already been paid at source by the life assurance fund managers to the Revenue Commissioners.

For products issued after the 1 January 2001 the life assurance company is obliged to deduct exit tax on any gains either every eight years or on encashment if earlier, at a rate of 41%. This tax will be a final liability tax for Irish residents. No tax will be deducted from payments to a person who is neither resident nor ordinarily resident here provided they have complied with the Revenue declaration requirements.

Tax on death or disability

The proceeds payable on death or disability are liable to the same level of exit tax as if the product had been surrendered at that date.

Example - Lump sum investment

An individual invests €100,000 in an Investment Bond on 4 January 2012. They die on 13 March 2018 when the gross value of their bond is €110,000. They made no withdrawals from the investment over the term. The "taxable gain" is the reduction in the surrender value of the bond as a result of the payout i.e. €150,000 less allowable premiums paid.

Taxable gain	=	€110,000 - €100,000	=	€10,000
Exit tax @ 41%	=	€10,000 x 41%	=	€4,100

Example 2 - Protection plan

You took out a long term savings/protection plan on 5 March 2015. Annual premiums are €1,000, Life cover is €30,000. This gross surrender value after 15 years is €20,000 (at 5 March 2030).

In the event of a full encashment, exit tax is charged on the difference between the surrender value (€20,000) and the total premium paid (€15,000). Assuming an exit tax rate of 41%, this would amount to €2,050. The net encashment value payable is €17,950.

Note: If any exit tax had been paid on the eight year anniversary of the policy this would be deducted from the final exit tax due.

Death

Using the example above and assuming the individual dies before 5 March 2030, the life company would pay the life cover sum (€30,000) less the appropriate exit tax. This tax would be calculated as follows - the surrender value of the plan after the payout is nil. Therefore, the reduction in surrender value as a result of the payout is € 20,000. So, exit tax is calculated on the difference between total premiums paid and the reduction in the surrender value after the payment of the sum assured is agreed (€20,000 less €15,000 = €5,000). Assuming an exit tax rate of 41%, the tax payable on the individual's death would also be €2,050.

Alternative investments

The case for gold

High demand for commodities in developing economies has resulted in the creation of a huge range of managed investment funds, index funds and ETFs that represent either the commodities themselves, such as oil, coal, iron, steel, base metals of all kinds, 'soft' agriculture-based commodities as well as commodity-related companies.

Precious metals, like gold, silver and platinum have also become widely traded commodities over the past several years, not just because of their growing industrial applications, but especially in the case of gold, and increasingly, silver because of their historic role as a store of value in tumultuous financial times. Very simply, more and more people are learning that gold and silver is 'real money'.

Whereas paper currencies lose their value over time when their supply is increased by governments and central banks, gold keeps its intrinsic value: an ounce of gold could buy a Roman tribune a fine set of clothes 2000 years ago - as it can today. Thirty years ago, an ounce of gold could buy an adult Irish private health insurance policy; today, that same ounce can still buy an adult private health insurance plan.

The average price of gold peaked in 1980 at $612.56 an ounce for that year and then more than halved in price until the end of the 1990s. It rose steadily from 2001, when global central banks began reducing interest rates to historically low levels and flooded the financial markets with credit in order to offset the double effects of the dot.com crash and the 9/11 attacks.

"An ounce of gold could buy a Roman tribune a fine set of clothes 2000 years ago - as it can today."

After more than a decade of steady growth, by the Autumn of 2015 the price of gold had fallen back to levels last seen in 2009-10 when it was just over $1,000 an ounce. Growing concerns about trade wars, the sluggish global economy and the impact of Brexit in the UK all contributed to strong gold prices in the Autum of 2019 when it peaked at c$1,550 an ounce.

The attraction of including gold as a small part of an investment portfolio, especially in times of political turmoil or when central banks are inflating the money supply, is that it provides a safe harbour - a hedge - against the falling value of a currency and because even though physical gold is not a tradeable currency, it is a convertible asset of value.

The demand for gold by both individuals and corporate investors has been facilitated by easier ways to buy it: huge trading now takes place in gold Exchange Traded Funds (ETFs), which can be purchased by Irish investors like a share on a stock market and which track the price of an ounce of gold in US dollars.

Another popular method is to buy gold coins and bullion from bullion dealers and allocated coins and bullion by way of certificates issued by the Bank of Western Australia in Perth and sold by the Irish gold bullion dealers , Goldcore. (see www.goldcore.com)

Investors need to be clear about their motives for buying gold: are they strictly speculating on its price, or do they want to add gold as a longer term hedge against the risk of other assets falling in value?

Gold may keep its intrinsic value, but investors need to remember that it pays no dividends and its price - as the table on page 58 shows -is subject to market forces that can push it down as well as up.

The price of silver is more volatile than gold because it has industrial as well as historic monetary uses. In the spring of 2011 it rose to an all time high of $50 an ounce, but fell back sharply and was an average price of $15.75 an ounce in 2018 compared to about $1,250 an ounce for gold. It too has crept up in price during the latter quarter of 2019.

Many commentators continue to believe that silver has fallen far outside its historical 1:16 sync with gold (whereby it took 16 silver ounces to buy one ounce of gold.)

Bitcoin

The 'virtual' currency, Bitcoin – and many other crypto-currencies - have emerged as a relatively recent internet phenomenon. The original Bitcoin, with its mysterious origins, allegedly at the hands of a Japanese software genius back in the late 2000's, is 'mined' using complex computer algorithms that control not just the (finite) number of coins in existence, but the number that are released into the virtual marketplace.

Denominated in American dollars, but backed by no physical assets and operating entirely outside of conventional US or global monetary regulatory or pricing controls, the price of individual Bitcoin on trading platforms is highly volatile, rising and falling over short periods of time.

There are now nearly 17.3 million Bitcoin in operation (out of a total of no more than 21 million that will be mined out by no later than 2040), and they are widely accepted by retailers and service providers worldwide. The main attraction of a crypto-currency, claim supporters is that each 'coin' or unit is worth exactly what willing buyers and sellers are willing to pay, mainly devoid of interference by third party states or central banks, though that may also come to an end: regulators and revenue authorities are showing increasing interest in them especially since they remain an untraceable currency within both the criminal underworld and amongst terrorist groups.

Price of Gold

Year	London Market Price (British £[1718-1949] or U.S.$. [1950 - 2006] per fine ounce)
1979	$307.50
1980	$612.56
1981	$459.64
1982	$375.91
1983	$424.00
1984	$360.66
1985	$317.66
1986	$368.24
1987	$447.95
1988	$438.31
1989	$382.58
1990	$384.93
1991	$363.29
1992	$344.97
1993	$360.91
1994	$385.42
1995	$385.50
1996	$389.09
1997	$332.39
1998	$295.24
1999	$279.91
2000	$280.10
2001	$272.22
2002	$311.33
2003	$364.80
2004	$410.52
2005	$446.00
2006	$610.00
2007	$696.00
2008	$871.96
2009	$972.35
2010	$1,225.94
2011	$1,565.67
2012	$1,650.00
2013	$1,407.00
2014	$1,266.00
2015	$1,150.00
2016	$1,200.00
2017	$1,257.00
2018	$1,268.00

4 Borrowing and managing debt

"Neither a borrower nor a lender be" may be sound advice, but few of us can afford to be so virtuous. Yet borrowing money, as so many people have discovered to their detriment, can be a perilous activity, since there are so many things that can go wrong when it comes to repaying the loan - illness, unemployment, other unexpected events, even happy ones like having a baby and having to interrupt a career.

No matter what form of credit you seek – a personal loan to buy a car, a mortgage for your first home or a short term line of credit from a credit card company, you need to consider the following:

- The amount.
- The type of loan.
- The rate of interest charged.
- The duration of the loan.
- Your ability to pay, especially should interest rates rise.
- Your personal circumstances.
- Borrowing outlets.

Loans

Borrowing money for a long-term purpose, such as a mortgage or to finance a business is very different from borrowing to buy a car, household goods or even a holiday. For one thing, the interest rate you pay and the repayment period are going to be very different. So try and match the loan with the right lender from the start.

In the recent past, if you wanted to borrow money for a home, you went to go to a bank or building society, but now that their lending rules are being eased by the Central Bank, certain credit unions have become a source of mortgage loans. Overdrafts that you dip in and out of, have tended to be the preserve of the bank, building society or credit union with which you have your current account.

But the lending pool for personal loans has been widening to not just include finance houses, credit unions and even life assurance companies but also the growing selection of entirely on-line banks that not only offer deposit and payment facilities accessed from mobile phone apps, but lending facilities as well.

Amidst this proliferating high tech banking world are moneylenders, who are the keenest of all to lend, but should be avoided by all but the most desperate because of the crippling interest rates they charge – up to 287% per annum.

Most licensed moneylenders charging an Annual Percentage Rate (APR) of interest above 23% have to include a warning notice saying "This is a high-cost loan" in any agreement with customers. The advent of credit union micro-loans for social welfare recipients has had limited success in their effort to break the grip that moneylenders have on many deprived communities.

Standard variable rate mortgage interest rates are relatively low by longer historic standards at c3% in 2019, but remain nearly twice the average rate in the rest of the eurozone. Nevertheless, the cheapest terms are still provided by mortgage lenders, who are counting on you borrowing over a period of many years.

The most expensive interest rates are charged by credit card providers and moneylenders whose lines of credit are designed to be paid off ideally in a short amount of time. Credit card "loans" should be used sparingly and ideally by people who can pay off the amount borrowed each month; that way they will incur no interest at all.

An upward change in interest rates will not normally change the amount most people pay back each month for personal short-term loans, even if the rate is a variable one. However any adjustments that have worked against you over the period will have to be settled up at the end - usually with a final balancing payment(s).

Variable rate mortgages don't work this way. Any rate hike or fall is usually applied to the homeowner's next repayment. If rates go up by a quarter or half percent, you will have to pay more each month until they go down again. Fixing your personal loan or mortgage interest rate is one way to avoid this kind of volatility, but it is difficult to predict interest rate movements: if you fix your rate and interest rates fall, you must

"Credit cards should be used sparingly and ideally by people who can pay off the amount borrowed each month."

continue to pay the fixed rate for the agreed term or incur penalties to break the contract.

Many term loan borrowers are keen to stretch their repayments over a longer number of years because the monthly repayment is smaller. But they sometimes forget that ultimately they will pay more interest on this loan. See example below.

Example

APR	Amount borrowed	Loan term	Repayment each month	Total to be paid back	Total cost of credit (total paid less original loan)
9.99%	€10,000	3 years (36 monthly payments)	€309.09	€11,127.24	€1,127.24
9.99%	€10,000	4 years (48 monthly payments)	€239.79	€11,509.92	€1,509.92
9.99%	€10,000	5 years (60 monthly payments)	€198.34	€11,900.40	€1,900.40

Source: www.bonkers.ie KBC Bank

Term loans

Before you take out a term loan with a bank or building society you need to determine the real cost of the loan, the Annual Percentage Rate (APR) and the total repayments. The APR is the true interest rate and is calculated based on the duration of the loan and any fees that may fall due. The APR is inevitably higher than the published flat rate. Along with the APR rate you should also ask for the cost per thousand per month which will tell you how much every €1,000 borrowed will cost. You then multiply this amount by however many thousands of euro you borrow and by the number of months over which you are repaying the loan. This figure represents your total repayment.

Overdrafts

Arranged on your current account, overdrafts are a way to arrange extra credit as you need it. Interest rates are usually higher than the personal lending rate, but not as high as a credit card rate, and payable only as you use the facility. If you exceed your overdraft limit without permission, the bank is entitled to charge extra interest and a "referral charge" which can amount to several euro per event.

Budget account

This is a type of overdraft which smoothes out the annual cost of running your current account. It allows you to borrow a multiple of your monthly pay cheque (paid directly into the account) to cover large once-off outgoings like school expenses in September, Christmas spending in December or the cost of a summer holiday. Interest is charged only as you draw down the facility.

Credit Union loans

Credit Unions do not seek collateral before lending money. Your record as a regular saver and whether you are employed or not, is how they judge your ability to repay. The unsecured loan amount is usually a multiple of the value of shares you hold.

In the past, credit unions, which calculate the interest on the diminishing balance of the loan, showed more repayment flexibility than conventional lenders. Few credit unions have been able to maintain this flexibility after being left with high rates of loan arrears, but the sector has been enjoying a period of recovery; many credit unions have been merged to form larger stronger unions, and are in a far stronger lending position. There has also been considerable investment in training and technology, and the rolling out of comprehensive current accounts and mortgage products. Dividend payments on savings remain low but can be higher than high street banks.

A positive development is the rolling out of "It Makes Sense" micro credit loans to members in receipt of social welfare payments, who also qualify for the Household Budget Scheme and cannot raise a loan with conventional banks. Loans worth between €100 and

€2,000 can be borrowed at a maximum APR of 12.68%. Repayments are deducted directly from weekly social welfare benefits. (See www.itmakessenseloan.ie for participating credit unions.)

Life assurance

Life assurance companies may seem like an unusual source from which to borrow money, but there is provision for lending up to 80% of the cash value of a with-profits policy. Interest rates are usually competitive and borrowing against the fund value may be better than encashing the policy. Investment policies like this should always be allowed to run their course - since a significant part of the total value of the policy may be paid in the form of a final bonus which only comes into effect on the maturity of the policy.

Life assurance policies are frequently used as security against conventional loans eg - if you renege on your debt the bank will simply encash the policy.

Credit cards

These are among the most expensive but convenient forms of borrowing. Designed for short-term purchases, the APR can be as high as 22.9% for cardholders who don't clear their monthly balances in full. The highest rates of interest charged immediately on cash withdrawals is now slightly lower at about 20%. Disciplined cardholders can take full advantage of up to 56 days of free credit available, but those who don't can run up large balances very quickly. The most popular credit cards are Visa and Mastercard which now come in different guises - such as affinity cards for professional groups who can benefit from a slightly lower interest rate and a donation to their college or charity or in the form of a loyalty card with which you can build up cash discounts with a series of retailers. With penalty charges for spending over your credit limit or not paying your bill on time and other conditions and interest rates varying so much between card providers, you need to shop around for the best rate and conditions. - see comparison tables on the Competition and Consumer Protection Commission (CCPC) website, www.consumerhelp.ie or at www.bonkers.ie

Debit cards

Debit cards are expected to overtake the use of cash in a few years. Equipped with a 'contactless' chip, debit cards are nearly universally accepted by merchants and more on-line security features. It does not replace a conventional credit card because the funds you spend will still be deducted from your current account, but it can also prevent the reckless borrowing that can happen with credit cards. Debit cards are subject to an annual ATM/debit stamp duty of €5.

Type of loan	Amount you owe	Term left to run	APR	Monthly Payments	Overall cost of credit
Existing mortgage	€100,000	20 years	4.60%	€634	€52,160
Home improvement loan	€30,000	7 years	9.90%	€490	€11,160
Car loan	€20,000	5 years	8.60%	€408	€4,480
Personal loan	€13,000	3 years	13.20%	€435	€2,660
Total	€163,000			€1,967	€70,460
New re-finance mortgage	€163,000	20 years	4.95%	€1,061	€91,640

Extra cost of debt -consolidation loan	
Total (€91,640) less €70,460)	€21,180

Although your repayments fall from €1,967 a month to €1,061 a month, you will end up paying €21,180 extra over the life of the new loan.

Charge/store cards

These include the likes of American Express and Diners Club as well as popular store cards like Arnotts, or Brown Thomas. Charge cards may involve an annual membership and require you to clear your balance off monthly within a set time frame or face hefty interest penalties. Unlike store cards, however, American Express and Diners Club do not have spending limits. The store cards are handy and convenient but interest rates can be very high (sometimes higher than ordinary credit cards) if you do not clear your balance each month.

Consolidation loans

These loans were much in demand in recent years as borrowers discovered that they could reduce the size of their overall monthly loan repayments by consolidating their credit card, overdraft, car loan, hire purchase payments into a new single super-loan. Ideally, many people wanted to consolidate these debts as part of an existing mortgage, since home loans carry the lowest annual interest rates.

However, the credit crisis made it more difficult to arrange consolidated mortgage loans; the option then is to seek personal loan consolidation finance.

The danger of re-financing all your debt is that the total, final repayment could end up much higher if you stretch your new repayment over an extended period, even if your monthly payment appears lower than the total of all the individual ones. The table on page 64 shows how this expensive effect can occur.

Budgeting

Whether you are single, married or a parent with family responsibilities, most of us need some help controlling our finances, especially in tight economic times.

With many people still burdened with relatively high levels of personal debt and the range of higher taxes, levies and cutbacks in social services that have been introduced after 2008, making our incomes stretch is still a priority.

You need an annual budget that sets out your household's income and outgoings and allows you to plan your immediate and longer term financial needs in an ordered and, hopefully, stress-free way.

This exercise will also be useful if you need to approach MABS (www. mabs.ie), or Step Change (www.stepchangedebtcharity.ie) for help in presenting a budget statement to a creditor from whom you are seeking informal debt restructuring. The Standard Financial Statement, or SFS, meanwhile, must be filled in by anyone applying to their lender for debt restructuring under the Central Bank's Mortgage Arrears Resolution Process (MARP). It can also be a very useful document for anyone who wants to get a better handle on their finances, before it becomes a much more serious issue.

Debtors should always seek the free assistance of MABS or Step Change from the outset. They may be able to help you negotiate a fair repayment arrangement with your creditors if you are not confident enough to do so on your own. People who are insolvent should approach either MABS, Step Change of the Insolvency Service of Ireland (www.isi.gov.ie) directly in order to engage the services of a properly regulated and supervised debt adviser or PIP (Personal Insolvency Practitioner.) A free service 'Abhaile', from the Mortgage Arrears Resolution Service has been launched by the ISI in association with MABS and is aimed at mortgage holders who are in arrears and insolvent but who have not been engaging with their lender.

Debtors are no longer required to pay any fees or charges to become insolvent, and should avoid the use of any so-called debt managers. Instead, the ISI provides a nationwide panel of free Personal Insolvency Practitioners whom debtors can engage. (www.isi.gov.ie)

So where do you start?

If you are conducting your own personal finance review, begin by setting aside a couple of uninterrupted hours for yourself or with your spouse/ partner. The time you spend sorting out all your bills, accounts and receipts will also be invaluable if later, you call in a professional adviser, enter into the MARP process or should you pursue a personal insolvency or bankruptcy action.

Step 1:   Buy a large copybook or ledger or download an on-line budget planner.

Step 2:   Gather all your financial documents together, such as pay slips, P60s, social welfare books, bank and credit card statements, loan statements, utility bills, insurance policies, savings books, investment and pension accounts/ statements. Copies of weekly grocery bills, for example, will also be useful to get a picture of how much you spend on food.

Step 3:   On one page, under the heading, "income" itemise all gross annual earnings and income coming into the household and then calculate the monthly, after-tax, figure. In addition to salaries and wages and/or pension income, this should include commissions and bonuses, share dividends, anticipated capital gains, rental income, etc. Don't forget to include any social welfare payments, such as monthly child benefit.

On the opposite page, under the heading "essential spending", list your annual outgoings, beginning with the amount of tax, PRSI, universal social charge (USC) and property tax you pay and any automatic deductions from salary or direct debits for pension/PHI or health insurance contributions. Prioritise the rest of your spending according to value, usually beginning with mortgage or rent payments and childcare costs if they apply. Leave two spaces for the annual amount, and the monthly average. Next, mark down your annual/monthly food bill, not forgetting to include the amount spent in addition to the large weekly shopping visit to convenience stores. Your food bill may be higher during the Christmas season and perhaps a bit lower over the summer if you are away on holidays. Utilities - gas, electricity, telephone/mobiles, television and solid fuel - are often the next largest outgoing, followed by on-going transport, essential clothing and insurance costs, annual education fees/costs. Bank charges on current accounts should also be included.

Step 4:   Underneath your list of "essential spending", mark down another heading, "non-essential spending" or "discretionary spending". This category should include occasional savings, personal loans, credit card balances, entertainment and hobbies, holidays and travel, miscellaneous shopping.

Again, the Standard Financial Statement (see www.mabs.ie) is an excellent template that includes a long list of household assets and liabilities.

Discretionary spending

While most of us have a pretty good idea of the size of our essential outgoings, too often we underestimate how much we spend for discretionary purposes. The best way to get a clear picture of exactly how much you are overspending is to keep a spending diary for one month.

This diary should be small enough to fit into a handbag or inside jacket pocket so that your daily purchases - from newspapers and magazines, cigarettes and coffee, milk and bread, petrol and flowers, evening drinks at your local pub, can all be marked down. (Smart phones make excellent ledgers).

Bigger spontaneous items you believe you can still afford can also be recorded in your ledger: those must-have shoes, the lunch out with a friend, the no-frills weekend flight to somewhere warm. Keeping a spending ledger will be an eye-opener. It will point out exactly why your income is not stretching as far as it should; it will probably reveal your spending patterns and triggers, especially concerning indiscriminate credit card or debit card usage. Ideally, it will make you more conscious of just how much you can afford for discretionary purchases.

Prepare your budget

You are now ready to create a budget for yourself or your family, to which you can refer as the year progresses. By knowing how much you spend for housing, utilities, food and transport, clothing and insurance, entertainment and holidays, you can try and make some savings by eliminating waste or unnecessary purchases.

For example, could you convince your existing lender to offer a better mortgage or personal loan rate; if not, is there another who will? Is there any cheaper credit card on offer? Are your savings enjoying the highest deposit rate on the market? Are you paying over the odds for motor, home, life or health insurance? You should refer to the surveys posted on the Competition and Consumer Protection Commission (CCPC) website, www.consumerhelp.ie or www.bonkers.ie for the best deals, or contact a good non-life broker to compare products and prices on your behalf.

Is there room to cut your food and waste charges bill, either by eliminating wastage or by switching to a better value supermarket? By only shopping with a list, and avoiding any impulse purchases, you could actually reduce your weekly bill. Are you and your family paying too much for energy, telephone, internet and mobile phone bills? This is one area of expenditure that has exploded in recent years and deserves being carefully scrutinised. If you have children in the family a spending and time limit should be placed on internet usage. What about bank charges and interest repayments? Is your bank providing good value? Would it pay you to switch to another bank?

Once you have trimmed your expenditure page of wasteful and unnecessary spending you can now allocate to your budget all the different categories of spending events and purchases. Some will be pretty immutable: the mortgage, car loans, utilities and insurance. Others will be a moveable feast, depending on the month or season. For example, you may need to budget for higher spending in August and September to accommodate the children going back to school and in December for Christmas. The month in which a summer holiday is booked will also eat into your (usually) fixed income more than non-holiday months.

A good way to tackle this is to set up a payment plan at your bank or Credit Union, in which all your major outgoings are estimated. The bank then averages this expenditure over a year and arranges for an overdraft facility to cover those months when your expenses are higher than usual - but which have been budgeted for. Over the course of the year, your income and expenditure usually balance out, with only a small drawdown on the overdraft. Costs are kept to a minimum, and there are no monthly money crises to deal with.

Savings and investments

An important part of any personal budget exercise is the review of your savings and investments. Everyone needs a good savings account, into which you hold sufficient cash reserves to see you over any short-term financial emergency, such as illness, temporary unemployment. Ideally, such a fund should amount to between three and six months net income. It might take you some time to build up this fund, so start making steady contributions as soon as you can, ideally from the moment you start drawing your first pay cheque.

If you have achieved any savings over the year, you should prioritise how it can be allocated: expensive debt like credit card and store card balances should be paid off first. Paying off a higher portion of your mortgage each month will have a disproportionate positive impact on the capital sum because of the effect of compound interest on long term debt.

If debt is not an issue you can use your budget savings to increase your pension contributions, to build up your emergency fund, to start a longer term investment fund or to even buy individual stocks and shares or some gold or silver.

An investment fund is aimed at longer term financial goals - the purchase of a house, to cover education costs for your children, early retirement.

"Everyone needs a good savings account into which you hold sufficient cash reserves to see you over a short-term emergency."

The 2008 economic and stock market crash frightened many investors out of the stock markets, but carefully selected investments, over the longer term, always outperform deposits, which are not only vulnerable to inflation but are providing near zero yields for most savers.

Many people still have to make significant changes to their spending patterns and lifestyle. We need to also take into account factors like currency risk and Ireland's position within the wider eurozone.

Every year going forward, on your personal Budget Day, you should review the state of your savings/investments and occupational pension fund. If you are unhappy with its performance, find out why it has under performed and research the affordable alternatives.

Once your budget is in place, you can hopefully rest more easily: your income and expenditure is under control for the time being. You have reviewed the important financial contracts - mortgages, loans, insurance policies - and have made savings on other essential purchases like food, clothing, utilities and transport costs.   If you budget for an annual holiday and Christmas spending, there is less chance for mad overspending.

Children, of course, learn by example. When they see how you keep control of your spending, and having a responsible attitude towards debt and savings, chances are they will develop the same good habits. Their own savings account and a spending ledger could be one of the best gifts you give them this year.

What goes into your personal budget		
Annual Income		**€**
Salary		
Commissions		
Bonuses		
Pensions		
Part-time earnings		
Total Income		
Annual Expenditure - Essential Spending		
Income tax/PRSI/USC		
Mortgage/rent		
Childcare costs		
Pension contributions		
Utilities:	Gas/oil	
	Electricity	
	Telephone	
	Mobile	
	Internet (ISDN/Broadband)	
	TV and cable	
	Local property tax (LPT)	
Insurance:	Life insurance	
	Health	
	Home and contents	
	Motor	
	Travel / pet	
Food:	Grocery (weekly/daily)	
Clothing:	Essential purchases and uniforms	
Transport:	Bus or train tickets,	
	Car tax, petrol and maintenance	
Bank account charges & loan repayments		
Charitable donations		
Christmas:	Gifts	
	Food	
	Alcohol	
	Entertainment	
	Savings and investments	
Total expenditure		

Annual Expenditure - Non-essential or discretionary spending	€
Private education fees/expenses/donations	
Holidays: Transport	
Accommodation and food	
Travel insurance	
Entertainment	
Souvenirs	
Kennel fees	
Hobbies & Entertainment:	
Eating and drinking	
Entertainment	
Memberships and equipment	
DVD's, CD's	
Books, cinema, theatre, sports	
Tickets	
Collector's items	
Pets	
Gifts - birthday, weddings anniversary etc.	
Consumables: Clothing	
Jewellery	
Personal grooming products & services	
Electrical equipment	
Gadgets	
Newspapers & magazines	
Snacks, food, drink	
Total Non Essential expenditure	

Personal insolvency and bankruptcy

The Insolvency Service of Ireland (www.isi.gov.ie) has been in operation since the Autumn of 2013 and there are now 110 PIPs or authorized Personal Insolvency Practitioners who have returned over 8,000 people to solvency and have arranged over 120,000 informal deals between debtors and creditors. Over four billion euro worth of debt has been written off by creditors in the successful settlements.

To encourage more debtors to come forward, the ISI waive all its fees and charges for the application of a Debt Relief Notice certificate, Debt Settlement Arrangement certificate and for a Personal Insolvency Arrangement certificate.

Personal Insolvency Practitioners are also remunerated within the ISI process; debtors seeking insolvency protection will not be required to pay any fees or charges.

The purpose of the insolvency regime is to provide much needed financial debt relief for the tens of thousands of Irish borrowers who accumulated too much debt, especially mortgage debt, during the economic boom. The Irish property market has still not fully recovered from its collapse a decade ago but the number of homeowners in arrears continues to fall. Just under 62,000 residential mortgage homeowners remain in arrears, with about 43,300 in arrears of more than 90 days. Over 94,000 other mortgage holders are categorised as having been restructured.

Informal debt repayment arrangements do not suit everyone, and these debtors may be better served applying for a

- A Debt Relief Notice (DRN).

- A Debt Settlement Arrangement (DSA).

- A Personal Insolvency Arrangement (PIA).

Debt Relief Notice (DRN)

Its purpose is to give relief from debt to people who have little or no disposable income or assets to use to repay what they owe. The qualifying debt can be worth up to €35,000. The DRN process, which involves the assistance of a registered approved intermediary with the Money Advice and Budget Service enables eligible insolvent debtors to write off their debts where they can prove they are not in a position to repay them and it is unlikely their financial situation will improve in the next three years. At the end of the three years the debtor will be discharged of their debt.

Debt Settlement Arrangement (DSA)

A DSA only includes most unsecured debts without a limit on the amount of debt. It differs from a Personal Insolvency Arrangement (PIA) as it only includes unsecured debts that are not backed by an asset of value, like a property. A DSA requires the engagement of a Personal Insolvency Practitioner (PIP) and it must be agreed by the debtor and approved at a creditor's meeting by 65% of creditors (in value). In addition it must be processed by the Insolvency Service of Ireland (ISI) and approved by the Court.

Under a DSA, a debtor's unsecured debts subject to the DSA, will be settled over a period of up to five years (extendable to six years in certain circumstances). If the arrangement is successful, the debtor will be discharged from debts specified in the DSA at the end of the period.

Personal Insolvency Arrangement (PIA)

A PIA can include most secured and unsecured debts, to a limit of €3 million unless all secured creditors consent to the inclusion of a higher amount. The PIA requires the engagement of a PIP, but it differs from a Debt Settlement Arrangement (DSA) as it includes secured debt, backed or secured by an asset, such as a mortgaged property. A PIA must be agreed by the debtor and approved at a creditors' meeting by a qualified majority of creditors. In addition it must be processed by the ISI and approved by the Court.

Under a PIA, a debtor's unsecured debts will be settled over a period of up to six years (extendable to seven years in certain circumstances) and the debtor is released from those unsecured debts at the end of that period.

Secured debts can be restructured under a PIA, for example, to provide for payments for a certain period or a write-down of a portion of negative equity. Depending on the terms of the PIA, the debtor may be released from a secured debt at the end of the PIA period or the secured debt can continue to be payable by the debtor (although perhaps on restructured terms).

Bankruptcy

Bankruptcy is no longer a lifelong sentence in Ireland. Instead it has a discharge date, usually within 12 months, whereby the property or assets of the debtor who is unable or unwilling to pay their debts is transferred to a person, (called a trustee or Official Assignee), given charge of the property by the High Court to be sold. This is the person who administers the estate of bankrupt persons.

When the property or assets are sold, the costs, expenses, court fees and certain priority debts are paid. After this, the net proceeds are distributed to those owed money (the creditors).

Bankruptcy proceedings begin with the filing of the application in the Office of the Examiner of the High Court. Following this, the proceedings are dealt with by the High Court. At the end of the now one year discharge period (it had been three years up to December 2015), the person is entirely debt free.

Personal Insolvency Practitioner (PIP)

Anyone who believes they may qualify for a DRN should contact an Approved Intermediary (AI) to begin proceedings. A register of 13 AI's appears on the ISI website. A register of 110 Personal Insolvency Practitioners is also available on the ISI website. There is no charge to the debtor for their services. All three options carry certain costs and fees. To be a successful applicant for a DSA or PIA, the debtor must have a certain level of income or assets to offer creditors over and above their own monthly Reasonable Living Expenses, as set out in the ISI guidelines. Where the debtor is already living below those living expenses, they may be unable to pay their debts and they may be advised to consider bankruptcy.

PIA applicants with secured mortgage debt must also have undergone a Mortgage Arrears Resolution Process before they can apply for a PIA.

The consequences of going insolvent or bankrupt can be onerous. The five or six year period of insolvency supervision and living under a strict budget will be difficult and the debtor may not be able to remain in their family home, though every effort is expected to be made to allow them to do so.

Any increased income, bonuses and inheritances received during the term of an insolvency can be paid to your creditors in part or full. Creditors may be able to claw back the growth in the value of your family home for up to 20 years after a discharge of a PIA if there has been debt writeoff. The debtor will need to inform their PIP of applications for credit or new bank accounts during the arrangement.

Where someone goes bankrupt, the person will not be allowed to hold a company directorship, hold certain public offices and some employment contracts could be compromised. Assets may be sold, including the family home...or not, depending on the amount of negative equity. In that case, the Official Assignee is unlikely to dispose of the property.

What the insolvency and bankruptcy process is expected to do, is to provide considerable or full debt relief and provide debtors with a chance to rebuild their lives and start again with a clear, debt-free financial state.

See www.isi.gov.ie or www.backontrack.ie for more information about the Insolvency Service of Ireland.

5. Buying a home

Buying a home is a big investment and an anxious time for most of us. Property prices have been recovering strongly from their 2013 post-boom floor, but our history of property booms and busts should be proof enough that there are few guarantees when it comes to house prices. For one thing, there remains the problem of attaining a mortgage especially if you are also struggling to pay record-high rents. To buy a home today you will need to have a 20% minimum deposit unless you are a first-time buyer.

The introduction of a limited Help to Buy tax incentive scheme for first time buyers of new homes further eased the deposit pressure, but long gone are the controversial 100% or interest only loans. There are also fairly rigid income to debt multiples of just three and a half times earnings. Buy-to-let borrowers must also have higher down payments – up to 30% in some cases - and existing ones have discovered that interest-only terms are not being extended once their initial term expires.

The most competitive mortgage of all, the tracker mortgage, which 'tracks' the European Central Bank (ECB) rate, has long gone, but most borrowers who secured trackers and did not switch to a fixed rate before they were withdrawn, continue to enjoy its security. The cost of their loan is priced based on the ECB lending rate plus an agreed interest premium, typically an extra 1%. With the ECB base rate still at zero percent, under no circumstances should holders amend their payment method if it means the loss of this valuable payment product.

Start saving

If an average new home costs in the region of €250,000, and you have already been a property owner, you will typically need a minimum of €50,000 as a down payment according to the Central Bank's revised lending criteria. First time buyers will only need a 10% down payment, or €25,000 in order to purchase the €250,000 value property. The 3.5 times income to loan limit means a first-time buyer couple would need to have joint income of about €64,300 to qualify for a mortgage of €225,000. Lenders are permitted to exceed these borrowing limits in up to 20% of the euro value of all their residential housing loans, but only to borrowers who can completely satisfy the risks associated with higher repayments.

To meet the higher downpayment and tighter lending conditions savers face very challenging obstacles, particularly as interest rates remain at historic lows across all deposit institutions and prospective buyers need to choose with care the highest yielding accounts possible, though they are not usually required to save with any particular institution in order to secure a mortgage from them at a later date.

Choosing a lender

Once you have the appropriate minimum capital and have found the home of your choice, you need to start shopping around for the best mortgage. All the lenders include up-to-date mortgage offers on their websites plus lending calculators that help you work out what your loan will cost you. The property supplements in the major newspapers publish updated rates from all the leading lenders and sometimes these lists also include a column which shows the cost per thousand euro borrowed so that you can quickly calculate the monthly repayment of the mortgage you have in mind. There are also cost comparison websites – www.consumerhelp.ie (the Competition and Consumer Protection Commission) and www.bonkers.ie that also list the various offers.

The banks have increased mortgage lending, but large numbers of mortgage applications are still being refused or discouraged, and you may want to use the services of a reliable mortgage intermediary to help secure a loan.

Income conditions

All lenders require certain income conditions before they will give you a mortgage. Lending conditions were very relaxed during the boom years, when credit was cheap and plentiful and property inflation was high. But the bursting of the property bubble and the collapse of the banks has meant that conservative lending is back. Buyers cannot borrow the five, six, seven times multiple of income that banks had been extending, even with substantial down payments. Instead, under the Central Bank's revised lending criteria a couple earning just over €40,000 and €24,300 respectively, or €64,300 per annum who are existing or previous owners, will be faced with a price ceiling of approximately €250,000 out of which €50,000 will be the downpayment and €200,000 the mortgage.

House purchase related costs

Other costs which may be connected with home purchase include: application or arrangement fees, legal and valuation fees, administration fees, indemnity bonds (which are now being required again by some lenders) and stamp duty as well as the cost of furnishing your new home.

Stamp duty

One of the most significant costs for anyone buying a home is Stamp Duty. The Stamp Duty rate for all residential properties is;

Aggregate consideration	Rate of duty
First €1,000,000	1%
Excess over €1,000,000	2%

The stamp duty rate for non-residential properties is a flat 7.5% rate in respect of instruments executed after 9 October 2019.

Fees

Home buyers can expect to pay up to 1.5% of the purchase price of the property plus VAT, in legal fees. But competitive rates can be found with solicitors reducing their fees for this type of business, so you should shop around.

Lenders vary considerably in the way they apply charges. Some, for example, insist on charging you their legal costs, calculated as a percentage of the loan up to a maximum amount. It could amount to as much as €250 to €350. If a lender's fees seem low in comparison to another, take a good look at the interest rates being charged. Both in the first year when a discount of half to one percent may apply and over the longer term, when you will revert to the normal interest rate.

Mortgage interest relief

Mortgage interest relief is a tax relief based on the amount of interest you pay in a tax year on a qualifying mortgage loan. Mortgages taken out after 31 December 2012 are not eligible for mortgage interest relief. Mortgages taken out between 1 January 2004 to 31 December 2012, are eligible for mortgage interest relief until 31 December 2020. Your lender applies tax relief on your qualifying mortgage loan directly through the Tax Relief at Source (TRS) scheme. This means that your mortgage provider will reduce your monthly mortgage repayments or make a direct payment into your bank account equal to the amount of tax relief you are entitled to.

A qualifying loan, is a secured loan which was used to purchase, repair, develop or improve your principal private residence situated in Ireland.

You can also claim tax relief, subject to the maximum allowance, in respect of interest paid by you for your separated/divorced spouse or former partner in a dissolved civil partnership, or a dependent relative for whom you are claiming a dependent relative allowance.

Amount of mortgage interest relief /tax relief at source (TRS)

Mortgage interest relief was due to cease at the end of 2017. It was extended on a reducing basis for a further three years. If you were entitled to the relief at the end of 2017 then it automatically continues on a reduced basis until the end of 2020.

The table below shows how the qualifying interest reduction will take effect:

Qualifying interest			
2017	2018	2019	2020
100%	75%	50%	25%

The ceilings or upper thresholds on the amount of interest paid that qualifies for tax relief are dependant on -

- The status of the individual, that is, whether they are married, in a civil partnership or single; **and**

- Whether they are a first time buyer

The ceiling or upper thresholds on the amount of interest allowable are also reduced for each of the three years as follows;

First time buyers				
	2017 €	2018 €	2019 €	2020 €
Single	10,000	7,500	5,000	2,500
Married, in a civil partnership, widowed or surviving civil partner	20,000	15,000	10,000	5,000

Non-first time buyers				
	2017 €	2018 €	2019 €	2020 €
Single	3,000	2,250	1,500	750
Married, in a civil partnership, widowed or surviving civil partner	6,000	4,500	3,000	1,500

"A loan for the purchase of an investment property does not qualify for mortgage interest relief."

First time buyers

The rate of relief payable for the first seven years is currently;

● 25% for years one and two.

● 22.5% for years three, four and five.

● 20% for years six and seven.

Lower rates apply if you bought your first home before 2009. After year seven, the rates and thresholds for relief revert to those of a non-first time buyer.

If you bought your first home between 2004 and 2008 inclusive, the rate of relief for the tax years 2012 to 2020 is 30%.

You can claim the full amount of relief due if;

● A parent acts as a co-mortgagor or guarantor for a first time buyer.

● The parent does not pay any of the mortgage.

Non-first time buyers

The rate of relief paid on qualifying home loans is currently 15%.

How to claim mortgage interest relief (TRS)

Mortgage interest relief must be claimed online at www.revenue.ie/en/online/mortgage-interest-relief.html.

You can contact the TRS Help Line on 1890 46 36 26 or by email at trsadmin@revenue.ie.   You can claim mortgage interest relief for previous years up to a maximum of four years.

De-registering your loan for mortgage interest relief (TRS)

If your property ceases to be your principal private residence, if you decide to rent the property and the mortgage is not paid off, or if your loan's qualifying percentage changes you must notify Revenue immediately. You can do this by using a TRS 4 form (available on www.revenue.ie) or by contacting the Revenue TRS help line on 1890 46 36 26.

Help to buy scheme (HTB) for first time buyers

In an effort to help first time buyers accumulate a big enough deposit under the Central Bank mortgage rules to buy a home, a Help to Buy Scheme was introduced. From January 2017, under this scheme first time buyers are able to claim a tax rebate equal to 5% of the value of the newly built property (including self-builds). The rebate is capped at €20,000. The rebate can be claimed on new homes bought between 19 July, 2016 and 31st December 2021.

The total tax rebate is limited to the total income tax and DIRT paid over the previous four tax years and is capped at €20k. The 5% only applies to properties valued at up to €600,000 for contracts signed in the period 19 July to 31 December 2016 or in the case of self-builds where the first tranche of mortgage drawdown was between those dates. From 1 January 2017, the maximum property value is €500,000. The maximum refund available is €20,000.

To claim HTB you must;

- Be a first time buyer.
- Buy or build a property between 19 July 2016 and 31 Dec 2021.
- Live in the property as your PPR for five years after you build/buy it.
- Be tax compliant, if you are self assessed you must also have a tax clearance.

Also, you must not have previously bought or built a house or apartment either on your own or jointly with another person.

The first time buyer applicants must take out a mortgage of at least 70% of the purchase price, or in the case of a self-build, at least 70% of the valuation approved by the mortgage provider.

Examples of rebate amounts from 1 Jan 2018

Purchase price €	Maximum tax rebate
€200,000	€10,000
€250,000	€12,500
€300,000	€15,000
€400,000	€20,000
€500,000	€20,000
€501,000	NIL

"Gone are the easy mortgage based loans which allowed the homeowner to extend the kitchen and buy a new SUV."

Interest rates and the cost of borrowing

The cost of borrowing for a mortgage in Ireland is nearly twice that of continental Europe, a legacy of the catastrophic collapse of the property bubble and banks and the large number of restructured mortgages and ongoing arrears. Nearly a decade later, tens of thousands of properties remain in negative equity.

The average standard variable interest rate in 2019 was c3.1%, and while the ECB base rate has fallen to zero percent these relatively low current mortgage rates and especially tracker rates of as little as 0.5%-0.75% are not sustainable over a typical 25 or 30 year repayment term.

The important thing for every prospective homebuyer is to take account of as many unforeseen circumstances as possible.

Although many couples are dual earners, an unexpected event, like illness, redundancy or even the arrival of a new baby, can put considerable strain on a family budget. A €250,000 mortgage being repaid at 3% interest will result in monthly repayments of €1,054 over 30 years; if it rises 2% to 5% - and all mortgages must now be stress-tested by 2% - the repayment will rise to about €1,350 per month.

	Repaying a €250,000 annuity mortgage @ 3% x 30 yrs					
End of Year	Annual repayments	Capital repaid	Cumulative capital repaid	Interest paid	Cumulative interest paid	Loan outstanding at end of year
€	€	€	€	€	€	€
1	12,649	5,220	5,220	7,429	7,429	244,780
2	12,648	5,378	10,598	7,270	14,699	239,402
3	12,648	5,542	16,140	7,106	21,805	233,860
4	12,648	5,710	21,850	6,938	28,743	228,150
5	12,648	5,884	27,734	6,764	35,507	222,266
6	12,648	6,063	33,797	6,585	42,092	216,203
7	12,649	6,248	40,045	6,401	48,493	209,955
8	12,649	6,438	46,483	6,211	54,704	203,517
9	12,648	6,633	53,116	6,015	60,719	196,884
10	12,648	6,835	59,951	5,813	66,532	190,049
11	12,648	7,043	66,994	5,605	72,137	183,006
12	12,648	7,257	74,251	5,391	77,528	175,749
13	12,648	7,478	81,729	5,170	82,698	168,271
14	12,648	7,705	89,434	4,943	87,641	160,566
15	12,648	7,940	97,374	4,708	92,349	152,626
16	12,648	8,181	105,555	4,467	96,816	144,445
17	12,648	8,430	113,985	4,218	101,034	136,015
18	12,649	8,687	122,672	3,962	104,996	127,328
19	12,648	8,951	131,623	3,697	108,693	118,377
20	12,648	9,223	140,846	3,425	112,118	109,154
21	12,649	9,504	150,350	3,145	115,263	99,650
22	12,649	9,793	160,143	2,856	118,119	89,857
23	12,648	10,090	170,233	2,558	120,677	79,767
24	12,648	10,397	180,630	2,251	122,928	69,370
25	12,649	10,714	191,344	1,935	124,863	58,656
26	12,648	11,039	202,383	1,609	126,472	47,617
27	12,648	11,375	213,758	1,273	127,745	36,242
28	12,648	11,721	225,479	927	128,672	24,521
29	12,648	12,078	237,557	570	129,242	12,443
30	12,648	12,445	250,000	203	129,445	0

Below we illustrate the typical monthly repayments on a €250,000 loan, assuming annual interest rates of 3.0% 4.00%, 4.50%, 5.00% and 5.50% p.a. over four lending periods:

Monthly repayments - €250,000 loan *				
Rate	20 yrs	25 yrs	30 yrs	35 yrs
3.00%	€1,387	€1,186	€1,054	€962
4.00%	€1,515	€1,320	€1,194	€1,107
4.50%	€1,582	€1,390	€1,267	€1,183
5.00%	€1,650	€1,461	€1,342	€1,262
5.50%	€1,720	€1,535	€1,419	€1,343

* Repayments do not include mortgage interest relief

The longer your mortgage term, the cheaper the monthly repayment will be. But when the total cost of interest and capital repayments are added up, an extra five or ten years will cost you thousands of extra euro over the entire term.

Total repayments over mortgage term - €250,000 loan				
Rate	20 yrs	25 yrs	30 yrs	35 yrs
3.00%	€332,800	€355,800	€379,440	€404,040
4.00%	€363,600	€396,000	€429,840	€464,940
4.50%	€379,680	€417,000	€456,120	€496,860
5.00%	€396,000	€438,300	€483,120	€530,040
5.50%	€412,800	€460,500	€510,840	€564,060

Example

Using the figures from the above charts you see that a €250,000 loan arranged over 25 years at 3.0% interest will cost €1,186 per month, but the same loan stretched out over a further five years will only cost €1,054 per month, a "saving" of €132 per month. However, the extra five year lending term, will amount to an extra €23,640 in mortgage payments overall.

Anyone who finds a lender that agrees to a 30 or even 35 year mortgage should try to accelerate their payments after a few years, when their income has increased and the high early costs associated with home ownership have diminished.

Mortgage lenders: choose carefully

Although lending is still very tight in Ireland as the banks continue to try and repair their balance sheets, choosing a mortgage lender that offers the best, long-term interest rate, is very important. By carefully shopping around, you may be able to save yourself a considerable sum of money over the term of your loan.

Mortgage repayment methods

Annuity based

The annuity method, also known as a repayment mortgage, is the most common way to pay off a mortgage. Annuity mortgages involve the payment each month of interest and some of the principal of the loan. In the early years, the bulk of the payment is interest, on which tax relief at source may be available. Although mortgage interest relief is no longer available to purchasers after the end of 2012, it will be finally abolished by the end of 2020 (see page 79 for more details).

As the years progress, you will pay less interest and more capital until eventually your entire loan will be cleared. A typical repayment mortgage will be repaid as illustrated on page 84, over a 30 year term.

Endowment mortgage

Endowment mortgages are rarely negotiated anymore, mainly because of high costs and their being reliant on the performances of investment markets.

Unlike conventional annuity mortgages, in which you repay both interest and capital each month, an endowment mortgage, also known as an 'investment' mortgage, involves only the repayment of interest and also an additional investment into a life-assurance based unitised or with profits funds. The interest payment attracts full mortgage interest relief subject to the normal limits (although mortgage interest relief is no longer available to purchasers after the end of 2012 and will be finally abolished by the end of 2020 see page 79 for more details) but the high costs associated with these types of mortgages have had the effect of eating into the investment fund, especially during periods of stock market volatility. Any performance shortfall has to be made up with higher endowment contributions either during the lifetime of the mortgage or at maturity in order to pay off the capital sum.

Pension mortgage

A pension mortgage is similar to an endowment mortgage, in that only interest is paid on the loan during the term of the contract. In this case, the investment vehicle which is used to pay off the capital is the homeowner's personal pension plan. Under Revenue rules, a quarter of the final pension fund value can be paid out as a tax-free lump sum up to a maximum of €200,000 and it is this sum which is used to repay the mortgage capital. Pension mortgages are subject to the investment performance of underlying assets in the pension fund and should be regularly reviewed.

Variable or fixed rate?

Should you arrange your mortgage on a variable interest rate basis or fix the interest for a period of years? Nearly all new borrowers are offered a discounted fixed rate for the first year of their loan, which usually amounts to a saving of a couple of hundred euro. In year two, you immediately revert to the variable rate of interest, which can go up and down over the term of the mortgage.

A fixed interest rate can provide considerable peace of mind and protect the borrower from the volatility of world money markets, but you can also suffer financially - if rates fall and your rate is fixed at a higher level for a few more years. The cost of breaking a fixed rate mortgage can be very high. Some banks charge nearly the entire interest balance that they could have expected to earn if you had seen out the contract.

Trackers

A tracker mortgage, whereby the cost of the loan for the entire repayment term is linked to the current ECB bank rate plus a premium rate, typically 1%, has proved to be advantageous to those borrowers who were able to secure one before they were withdrawn by the main lenders. These loans are costly for the banks, and their policy is to discourage tracker customers from keeping them by recommending that in some cases they fix their loans instead, in an effort to avoid what may or may not be higher ECB rates in the future. Existing tracker contracts are protected under Consumer Credit legislation and cannot be arbitrarily withdrawn by the lender as a result of the restructuring of a mortgage, though thousands of trackers were treated this way. This tracker scandal is still under investigation and has resulted in monetary compensation and in some cases, reinstatement at the direction of the Central Bank of Ireland.

No one should transfer their tracker to a variable rate loan unless the lender offers substantial capital write off. Always refer to the tracker lending terms in your original mortgage contract.

Mortgage and home insurance

The monthly mortgage repayment is not the only one you have to make. Mortgage protection and buildings insurance are compulsory in most cases and can cost up to 10% of your gross monthly mortgage repayments.

Mortgage protection insurance is a life assurance policy that covers the value of the mortgage and ensures that your debt to the bank or building society is repaid in the event of your death or that of your spouse. Rates are based on age and the premiums can be paid monthly or annually. You are not obliged to purchase the policy from the lender and you should shop around for the best market rate, especially if you are a smoker.

Many new home owners arrange serious illness cover as part of their mortgage protection policy, in order that the loan can be paid off not only if they die but also in the event of a life-threatening illness. The cost is higher, but can be mitigated against by arranging the policy on a decreasing term basis.

Example

You and your spouse have a mortgage of €225,000 over 30 years. You are both age 29 and non-smokers. The monthly cost of a conventional mortgage protection plan which includes accelerated serious illness cover,(the benefit of which will pay out once on the earlier event of either serious illness or death), will work out approximately as follows:

Plan type	Monthly cost
Conventional mortgage protection plan	€18.44
Mortgage protection plan plus accelerated serious illness cover	€80.73

* Based on rates December 2019

Protect your mortgage repayments

If you are concerned about how your mortgage would be paid if you became ill or were made redundant, even for a short period of time, you could take out mortgage payment protection cover, but 'buyer beware'! This type of insurance can work out very expensive, relative to any benefits and there has been widespread misselling of this insurance. An investigation by the Central Bank has resulted in tens of millions of euro of compensation paid to consumers who were missold PPI.

"Mortgage protection and building insurance are compulsory"

Available from all the major lenders, it costs about €5 - €6 for every €100 cover required per month and may pay out benefits if you become ill or disabled and are unable to work, or have been made redundant. You cannot be self-employed to make a claim or work fewer than 18 hours a week. You will need to have been out of work for at least 30 days before your first claim can be made. Some firms impose up to a six month exclusion period, and there is generally a 12 month payment limit per claim. You need to very carefully read the terms and conditions under which benefits are paid before you take out such a policy and if you already have permanent health insurance (PHI) or serious illness cover, this type of policy may be unnecessary.

Protect the building

Building insurance is also compulsory if you take out a mortgage. Again, the lender wants to protect their share of the property in the event of a fire or another disaster. The premiums are based not on the market value of the property, but on the cost of rebuilding. It is important that you have the property surveyed to ensure the rebuilding cost is correct and any changes in the cost of materials and labour are taken into account.

Most general insurance companies offer combined buildings and contents policies. Some automatically provide contents cover worth up to half the value of the building cover. With the price of buildings insurance rising sharply in recent years it is advisable to shop around at every renewal date or engage an independent financial advisor to help you find the right policy for you and to ensure you put a correct value on your fittings and personal belongings. Premium discounts may be available, which will depend on your age, whether the house is occupied during the daytime and if it is fitted with approved locks, fire and burglar alarms etc. Accepting a higher 'excess' payment can also reduce your annual premium.

Coping with mortgage debt

House prices have made a substantial recovery and while the demand for family homes in desirable neighbourhoods with good schools, public transport and other amenities, is very high, price growth has slowed due to the Central Bank mortgage lending restrictions. (The tax incentivised Help to Buy scheme has been extended to the end of 2021 for first time buyers struggling to put a down payment together. See page 82).

The most serious consequence of our extraordinary property boom and bust has been the large number of borrowers still in negative equity - where the balance of their mortgage continues to be greater than the market value of their property.

Efforts continue, however to restructure distressed loans and it is now estimated that fewer than 62,000 households were still in arrears at the end of June 2019, 43,300 of those in arrears of more than 90 days. Over 94,000 other loans have seen their arrears capitalised, have had repayment terms or interest- only facilities extended and a small number have had half the loan "warehoused" with the owners only servicing the other half. The balancing payment in this 'split mortgage' must be repaid at the end of the original mortgage term.

Negative equity

Negative equity, some commentators believe, is less of a problem now than it was, especially if you have no intention or need to sell your home. House prices are cyclical and temporarily depressed house prices are only one aspect of the problem.

What if you happen to have a fixed rate interest arrangement that is maturing and your lender is adamant that you must pay a higher than average annuity interest rate? Negative equity means that you are now tied to your lender - other banks are not interested in taking on a customer with a property that has devalued.

Negative equity becomes a personal financial disaster and not just an unfortunate financial setback, when the mortgage holder struggles to make their repayments or they lose their job. A build up of arrears, default and foreclosure can become a real possibility in such a scenario.

Code of conduct on mortgage arrears (CCMA)

The CCMA requires mortgage lenders to adopt special procedures when dealing with borrowers who are experiencing arrears and financial difficulties. The CCMA requires lenders to wait eight months before taking legal action on mortgages in arrears. However, this requirement will not apply if the borrower is deliberately not co-operating with the lender.

The revised code states that borrowers deemed to be not co-operating may also find that they will not be eligible for a Personal Insolvency Arrangement in accordance with the Personal Insolvency Act 2012.

However, mortgage holders who are in arrears and insolvent and have not been cooperating with their lender can seek free insolvency and legal assistance from the 'Abhaile' Mortgage Arrears and Resolution Service scheme, launched in conjunction with MABS, Flac, the free legal aid service and the Insolvency Service of Ireland. (see www.MABS.ie; www.isi.gov.ie)

The revised Code requires that

- Lenders have in place an Arrears Support Unit (ASU), established in accordance with Provision 17, in respect of these cases.

- Has in place the correct procedure for dealing with each type of borrower - those in mortgage arrears, those in pre-arrears and those who fall under the MARP.

Such procedures must:

- Allow for a flexible approach in the handling of these cases;

- Be aimed at assisting the borrower as far as possible in their particular circumstances;

- Set out how the lender will implement the four steps of the MARP; **and**

- Set out how the ASU will assess cases referred to it, including the types of alternative repayment arrangements or any other relief method that may be offered to borrowers by the lender.

Significant changes in the revised code include the commencement of legal proceedings against borrowers in 90 days arrears who have been deemed by the lender to have not co-operated with the Mortgage Arrears Resolution Process within 20 days of receiving a notice to that effect. In such circumstances legal action can proceed immediately. Other options may also become available, including voluntary surrender of the property, trading down, mortgage to rent or a voluntary sale.

The revised code also allows for unsolicited personal visits, by the lender when all other attempts at contact in relation to the borrower's arrears have failed and immediately prior to classifying a borrower as not co-operating.

For a copy of the revised CCMA:
http://www.centralbank.ie/publicinformation/Documents/2013%20CCMA.pdf

Local property tax (LPT)

Residential property owners are liable for local property tax (LPT) based on the self-assessment market value of their property on 1 May 2013.

Property values are grouped into value bands. A rate of 0.18% applies to the midpoint of the value band up to €1m. Payments relate to the market value of your property on 1 May 2013 and have now been extended a further four years, from 1 November 2016 to 2020. (See Chapter 3, page 50 for the LPT valuation table). The LPT liability for property valued at over €1m will be calculated as 0.18% on the first €1m and 0.25% on the portion over €1m.

Exemptions

Certain properties are exempt from LPT if they meet the relevant qualifying conditions. Exemptions apply to all properties purchased in 2013 and to new and previously unused properties purchased from a builder or developer between from 1 January 2013 to 31 October 2016. Properties that have been certified as having significant pyritic damage are also exempt from LPT (see revenue.ie for a full list of exemptions). When LPT was introduced in 2013, property owners who qualified for an LPT exemption were required to claim the relevant exemption by filing an LPT Return. In most cases a residential property that was exempt from LPT on 1 May 2013 continues to be exempt until the end of the current valuation period, even where the property is sold or ownership is transferred by way of gift or an inheritance.

Deferrals

A system of deferral arrangements for owner-occupiers where there is an inability to pay the LPT under specified conditions (e.g. where the gross income does not exceed €15,000 - single and €25,000 - couple). Some owner-occupiers may be eligible to apply for marginal relief, which will allow them to defer up to 50% of their LPT liability. It should be noted that interest will be charged on deferred amounts at a rate of 4% per annum.

6 Insurance

Everyone has something to protect - your wealth, your health, your life and those dearest to you. Insuring your own life against sudden serious illness or unexpected death relieves the financial burden on your dependents. Insuring your car, home and contents is yet another way for you to avoid financial disaster should anything unexpected happen to you.

There are a number of different ways for you to arrange your insurance. You can either contact an insurance company of your choice directly or you can arrange insurance through your bank, building society, through a service provider like a motor association or on-line. Alternatively, you can contact an independent financial advisor or broker who can offer you advice on the type of insurance protection that best suits your needs and your budget. Keep in mind that on-line purchases are usually based on execution-only service and you may need to do your own research.

"Ten times the size of your net after tax salary is a standard gauge for the amount of life cover you should have."

Life assurance

The purpose of life insurance is to make sure that your dependents are financially secure in the event of your death. As a general rule, the younger you are, the better your health and the safer your lifestyle, the cheaper the cost of your insurance. You may not be able to obtain any life assurance cover at all if you are suffering from a serious illness. Alternatively, you could be offered insurance at a premium price - which, in insurance jargon is called 'loading'. For example, a 50% loading could mean you pay 50% more than the average insured person of your age for the same amount of life cover.

How much cover do you need?

Ten times the size of your net, after-tax, salary is a standard gauge for the amount of life insurance cover you should have. A good rule of thumb when trying to decide your total level of cover, is to aim to provide a fund to adequately replace your income in the event of your premature death. This means that your income, the number and ages of your dependents, your assets and outstanding loan commitments etc. all have to be carefully considered. You may find that you don't need as much 'stand-alone' life cover as you might initially think if your employment benefits package includes a 'death-in-service' benefit and a spouse's/dependent's pension, or if your mortgage is covered by mortgage protection insurance. This is invaluable advice that an independent financial advisor or broker will be able to offer you.

Life assurance is arranged for a fixed number of years and comes in a number of forms:

Level term cover

This type of cover is relatively inexpensive, and it only pays out at death and has no underlying investment value. Quite simply, when you take out a term assurance plan, you agree to pay a specific or level premium over a pre-agreed number of years. Every year, as you get older, your risk of death increases so your level premium is based on the average risk of death.

'Averaging' means that in the early years of your plan you will pay too much in proportion to the actual risk of death involved, and this extra premium in the early years is used to 'subsidise' the cost of your life assurance benefit in later years. If your plan is discontinued, or in the event of an early claim before your pre-agreed number of years have elapsed, this surplus will not be repaid.

Convertible term cover

This is slightly more expensive than level term cover but it gives you the flexibility, without any further medical test or examination and regardless of any change in your health circumstances, to convert into another type of policy at any future date in your contract. This could include converting to a guaranteed 'whole of life assurance plan' which could be a very valuable option for you to have because, regardless of any changes in your health, no unexpected 'loadings' are applied to your premium payable at conversion. Like all 'term' covers, this is a protection policy only and it will never acquire a cash value.

Decreasing term cover

This is a variation on the basic 'term' cover, which means that it is a protection policy only. Decreasing term cover is often taken out as a mortgage protection policy where both the requirement and the amount of cover decreases as your mortgage is repaid and your need for protection recedes.

Guaranteed 'whole of life' cover

Effectively 'whole of life' is a term cover protection policy which guarantees to pay a specific sum of money whenever you die, provided of course, that you continue to pay the premiums. Because of 'averaging', your premiums are relatively high at the outset, but they remain unchanged for the entire duration of your life. As you might expect, these policies do not have any residual or investment value but the cost is relatively cheap, particularly when you are young and healthy. They are very suitable if, for example, you are self-employed and don't have a pension plan but you want to provide long term financial protection for a dependent spouse or partner in the event of your death. They are also very useful if you have a disabled child or relative who will need financial protection after your death.

Monthly cost of a male, non-smoker, obtaining €350,000 life assurance cover (Different plan types)

Age next birthday	25	35	45	55
Decreasing Term over 20 yrs	€12.00	€17.48	€35.12	€90.64
Level Term over 20 yrs	€17.62	€25.21	€51.99	€140.75
Convertible Term over 20 yrs	€18.38	€26.34	€54.47	€147.66
Whole of life	€243.05	€325.09	€395.28	€599.34

Notes: The premiums quoted above include a 1% government life assurance levy and are not indexed.

*   Based on rates December 2019

Various life assurance providers often offer discounts on premiums, which are not included in the premium costs above, so be sure to check these with your Financial Advisor.

Unitised whole of life policies

Another type of whole of life policy is the unit-linked one, in which the life assurance company invests your premium in a managed fund that aims to grow at a certain rate and to increase in value over time.

The fund value is not guaranteed and it may grow by enough to pay for your life insurance throughout your life or it may fall short of the amount that is needed to pay for your life insurance. In that case, you may have to pay a higher premium to keep the sum assured at the agreed level and prevent what is commonly known as a "bombing out" effect. Whole-of-life policies have ongoing charges, such as yearly charges for managing the investment fund and sometimes monthly charges for handling your premium. These charges, which can be very high, have the effect of reducing the value of the policy fund so the amount of any benefit paid out on your death is not guaranteed.

For a unitised whole-of-life policy to build up a cash lump sum over and above what is needed to pay for your life insurance, the investment fund will need to provide strong, steady growth. Too often, policy holders have found that their policy has little or no cash value at any time. A better arrangement is usually to de-couple life insurance from savings and buy separate policies.

"Too often, policy holders have found that their policy has little or no cash value."

Changing circumstances

There is a saying among life assurance professionals that 'a little life assurance can be a dangerous thing'. Effectively, what this saying means is that, all too often, the very fact that you know you have 'some kind' of a life assurance cover lulls you into a false sense of security. The years slip by without you ever feeling the need to check and make sure that your 'fixed' level of protection is still sufficient for your 'changing' requirements. It is always good advice to discuss your changing requirements with an independent financial adviser on a regular basis.

Own life / joint life policies

If the policy is an 'own life' plan, effectively you are both the 'life assured' and 'the assured'. This means that the lump sum that is payable from the policy upon your death will form part of your estate and may be subject to inheritance tax. In the case of a joint-life policy, usually taken out by spouses, the death benefit is normally paid to the surviving spouse.

If your policy is arranged on an 'own life' basis, your legal representatives, (i.e. your 'executor' if you have made a Will) may be required to produce a grant of probate and proof of title before the insurance company can pay out the sum assured. However, if no Will exists, the policy benefits will be subject to the law of intestacy and the payments of the proceeds of the life assurance policy will be as set out in the legislation which may not be in accordance with your wishes.

If your life assurance policy is arranged on a 'life of another' basis, then, when you die, that other person becomes the owner of the policy. They can claim the encashment value of the policy from the insurance company by simply producing the policy document, together with your death certificate.

Life assurance under trust

Setting up a life assurance policy under trust is an increasingly popular way of making sure that your policy proceeds will not become part of your estate when you die. In addition, a trust ensures:

- Quick and easy payment of the death benefit. The insurance company will pay the surviving trustee(s), usually your spouse or children, on proof of death and the production of the policy document.

- By being a Trustee of the policy yourself you can maintain a degree of control over the policy during your lifetime. The trust must be set up, by completing a standard trust form and nominating Trustee(s) and the beneficiaries, before you commence the policy.

Exit tax

No tax relief is available for life assurance premiums unless it is set up as part of your pension scheme. The returns from life assurance products funds taken out before 1 January 2001 are paid tax-free. All taxes that were due on profits earned will have already been paid at source by the life assurance fund managers to the Revenue Commissioners.

For products issued after the 1 January 2001 no tax will be imposed within funds on certain 'chargeable events'. However the life assurance company is obliged to deduct exit tax on any gains or investment income generated during the term of the product. This tax will be a final liability tax, for Irish residents. The rate of exit tax is 41%.

Is anyone exempt from exit tax?

- Non-resident individuals.
- A life assurance company.
- An investment undertaking.
- A Revenue approved charity.
- A PRSA provider.
- A credit union.
- The court service.

What is a chargeable event

- A claim, maturity or the full surrender of a policy, including a payment on death or disability.
- A partial encashment, including an automatic income payment.
- An assignment of a life policy in certain circumstances.
- Every eighth anniversary of the policy.

A credit will be given for the tax deducted in year eight against any tax payable on a subsequent chargeable event. Also, where the tax payable on a subsequent chargeable event is lower than the tax deducted on the 8th anniversary the customer will receive a refund of the "overpaid" tax.

Example

€25,000 invested on 1 March 2011.

Deemed encashment 8th anniversary i.e. 1 March 2019.

Cash value at 1 March 2019 is €37,000.

The policy is deemed to be "encashed" and so the gain of €12,000 liable to exit tax @ 41%, is €4,920.

This amount is deducted and paid to Revenue, so the value of the bond immediately after is €32,080.

The bond is then fully encashed on 1 March 2020 with a gross value of €37,750.

In order to calculate the 'chargeable gain' on the encashment, the gross policy value is first increased by the exit tax deducted on the deemed disposal i.e. €4,920.

The gain liable to exit tax of 41% is	€37,750 + €4,920 - €25,000 = €17,670
The exit tax at 41% is	€17,670 x 41% = €7,244
But the previous exit tax deducted of €4,920 is deducted	€7,244 - €4,920 = €2,324

The total exit tax on this policy is €7,244 which is comprised of €4,920 paid on the 8th anniversary plus €2,324 on the subsequent encashment.

Income protection insurance / disability insurance

Unlike life assurance, which only pays out benefits on death, disability or Income Protection Insurance, also known as permanent health insurance (PHI) pay benefits, if you become ill or injured and cannot work. Its aim is to replace your current income - up to retirement age if necessary. It may also be included as part of your pension scheme.

If it is not provided as a benefit of your pension scheme - there is no obligation for employers to provide this benefit, though many workers think they do - you can buy a policy yourself.

How much does it cost?

The cost varies with age, occupation and with the 'deferred period', which is explained in more detail on the next page. Occupation is also a crucial factor in determining the cost of the risk involved and people who work in higher risk jobs and more likely to have an accident or illness and less likely to return to work than those in more sedentary jobs, normally have to pay more.

"There is no obligation for employers to provide this benefit."

Case study

Jack, 40, is an accountant currently earning €85,000 per year. He has chosen to protect 50% of his salary i.e. €42,500 per year until his retirement at age at 65. He selects a 26 week period (deferred period) before benefit becomes payable and chooses to index link his benefit and premiums. Jack's benefit is €42,500 per annum (or €817.31 per week) and he pays a premium of €66.36 net per month after tax relief based on a tax rate of 40% (gross €110.60, which includes the 1% government life assurance levy.

If Jack were to claim on his policy in two years time (aged 42) and his claim lasted for five and half years (benefits are typically paid for five and a half years) then the benefit payable to him would be over €265,513 including indexation. If he were unable to return to work before retirement then over that 23 year period the benefit payable to him would be a total of €1,463,000.

Deferred period

Most disability plans will not pay you any benefit until you have been out of work for at least thirteen weeks - the deferment period. The longer the deferment period, which normally ranges from 4 to 52 weeks, the cheaper the premiums. At the outset of your plan you can decide on the length of the deferment period that best suits your budget and financial protection requirements.

To ensure that you don't end up financially better off claiming benefit, which could leave these plans open to abuse, many disability contracts put a limit on the amount of benefit payable and this limit applies regardless of your maximum level of benefit insured. Normally, you will not be able to receive a benefit that is more than 75% of your average annual earnings in the year prior to your disablement. Many plans also include the value of State disability benefits within this 75% rule.

Tax relief

Disability or income protection insurance premiums are eligible for tax relief at your highest rate of income tax. However, the amount of relief granted cannot exceed 10% of your total income. All disability and income protection insurance benefits are liable to tax under PAYE.

Tax relief for such contributions made by PAYE taxpayers is normally given on a net pay basis i.e. the contributions are deducted from your gross salary prior to the application of income tax. However employee contributions to an income protection insurance scheme do not reduce the pay amount for USC or PRSI purposes.

Loan protection insurance

If you lose your job or become ill and are unable to work, any outstanding personal loans that you are committed to will still have to be repaid. Payment protection insurance, widely sold by the banks for everything from mortgages to credit cards and personal loans, was supposed to be an affordable way for borrowers to meet their obligations should they fall into financial difficulties.

Though still available, loan protection policies have been discredited as a result of widespread misselling.

Designed to cover usually no more than 12 months worth of monthly loan repayments, the polices were supposed to be activated if the holder ever became redundant, sick or disabled. An investigation by the Central Bank has, however, resulted in millions of euro of compensation being paid by the lenders to thousands of payment protection insurance holders who turned out to be unsuitable candidates for this kind of insurance, who were never fully informed of the often excessive costs, or were unaware of the restrictive terms and conditions.

If you already have adequate income protection cover, or a proper emergency savings fund in place, payment protection insurance may be completely unnecessary. After all, the whole purpose of income protection insurance is to provide you with a replacement income so that you can meet your regular outgoings and other financial commitments in the event of a financial setback.

This optional payment protection insurance should not be confused with compulsory mortgage protection insurance. Mortgage protection insurance repays the mortgage in the event of death only.

Serious illness insurance

Serious illness insurance that is linked to a mortgage pays your entire loan if you contract any one of a defined number of serious illnesses.

It is designed to alleviate the financial burdens of anyone who suffers a serious life threatening illness or condition. It does this by paying you a tax-free lump sum on official diagnosis of a serious illness. This lump sum can be used to meet your day-to-day living requirements, pay off your mortgage or even meet the cost of health care.

Illnesses and conditions

The main illnesses and conditions include cancer, heart attack, stroke, kidney disease, multiple sclerosis. However most policies will also pay out for organ transplants, rare ailments like motor neurone disease and CJD, and in the rare chance that you contract HIV by accident or injury. The better policies also pay out benefits in the event of permanent and total disability (PTD) (including loss of limbs, hearing or speech, Alzheimer's disease, etc.), and offer cash benefit options if you are hospitalised.

Every insurer includes a slightly different list of conditions so it is always prudent for you to check these in advance with an independent financial advisor. Although the lump sum benefit is tax-free, there is no tax relief available on serious illness policy premiums.

More recent hybrid serious illness policies now offer other options that can be added to serious illness insurance, such as hospital cash. This is a daily amount that will be paid to you for each complete period of 24 hours you are hospitalised. This limit is usually capped at approximately €200 per day.

Also accident benefit may be an option offered to you by the insurer at an extra cost. Accident benefit is similar to income protection but is only payable if you are temporarily disabled as a result of an accident and are unable to carry out your occupation. It is a weekly amount that is tax free and usually capped at approximately €400 p.w. The deferred period before the benefit is payable, is shorter than income protection, usually about two weeks but the benefit will only be payable for a maximum of 52 weeks.

Mortgage protection

Serious illness cover is a popular part of mortgage protection policies, and both the level of cover and the premium payments can be arranged either on a level or decreasing premium basis.

In the latter case, your cover decreases in value with the decreasing value of your outstanding mortgage. The drawback to this, however, is that although your benefits will clear your outstanding mortgage, there will be no extra cash available to ease any other financial burdens you may face. By arranging your cover on a level term basis, you will be guaranteed a lump sum (the size of the original mortgage) throughout the entire duration of your loan.

Serious illness policies are often arranged by companies for key members of staff or directors. In this context they are known as "keyman" insurance and the benefits are paid, not to the individual but to the company or partners, to lessen any financial burden that they may face because of the absence of that key employee or director.

Mortgage protection case study

Conor and Sinead have a mortgage of €300,000 over 30 years.

They are both age 29 and non-smokers. The monthly cost of a conventional mortgage protection plan and a mortgage protection plan, which included serious illness cover, will work out approximately as follows:

Plan type	Monthly cost
Conventional mortgage protection plan:	€23.84
Mortgage protection plan plus accelerated serious illness cover:	€106.80

Insuring your home and its contents

Your home and its contents are among your most valuable possessions. Insuring them against fire, theft and other damage should be an important priority. If you have a mortgage you must take out compulsory buildings insurance, which varies in price depending on the value of your property, the size, location and rebuilding cost of your property. Your lender requires this insurance, not for your benefit, but for theirs. Their major concern is to protect their financial interest vested in your property. You should take great care, therefore - especially once your mortgage is paid off - to ensure that your building and contents are properly valued and insured.

Proper valuation

The minimum insurance you require is the cost of rebuilding your home in the event of its destruction. Your rebuilding costs are not the same as your mortgage amount, or the market value of your property and rebuilding costs have fallen sharply in recent years. If you have any doubt about the rebuilding cost of your property you should arrange for an independent valuation or survey and check the chartered surveyors annual survey which is available from the Society of Chartered Surveyors at 38 Merrion Square, Dublin 2.

Also, take care not to underinsure your home or contents because most home insurance policies include what is known as an "averaging" clause which determines that if you under insure your property, for example, by 50%, the insurer is only obliged to pay you 50% of your claim.

Nowadays, the cost and the scope of benefits available in home and contents insurance policies vary widely. But with annual premiums rising by as much as 30% it pays to shop around to make sure that you get the best available value in terms of level of claim excesses, exclusions, discounts and risk cover. A good general insurance broker can help you assess the value of your buildings and possessions and carefully choose the right policy for your needs and budget.

The National Competition and Consumer Protection Commission (CCPC www.consumerhelp.ie) produces bi-annual home insurance surveys with several examples of different home values. If in doubt, seek out the best professional advice available.

Health and medical insurance

Over two million people have private health insurance in Ireland, mainly in response to their concerns about long delays in accessing specialist consultants for diagnosis and long hospital waiting lists.

Health insurance still attracts standard rate tax relief, credited at source by the insurer capped on a gross premium of €1,000 per adult, and €500 per student and children (under 21 years of age). A levy applies to health insurance plans as a risk equalisation subsidy to the state owned VHI. From April 1st 2018 the two levy rates for adults are €240 and €399; and two rates for children, €80 and €135. The rate applied depends on the level of insurance cover purchased, those on more advanced policies pay the higher levy.

There are over 400 different health insurance plans provided by the three providers, VHI, Laya Health and Irish Life Health, formerly Aviva Health and GloHealth. (The Gardai and ESB have their own private schemes). The main providers offer both individual and corporate plans that include access to out-patient and in hospital benefits, and to a growing range of other services like 24 hour health information, help lines with a nurse or general practitioner, GP video consultations and life and travel insurance.

All Irish health insurance plans include core, minimum benefits such as in-hospital treatment.

There are no penalties for switching health providers, and there is no age restriction for joining a health insurance plan. All plans are now "Lifetime Community Rated" which means that policyholders cannot be discriminated against, either on a cost or benefits level, because of their age so long as they become a policy holder by age 34.

Anyone who purchased a private health insurance policy for the first time after 1 May 2015 and was aged 35 or older, will be liable to a lifetime 2% price loading for each year over 34 years of age. At age 35 this will result in only a 2% annual higher premium for life, but a 44 year old, for example will pay 20% more.

Someone who was not insured on 1 May 2015 but previously had health insurance can be given credit for the time they were insured, reducing the number of years to which the loading applies.

If the person stopped their insurance cover for periods of unemployment since 1 January 2008, up to three years of credits can be provided and a person who is living outside of Ireland on 1 May 2015 but subsequently moves here, will not be loaded if they are insured within nine months and continue to be insured.

Meanwhile, under the Lifetime Community Rating system, members of private health insurance schemes can also ask for the corporate equivalent of individual plans, at some savings. However, if you decide to switch to a higher benefit plan with your existing provider or a different provider and you have a pre-existing medical condition, you may be subject to a period in which benefits will not be paid for that condition. Be sure to check all terms before you switch.

Private health insurance premiums have more than doubled since 2008 and annual increases are attributed not just to medical inflation, but to the €813 per night public hospital private room charge. This charge has no time limit and is charged to the insurance company even if the patient does not occupy a private room. The standard charge per night, for all patients admitted to a public hospital is €80 a night for a maximum of 10 nights.

The price and terms of all the private health insurance plans can be compared on the Health Insurance Authority website, www.hia.ie or you can hire a specialist health insurance advisor to do the comparison for you.

Hospital cash benefit plan

Sold by non-profit, charitable-status, companies like The Hospital Saturday Fund (HSF) these pay tax-free cash payments to members who need hospitalisation or a range of out-patient treatments.

Premiums, which can be as low as a few euro a week, are age related, but they provide reduced benefits for dependents at no extra cost. Benefits are also paid for routine optical, dental and alternative medical treatments that are not covered by the private health insurers. Daily cash benefits are not paid for routine maternity in-patient stays, but new mothers are paid upon delivery of their baby.

Hospital cash schemes are usually arranged on a group or company basis, but can also be purchased by individuals. There is no tax relief available on these premiums.

As we said at the outset of this chapter, your wealth, your health, your life and those nearest to you are important priorities when it comes to financial protection. Likewise, your home and its contents are among your most valuable possessions. That is why it makes such good sense for you to seek out the best available independent professional advice before making your final decision about what policies and protection arrangements suit your requirements best.

Keep in mind that as you get older, married, or your family commitments change, your protection requirements will change too. So you should regularly check your existing arrangements to ensure that they are still adequate to meet your changing needs and, indeed, to ensure that you are not 'over protecting' yourself in any areas, for example, as your children grow up and become financially independent.

7 Income tax

Individuals whose income is taxed under the PAYE system are obliged to make a return only when requested to do so by their Tax Inspector. Self employed individuals and proprietary company directors must submit a return on or before 31 October for the tax year ending the previous 31 December, whether they are requested to do so or not, under the self assessment system.

If your main income is taxed under the PAYE system and you have other income e.g. rental, dividend income, foreign pension etc., you may be regarded as a "chargeable person". This means that you are required to submit and pay your taxes under the "self assessment" system.

Chargeable person

An individual who is in receipt of income chargeable to tax under the PAYE system but who is also in receipt of substantial gross income from other sources, such as trading, professional or rental income, will be regarded as a "chargeable person" under the self assessment system unless the gross income from all non-PAYE sources is less than €30,000 and the net assessable income is less than €5,000 and the income is coded against PAYE credits.

Proprietary director

A proprietary director is a director of a company who is the beneficial owner of, or is able either directly or indirectly to control more than 15% of the ordinary share capital of the company.   All proprietary directors are "chargeable persons".

Classification of income

Income is classified under a number of headings. These headings are known as schedules and the income falling under each is as follows:

Schedule C:

Those who have deducted income tax from certain payments are assessed under this schedule e.g. banks.

Schedule D:

Case I:	Profits from a trade.
Case II:	Profits from a profession.
Case III:	Interest not taxed at source and all foreign income.
Case IV:	Taxed interest income not falling under any other case or schedule.
Case V:	Rental income from properties in Ireland.

Schedule E:

Income from offices or employments together with pensions, benefits-in-kind and certain lump sum payments arising from an office or employment.

Schedule F

Dividends and other distributions from Irish-resident companies.

Tax credits

	2018	2019	2020
Single person	€1,650	€1,650	€1,650
Married couple or couple in a civil partnership	€3,300	€3,300	€3,300
Widowed person or surviving civil partner			
Without dependent children	€2,190	€2,190	€2,190
In year of bereavement	€3,300	€3,300	€3,300
Widowed Parent			
First year after bereavement	€3,600	€3,600	€3,600
Second year after bereavement	€3,150	€3,150	€3,150
Third year after bereavement	€2,700	€2,700	€2,700
Fourth year after bereavement	€2,250	€2,250	€2,250
Fifth year after bereavement	€1,800	€1,800	€1,800
Single person child carer credit	€1,650	€1,650	€1,650
Home carer's credit - max	€1,200	€1,500	€1,600
PAYE credit	€1,650	€1,650	€1,650
Earned income tax credit	€1,150	€1,350	€1,500
Age credit			
Single/widowed/surviving civil partnership	€245	€245	€245
Married/civil partner	€490	€490	€490
Incapacitated child credit	€3,300	€3,300	€3,300
Dependent relative credit	€70	€70	€70
Blind Credit			
Blind person	€1,650	€1,650	€1,650
Both spouses/civil partners blind	€3,300	€3,300	€3,300

Computation of your income tax liability

Income tax is payable on your taxable income, i.e. your total assessable income for a tax year, less deductions for any, non standard rate allowances (not tax credits) to which you may be entitled.

Tax bands and rates

2019	2020
Single/Widow(er) or surviving civil partner First €35,300 @ 20% Balance @ 40%	**Single/Widow(er) or surviving civil partner** First €35,300 @ 20% Balance @ 40%
One Parent Family First €39,300 @ 20% Balance @ 40%	**One Parent Family** First €39,300 @ 20% Balance @ 40%
Married or in civil partnership - two incomes Note 1 + 2 First €70,600 @ 20% Balance @ 40%	**Married or in civil partnership - two incomes** Note 1 + 2 First €70,600 @ 20% Balance @ 40%
Married or in civil partnership - one income First €44,300 @ 20% Balance @ 40%	**Married or in civil partnership - one income** First €44,300 @ 20% Balance @ 40%

1. Transferable between spouses up to a maximum of €44,300 in 2019 and 2020 for any one spouse.

2. Subject to the lower earning spouse having income of at least €26,300 in 2019 and 2020.

Individualisation

In 2020 the standard rate tax band for a married couple, where both spouses have income, can be increased by the lower of

- €26,300

    or

- the income of the lower earning spouse.

The maximum standard rate band available to either spouse is €44,300.

Income exemptions limits

A person over the age of 65 whose income does not exceed the following limits, is completely exempt from income tax.

	2018 €	2019 €	20120 €
Person age 65 years or over:			
- Single / Widow(er) / surviving civil partner	€18,000	€18,000	€18,000
- Married / in a civil partnership	€36,000	€36,000	€36,000

Increased exemption/dependent children

If you have dependent children, the exemption limit can be increased, by €575 for the first and second child and €830 for the third and subsequent qualifying children.

Marginal relief

Marginal relief is available for those whose total income exceeds the exemptions limits, but is less than twice the relevant limit. It restricts the tax payable to 40% of the difference between your income and the appropriate exemption limit.

Example

A married man aged 70, has total income for 2020 of €40,000. His tax liability would normally work out as follows:

		€
	Total Income	€40,000
	Taxable	€40,000
	€40,000 @ 20%	€8,000
Less:	Tax Credits	
	Personal	(€3,300)
	PAYE	(€1,650)
	Age	(€490)
	Net tax payable	**€2,560**

However, marginal relief will restrict the overall tax liability to €1,600. (€40,000 - €36,000) x 40% = €1,600

Tax credits

An individual who is resident, ordinarily resident and domiciled in the State, is liable to income tax in respect of their total income, wherever it arises. They are entitled to claim certain tax credits and deductions.

Single credit

This credit is granted to the following

- Individuals who are single.

- Married couples or civil partners who opt for single/separate assessment - both partners receive a single tax credit.

- Separated couples who have not opted for joint assessment.

Married credit

This credit, which is double the single credit is granted to couples in a marriage or civil partnership who;

- Are assessed to tax under joint assessment (See Chapter 15 - Marriage, separation and divorce).

or

● Are living apart but one partner is maintaining the other and is not entitled to claim tax relief on the maintenance paid (for more details on this see Chapter 15 - Marriage, separation and divorce).

Single person child carer credit

This tax credit is granted to the primary carer who is either the parent, or to an individual who has a qualifying child in their custody and maintains that child for the whole or the greater part of a year of assessment. The credit is granted for a child up to the age of 18 years or, if over 18 years, where they are in full-time education.

The credit can also be claimed in the case of a permanently incapacitated child where the incapacity occurred before age 21, or if older, while the child was in full time education.

The child must reside with the claimant for at least six months of the year of assessment. If the child was born in the year of assessment, they must reside with the claimant for the greater part of the period from their date of birth. A child can only be the subject of one claim, and a claimant can only make a claim for one child for a year of assessment irrespective of the number of children that reside with him or her.

Where the primary carer has no tax liability the credit can be used instead by the non-primary carer.

Widowed parent credit

An additional credit is granted to widowed parents for the five tax years following the year of bereavement. The credit is €3,600 in year one, €3,150 in year two, €2,700 in year three, €2,250 in year four and €1,800 in year five.

Home carer's credit

The Home Carer's credit of €1,600 (€1,500 in 2019) may be claimed by a couple who are married or in a civil partnership, where one partner cares for one or more dependent people.

If the carer has income in their own right of less than €7,200 the full home carer's credit may still be claimed. If income is between €7,200 and €9,600 the tax credit of €1,500 is reduced by 1/2 the income of the home carer over €7,200. Only one credit is due irrespective of the number of dependents.

If your income exceeds €9,600 in the tax year no Home Carer's credit is due unless it was granted for the immediately preceding tax year and the other conditions for claiming the tax credit are met.

In order to qualify for the credit the following conditions must apply:

- The couple must be jointly assessed to tax - it does not apply where couples are taxed as single persons.

- The Home carer must care for one or more dependent persons. A dependent person is:

    - A child for whom child benefit is payable.   **or**

    - A person aged 65 years or over;   **or**

    - A person who is permanently incapacitated by reasons of mental or physical infirmity.

A dependent person does not include a spouse/partner.

- The dependent person(s) must normally reside with the couple for the tax year.

"If the Home Carer has income in their own right of less than €7,200 the full Home Carer's credit can be claimed."

You can also claim the carer's credit for a dependent relative who is cared for outside the home provided they live in a neighbouring residence or within two kilometres of the carer.

A couple cannot claim both the Home Carer's credit and the increased standard rate cut off point for dual income couples. However, they can claim whichever of the two is more beneficial. In practice, the tax office will grant the more beneficial treatment.

Incapacitated child credit

Incapacitated child credit can be claimed where an individual has a child who is permanently incapacitated either physically or mentally from maintaining themselves and is maintained by the claimant living with them at any time during the tax year.

- The child must have become incapacitated before reaching 21 years of age;   **or,**

- If over 21 years had become permanently incapacitated while still in full time education or full time training for a trade or profession for a minimum of 2 years.

For the tax year 2020 the tax credit is €3,300.

Age credit

A credit is available if you or your spouse/civil partner are over 65 years of age in the relevant tax year. In the case of a couple, married or in a civil partnership, the credit for 2020 is €245 and for a single or widowed person it is €490.

Dependent relative credit

This credit is granted to claimants who prove that they maintain at their own expense any person who is:

- A relative, who is incapacitated by old age or infirmity from maintaining themselves.

- Their or their spouse/civil partner's widowed mother or father, whether incapacitated or not.

- A son or daughter who resides with them and whose services they depend on by reason of old age or infirmity.

The credit of €70 p.a. in 2020, is reduced by the amount by which the income of the person whom the claim is made for exceeds the maximum rate of old age contributory pension payable to a single person over 80 €15,060 in 2020). If two or more people help maintain the relative the credit is divided between them in proportion to the amounts contributed by each.

Incapacitated person (employing a carer)

This allowance can be claimed if you employ a person to take care of yourself or a family member who is totally incapacitated, owing to old age or infirmity. The allowance can also be claimed if the services are provided by or through an agency.   The amount of this allowance is the actual cost of employing the carer up to a maximum of €75,000.

Any amount recovered from the HSE or a local authority in respect of the cost of employing the carer does not qualify for relief.

This allowance is granted at your highest rate of tax.

If two or more individuals are entitled to claim this deduction in respect of the same incapacitated individual, then

- The aggregate of the deductions granted to them cannot exceed the current maximum amount and

- The relief granted to each individual will be in proportion to the amount of the employment cost they have borne.

Blind person's credit

A credit of €1,650 is available during the tax year if you are blind. If both spouses/civil partners are blind, a credit of €3,300 may be claimed.

Mortgage interest relief

Mortgage interest relief is a tax relief based on the amount of interest you pay in a tax year on a qualifying mortgage loan. Mortgages taken out between 1 January 2004 to 31 December 2012, are eligible for mortgage interest relief until 31 December 2020. Mortgages taken out after 31 December 2012 are not eligible for mortgage interest relief. Your lender applies tax relief for your qualifying mortgage loan directly through the Tax Relief at Source (TRS) scheme. This means that your mortgage provider will reduce your monthly mortgage repayments or make a direct payment into your bank account equal to the amount of tax relief you are entitled to.

A qualifying loan, is a secured loan which was used to purchase, repair, develop or improve your principal private residence situated in Ireland.

You can also claim tax relief, subject to the maximum allowance, in respect of interest paid by you for your separated/divorced spouse or former partner in a dissolved civil partnership, or a dependent relative for whom you are claiming a dependent relative allowance.

Amount of mortgage interest relief /tax relief at source (TRS)

Mortgage interest relief was due to cease at the end of 2017. It was extended on a reducing basis for a further three years. If you were entitled to the relief at the end of 2017 then it will automatically continue on a reduced basis until the end of 2020. 100% in 2017, 75% in 2018, 50% in 2019 and 25% in 2020 and will cease from 1 January 2021.

The ceilings or upper thresholds on the amount of interest paid that qualifies for tax relief are dependant on -

- The status of the individual, that is, whether they are married, in a civil partnership or single; **and**
- Whether they are a first time buyer

The ceiling or upper thresholds on the amount of interest allowable are also reduced for each of the three years as follows;

First time buyers				
	2017	2018	2019	2020
	€	€	€	€
Single	10,000	7,500	5,000	2,500
Married, in a civil partnership, widowed or surviving civil partner	20,000	15,000	10,000	5,000

Non-first time buyers				
	2017	2018	2019	2020
	€	€	€	€
Single	3,000	2,250	1,500	750
Married, in a civil partnership, widowed or surviving civil partner	6,000	4,500	3,000	1,500

First time buyers

The rate of relief payable for the first seven years is currently;

● 25% for years one and two.

● 22.5% for years three, four and five.

● 20% for years six and seven.

Lower rates apply if you bought your first home before 2009. After year seven, the rates and thresholds for relief revert to those of a non-first time buyer.

If you bought your first home between 2004 and 2008 inclusive, the rate of relief for the tax years 2012 to 2020 is 30%.

You can claim the full amount of relief due if;

- A parent acts as a co-mortgagor or guarantor for a first time buyer.
- The parent does not pay any of the mortgage.

Non-first time buyers

The rate of relief paid on qualifying home loans is currently 15%.

A loan used for the purchase of an investment property does not qualify for mortgage interest relief. You can however, claim the mortgage interest paid as an expense against the gross rent received. (See page 44 for more details) If part of your mortgage is used to finance non-qualifying expenditure such as a holiday or a car, only the percentage applicable to your principal private residence qualifies for mortgage interest relief.

Example

A married couple have a €350,000 mortgage at a rate of 4.5%, and pay mortgage interest of €15,750 in the tax year. Their mortgage interest relief (TRS) will work out as follows;

| | 2020 | |
	A Less than 7 years mortgage holders	B More than 7 years mortgage holders
Mortgage interest paid	€15,750	€15,750
Maximum interest allowed for tax purposes	€5,000	€1,500
Tax credit €5,000/€1,500 @ 20%/15%	€1,000	€225

A   Assumes they were first time buyers in 2012.

B   Assumes they were not first time buyers.

Note: This tax relief will be granted at source by the bank or building society.

Help to Buy (HTB) Incentive

The Help to Buy incentive is a scheme designed to assist first-time buyers obtain the deposit required to purchase a home or, first-time home owners looking to build their own home (self-builds).

A first-time buyer of a house or apartment who purchases or self builds a new residential property between 19 July 2016 and 31 December 2021 may be entitled to claim a refund of income tax and DIRT paid over the previous 4 years. The rebate available is 5% of the purchase price of a new home, capped at a maximum refund of €20,000.

The incentive is available on properties valued at up to €600,000 for contracts signed in the period 19 July to 31 December 2016 or in the case of self-builds where the first tranche of mortgage drawdown was between those dates. From 1 January 2017, the maximum property value is €500,000. The maximum refund available is €20,000.

The incentive is only available in respect of principal private residences.

There is a requirement that the first-time buyer take out a mortgage of at least 70% of the value of the purchase price, or in the case of a self-build, 70% of the valuation approved by the mortgage provider. Cash-buyers are not eligible for the incentive.

Relief will be provided at deposit stage (signing of contract) or, in the case of a self-build, following the drawdown of the first tranche of the relevant mortgage.

Home renovation incentive

A scheme of tax relief for home renovation work was introduced for a period from 25 October 2013 to 31 December 2018 for homeowners and from 15 October 2014 to 31 December 2018 for landlords.

The Home Renovation Incentive (HRI) provides an income tax credit of 13.5% on qualifying expenditure on repairs, renovation and improvement works carried out on a main home or rental property by a qualifying contractor. Qualifying expenditure is expenditure which is subject to the 13.5% VAT return.

The credit is paid over the two years following the year in which the work is carried out and paid for. The first year for HRI tax credits is 2015 for homeowners and 2016 for landlords.

Payments made under deeds of covenant

A deed of covenant is a legally binding written agreement made by an individual to pay an agreed amount to another individual, without receiving any benefit in return. To be legally effective, it must be properly drawn up, signed, witnessed, sealed and delivered to the individual receiving the payments. Any amount can be paid under a Deed but only covenants in favour of the following individuals qualify for tax relief.

- People over 65 up to a maximum of 5% of the covenantor's total income;

- Permanently incapacitated individuals.

Payments by a parent to a son or daughter under 18 do not qualify for tax relief even if incapacitated.

If you pay tax at the higher rate you may reduce your tax liability and increase the disposable income of the covenantee. In addition, if the covenantee pays tax at a lower rate or is exempt from tax, a tax advantage may be gained.

Example

You have an income of €58,000 in the 2020 tax year and pay tax at 40%. Your spouse has no income. In 2020 you wish to supplement your widowed mother's (aged 81) income by €2,000 p.a. Your mother's income is a pension of €13,172 p.a.

You can do this in one of two ways:

- Hand over €2,000 to your mother each year.   **or**

- Complete a Deed of Covenant for €2,500 (it gets a little complicated here!) You deduct tax at the standard rate (20%) from this gross amount and pay the balance of €2,000 to your mother.

We have illustrated both positions below.   When all the paperwork is completed, under a Deed of Covenant you will be better off by €500 p.a. and your widowed mother is better off by €500 p.a.

A note of caution; if your mother's pension is a non-contributory pension, the covenant income will be taken into account for means-test purposes and may affect the amount of pension she will receive.

Your Mother's position as the covenantee

		2020 Tax Year	
		Without Covenant €	With Covenant €
A	Deed of Covenant	Nil	€2,500
B	Pension	€13,172	€13,172
	Total Income	€13,172	€15,672
	Taxable Income (Income Under Exemption limit)	Nil	Ni
	Tax Payable	Nil	Nil
C	Tax Refund Due (tax paid by you)	Nil	€500
D	Payment from you	€2,000	€2,000
	Disposable Income	**€15,172**	**€15,672**
		B+D	B+(C+D)

If your employer pays your medical insurance premium you will not have been allowed TRS. Any tax relief due in this case should be included on the employees tax credit certificate or claimed on their annual tax return.

Tax relief at source is capped on a gross premium of €1,000 per adult (€800 net) and €500 gross (€400 net) per student and child on all health insurance policies.

Medical expenses

"Tax relief for medical expenses is granted at 20%."

Relief is available at the standard rate of tax 20%, for qualifying health expenses paid by you in respect of any individual with the exception of nursing home fees which are allowed at 40%. You cannot claim relief for any expenditure that has been or will be reimbursed by any body such as VHI, Laya Healthcare, Irish Life Healthcare, HSF, or where a compensation payment is or will be made.

Tax relief is not available to expenses relating to routine dental and ophthalmical care

Qualifying health expenses cover a wide variety of matters and include:

- Doctors' and consultants' fees.

- Diagnostic procedures carried out on the advice of a practitioner.

- Drugs or medicines prescribed by a doctor, dentist or consultant.

- Maintenance or treatment in a hospital or nursing home provided the expenses are necessarily incurred in connection with the services of a practitioner or refer to diagnostic procedures carried out on the advice of practitioner.

- Supply, maintenance or repair of any medical, surgical, dental or nursing appliance used on the advice of a practitioner.

- Physiotherapy or similar treatment prescribed by a practitioner.

- Orthopaedic or similar treatment prescribed by a practitioner.

- Speech and language therapy carried out by an approved Speech and Language Therapist for a qualifying child.

- Transport by ambulance.

- Educational psychological assessments for a qualifying child, carried out by an Educational Psychologist who is registered with the Minister for Education and Skills.

- Certain items of expenditure in respect of a child suffering from a serious life threatening illness.

- Kidney patients' expenses, (up to a maximum amount depending on whether the patient used hospital dialysis, home dialysis or CAPD).

- Specialised dental treatment.

- "In vitro" fertilisation.

- Maternity care and IVF.

- Glucometre machine for a diabetic.

- The cost of food products manufactured specifically for diabetics is an allowable expense for the purpose of a health expense claim.

- The cost of gluten free foods for coeliacs. As this condition is generally ongoing, a letter instead of prescriptions, from a doctor stating that the taxpayer is a coeliac suffer is acceptable. Receipts from supermarkets in addition to receipts from a pharmacist are acceptable.

- Nursing care and maintenance paid to a nursing home, for a dependent relative.

Health expenses carried out abroad also qualify for tax relief provided the practitioner is qualified to practice in the county.

Where qualifying care is only available outside Ireland, reasonable travelling and accommodation expenses can also be claimed. In such cases the expenses of one person accompanying the patient may also be allowed where the condition of the patient requires it.

Certain non routine dental treatment also qualify for tax relief.

Dental treatments which qualify for standard rate tax relief are as follows:

- Crowns which are permanently cemented to the existing tooth tissue.

- Veneers/rembrant type etched fillings.

- Tip replacing where a large part of the tooth needs to be replaced and the replacement is made outside the mouth.

- Posts which are inserted in the nerve canal of a tooth to hold a crown.

- Inlays which are smaller versions of a crown. Relief will only be available if they were fabricated outside the mouth.

- Endodontics - root canal treatment: This involves the filling of the nerve canal and not the filling of teeth.

- Periodontal treatment which includes, root planing, curettage and debridement, gum flaps and chrome cobalt splint.

- Bridgework consisting of an enamel retained bridge or a tooth supported bridge.

- Orthodontic treatment which involves the provision of braces and other similar treatments.

- Surgical extraction of impacted wisdom teeth when undertaken in a hospital or dental surgery.

Non-routine dental treatment obtained outside Ireland may qualify for tax relief provided the dentist is a qualifying practitioner.

Exclusions

Health care specifically excludes expenses relating to routine ophthalmic treatment and routine dental treatment.

Routine ophthalmic treatment

This means sight testing and advice as to the use of spectacles or contact lenses and the provision and repair of spectacles or contact lenses.

Routine dental treatment

This means the extraction, scaling and filling of teeth, and the provision and repairing of artificial teeth and dentures.

How to claim

Relief for any income tax year is normally given by repayment i.e. a refund after the end of the relevant tax year. You can claim tax relief

- Online using Revenue's online service myAccount, see www.ROS.ie if you are a PAYE taxpayer.

- If you are a self assessed tax payer and you complete a Form 11 each year you can claim relief for health expenses on this form.

A claim for relief for the cost of dental treatment other than routine dental treatment must be accompanied by a certificate (Form Med 2 -this will be provided by your dentist) signed by a qualified practitioner.

Guide dog

A standard €825 per annum is allowed as medical expenses where a blind person maintains a trained guide dog and is the registered owner with the Irish Guide Dog Association.

Permanent health insurance (PHI)

Permanent health insurance (PHI) protects your income against accidents or illness for up to 75% of your normal earnings. After a specific period has expired, the benefits are paid for the duration of your incapacity or to a specific age, whichever is the earlier. Income tax relief may be claimed on the contributions made to a PHI scheme.

Contributions to a PHI scheme by PAYE tax payers are on a 'net pay' basis i.e. the contribution is deducted from your gross salary prior to the application of tax and PRSI. However employee contributions to a PHI scheme do not reduce the pay amount for USC purposes.

The amount of relief granted cannot exceed 10% of your total income for the year of assessment in which the premiums are paid. All receipts from a PHI plan are taxable, regardless of whether or not the relief is claimed on premiums paid.

Tuition fees

An individual can claim tax relief on tuition fees paid for certain full time and part-time undergraduate courses of at least two years duration.

Tax relief is available at the standard rate of income tax (20%) for qualifying tuition fees. The maximum limit on such qualifying fees is €7,000 per academic year, per individual per course.   The relief can be claimed by an individual who pays fees to publicly or privately funded third level colleges from themselves or any other individual.

Qualifying fees means tuition fees but not examination fees, registration fees or administration fees, in respect of an approved course at an approved college.

The first €3,000 of fees paid for full time courses and the first €1,500 paid for part time courses will be disregarded from fees paid before tax relief is applied.

Employment Investment Incentive (EII)

The Employment Investment Incentive (EII) is a tax relief incentive scheme that provides tax relief for investment in certain corporate trades.

The scheme allows an individual investor to obtain income tax relief on investments up to a maximum of €150,000 per annum in each tax year up to 2019. Relief is initially available to an individual at 30%. A further 10% tax relief will be available where it has been proven that employment levels have increased at the company at the end of the holding period (three years) or where evidence is provided that the company used the capital raised for expenditure on research and development.

For EII investments made on or after 8 Oct 2019 full income tax relief will be given in the year the investment is made.   The condition relating to the number of employees or expenditure on Research & Development will not apply to investments made after this date. The maximum annual investment limit is increased to €250,000 for 2020 and subsequent years. If you invest in EII for a minimum period of 7 years a limit of €500,000 applies from 2020.

An investor who cannot obtain relief on all their investment in a year of assessment, either because their investment exceeds the maximum €150,000 or their income in that year is insufficient to absorb all of it, can carry forward the unrelieved amount to following years, subject to the normal limit on the amount of the investment that can be relieved in any one year.

Universal social charge (USC)

The universal social charge was introduced from 1 January 2011. It is payable on gross income including notional pay, after relief for certain trading losses and capital allowances, but before pension contributions.

All individuals are liable to the USC if their gross income exceeds €13,000 per annum or €250 per week.

The rate of USC for 2019 and 2020 are as follows:

USC Thresholds 2019 and 2020			
2019		2020	
	Rate		Rate
Income up to €12,012.00	0.5%	Income up to €12,012.00	0.5%
Income from €12,012.01 to €19,874.00	2%	Income from €12,012.01 to €19,874.00	2%
Income from €19,874.01 to €70,044.00	4.5%	Income from €19,874.01 to €70,044.00	4.5%
Income above €70,044.00	8%	Income above €70,044.00	8%

Individuals whose Non-PAYE income exceeds €100,000 in a year are liable to an additional USC surcharge of 3% on any Non-PAYE income over €100,000.

A reduced rate of USC applies to

- Individuals aged 70 years or over whose aggregate income for the year is €60,000 or less.

- Individuals (aged under 70) who hold a full medical card whose aggregate income for the year is €60,000 or less.

Note 2: "Aggregate" income for USC purposes does not include payments from the Department of Social Protection.

Note 3: A "GP only" card is not considered a full medical card for USC purposes.

The reduced rates of USC for 2019 and 2020 are as follows;

USC Thresholds 2019 and 2020			
2019	Rate	2020	Rate
Income up to €12,012	0.5%	Income up to €12,012	0.5%
Income above €12,012	2%	Income above €12,012	2%

Exempt categories

2019	2020
Where an individual's total income for a year does not exceed €13,000.	Where an individual's total income for a year does not exceed €13,000
All Department of Social Protection payments.	All Department of Social Protection payments.
Income already subjected to DIRT.	Income already subjected to DIRT.

8 PAYE made easy

The Pay As You Earn (PAYE) system applies to you if you have income from employment or a pension that is taxed at source.

Tax credits

Tax credits are allowed at the standard rate of tax only, regardless of whether you are a higher rate tax payer or not. This means that tax credits benefit each individual by the same amount.

Tax credit system

Tax is calculated at the appropriate tax rates on gross pay and this tax is then reduced by any tax credits due, in order to arrive at the net tax payable.

Before the start of the new tax year, around December, your tax office will issue a notification of determination of tax credits and the standard rate cut off point.

The notification of determination of tax credit and standard rate cut off point will show the following information;

- Standard rate cut off point.
- Tax credit due to you.
- Your rate(s) of tax.

Standard rate cut off point

This is the amount of income you can earn at the standard rate. The amount will depend on whether you are married, in a civil partnership, single or widowed. Also if you have any allowances which are allowed at the higher rate of tax e.g. pension contribution, this will increase your "standard rate cut off point".

Standard tax rate band

	2020 €
Single or Widowed person or Surviving civil partner, without qualifying child.	€35,300
Single or Widowed person or Surviving civil partner, qualifying for single person child carer credit	€39,300
Married or in a Civil partnership, one spouse or Civil partner with income.	€44,300
Married or in a Civil partnership, both spouses or Civil partners with income * (both working -maximum)	*€70,600

*   Subject to lower earning spouse having an income of at least €26,300.

The tax credits and standard rate cut off point will vary depending on the circumstances of each individual.

Income tax is calculated for each pay period by applying the information supplied by the notification against the gross pay as follows:

The standard rate of tax (20%) is applied to your gross pay up to the standard rate cut off point for that week or month. Any balance of income over that amount in the pay period is taxed at the higher rate (40%). This gives the gross tax payable. The gross tax payable is reduced by the amount of tax credits as per the notification sent by your tax office, to arrive at the net tax payable.

Example

A married individual has gross earnings of €50,000, their spouse has no income. For 2020 a notice of determination of tax credits and standard rate cut off point issues showing:

Standard rate cut off point of €44,300 per annum of €851.92 per week.	Based on a standard rate band of €44,300 for a married couple - one spouse working.
Standard rate of tax is 20%	Based on standard rate of tax of 20%
Higher rate of tax is 40%	Based on a higher rate of 40%
Tax credits of €4,950 per annum or €95.19 per week	Personal €3,300 PAYE credit €1,650 Total €4,950

Income tax would be calculated as follows for the first week

Gross pay	€961.52	(€50,000/52)
Tax on €851.92 @ 20%	€170.38	(Standard rate up to a maximum of €851.92 which is the standard rate cut off point as advised by the tax office)
Tax on €109.60 @ 40%	€43.84	(Higher rate of tax in excess of income over the standard rate cut off point)
Gross tax	€214.22	Total of higher rate and standard rate tax.
Less: Tax Credits	€95.19	Tax credits as advised by the tax office
Total Tax due for this week	€119.03	Total tax less tax credit

Non standard rated reliefs

If you have deductions from income tax which qualify for tax relief at the higher rate of income tax, your tax credits will be increased by the amount of the relief at the standard rate of income tax and the standard rate tax band will also be increased by the amount of the relief in order to arrive at the standard rate cut off point.

Example

A married individual has a gross income of €50,000. Their spouse has no income. Personal and PAYE tax credits amount to €4,950. They have a standard rate tax cut off point of €44,300 and their rates of tax are 20% and 40%. They also pay €2,000 into a personal pension scheme, tax relief on which is allowed at the higher rate of tax. Their tax credit will increase by €400 (€2,000 @ 20%). Their standard rate tax band will also increase by €2,000 in order to arrive at the standard rate cut off point.

Calculation of tax credits	
	2020 €
Married	€3,300
PAYE	€1,650
Total	€4,950
Increased by pension	€400
Net tax credits	€5,350

Calculation of standard rate cut off point	
	2020 €
Standard rate band (married couple one spouse working)	€44,300
Increased by pension	€2,000
Standard rate cut off point	€46,300

Income tax would be calculated as follows for the first week

Gross pay	€961.52	(€50,000/52)
Tax on €890.38 @ 20%	€178.08	(Standard rate up to a maximum of €890.38 which is the standard rate cut off point as advised by the tax office)
Tax on €71.14 @ 40%	€28.46	(Higher rate of tax in excess of income over the standard rate cut off point)
Gross tax	€206.54	Total of higher rate and standard rate tax.
Less: Tax credits	€102.88	Tax credits as advised by the tax office
Total tax due for this week	€103.66	Total tax less tax credit

Summary

Tax credit system

- Gross pay is taxed at the appropriate tax rate(s) to give the gross tax.

- The tax office will advise you of the standard rate cut off point for each pay period. The standard rate of tax is applied to pay up to that limit. Any balance of pay over that amount in any pay period is taxed at the higher rate.

- The gross tax is reduced by a tax credit as advised by the tax office to arrive at the tax payable.

PAYE emergency tax

The emergency tax operates when:

- Your employer has not received a notification of determination of tax credits and standard rate cut off point for you for the current year or your Form P45 for the current tax year.

  or

- You have given your employer a completed form P45 with "E" written on it.

For the year 2020 the PAYE emergency tax credit for the initial period of employment and the rates at which tax will be deducted are set out below.

If paid weekly:

	2020	
	Tax credit €	**Rate** %
Weeks 1 - 4	€32.00 (1/52 of single persons tax credit)	20% up to €679 (1/52 of single persons standard rate cut off point) Balance @ 40%
Weeks 5 - 8	Nil	20% up to €679 (1/52 of single persons standard rate cut off point) Balance @ 40%
Week 9 onwards	Nil	40%

If you do not supply your employer with your PPS Number, your employer must deduct tax at the higher rate on your gross pay (less superannuation and permanent health contribution if applicable). No tax credits are due.

Emergency basis of USC

The rate of USC payable if you are on emergency tax is 8% of your gross income.

Tax refund during unemployment

If tax has been deducted from your pay since 1 January last, and you are now unemployed, you may be entitled to a tax refund. If you have not paid tax, you cannot claim a refund on becoming unemployed.

How do I apply

You can apply for this refund online if you are registered for myAccount, see www.revenue.ie.

myAccount

This is the Revenue On-Line Service for employees. It is an interactive systems which allows individuals who pay tax under the Pay As You Earn (PAYE) system, a quick, secure and cost effective method to manage their taxes online. It can be accessed through myAccount on Revenue.ie

Once registered, you can:

- View your tax record.

- Claim a wide range of tax credits.

- Apply for refunds of tax including health expenses.

- Declare additional income.

- Request a review of tax liability for previous years.

- Re-allocate credits between yourself and your spouse.

- Track your correspondence submitted to Revenue.

Changes requested are reflected in your PAYE record in two days. There is no need to submit paper claims when a transaction is submitted through myAccount, however you are obliged to retain receipts for six years as Revenue may ask to view them at a later stage.

The myAccount system is for PAYE employees only. If you are self-employed you should register instead for ROS. (see page 168)

Time limited for claiming tax refunds

There is a four year time limit for claiming income tax refunds. PAYE tax payers seeking an income tax refunds for 2016 must submit their claim to Revenue by 31 December 2020.

What is a P21 form

A P21 is a PAYE end of year statement which shows your total income, tax credits and tax paid for a particular tax year.

I need to get a P21 to apply for a grant, how do I get one?

You may need to get a PAYE end of year statement (Form P21) as proof of earnings for the purpose of obtaining an education grant, or a medical card. You can apply for a P21 through myaccount on Revenue.ie. A P21 gives details of your total income, tax credits and PAYE tax paid for a particular tax year. It also shows whether you have overpaid or underpaid tax for the year. If you have underpaid tax your tax office will indicate if, and how the underpayment will be collected - usually by reduction of your tax credits for a subsequent tax year. Any overpayment will be refunded either by cheque or directly into your bank account.

Allowable deductions incurred for your employment

For expenses to be allowable for tax purposes they must be incurred for your employment and must be "wholly, exclusively and necessary" for the purpose of performing the duties of your employment. This rule is very strictly interpreted.

Motor and travelling expenses

A mileage allowance agreed between you and your employer for the use of your car for business purposes is not taxable provided it does not exceed the civil service mileage rate. However, you are not entitled to claim the cost of getting to or from work but only expenses incurred in the actual performance of your occupation.

For employees who use their cars in the normal course of their duties the rates are as follows:

Cars (effective from 1 April 2017)

Official motor travel in a calendar year	Rates per kilometre		
	Engine capacity: Up to 1200 cc	Engine capacity: 1201 - 1500cc	Engine capacity: 1501cc & over
Up to 1,500 km	37.95 cent	39.86 cent	44.79 cent
1,501 - 5,500 km	70.00 cent	73.21 cent	83.53 cent
5,501 - 25,000 km	27.55 cent	29.03 cent	32.21 cent
25,001 and over	21.36 cent	22.23 cent	25.85 cent

Motorcycles (effective from 5 March 2009)

Official motor travel in a calendar year	Rates per kilometre			
	Engine capacity: Up to 150 cc	Engine capacity: 151 - 250 cc	Engine capacity: 251 - 600 cc	Engine capacity: 601 cc or more
Up to 6,437 km	14.48 cent	20.10 cent	23.72 cent	28.59 cent
6,438 km & over	9.37 cent	13.31 cent	15.29 cent	17.60 cent

Bicycles

Rates per kilometre	8.00 cent

Flat rate expenses

Special flat rate allowances are allowed to certain categories of workers such as teachers, nurses, journalists and building workers for expenses. The amounts are agreed from time to time between trade unions and professional bodies and the Revenue Commissioners. (Details of these expenses are listed on www.revenue.ie)

Round sum expenses

If you get round sum expenses from your employer they will be regarded as part of your salary and taxed accordingly, unless you can demonstrate that the expenses were incurred "wholly, exclusively and necessarily" in the performance of your duties. If your expenses actually exceed the sums reimbursed, you are entitled to an expense allowance for the excess.

Employee tax-efficient benefits

Here we list benefits which may be paid to you tax-free or tax efficiently by your employer:

1. If an employee is working away from normal base, daily and overnight allowances to cover the cost of lunch, evening meal, bed & breakfast etc. may be paid tax free provided it does not exceed the following limits.

From 1 July 2019

Overnight rate			Daily rate	
Normal Rate Up to 14 nights	Reduced Rate 15 to 28 nights	Detention Rate 28 to 56 nights	10 hours or more	5 hours but less than 10 hours
€147.00	€132.30	€73.50	€36.97	€15.41

Special rules apply to absences over 56 nights

The night allowance can only be paid where the employee is at least 100 kms away from their home or place of work and covers a period of up to 24 hours from the time of departure, and any further period not exceeding 5 hours. The day allowance may only be paid where the employee is at least 8 kms away from their home or normal place of work.

2. Canteen meals and refreshments, provided these are available to all employees or luncheon vouchers up to 19c per working day.

3. Rent-free or low rent accommodation provided this is necessitated by the job.

4. Non-cash personal gifts for reasons not connected with work but including retirement presents.

5. Share in an employer's Revenue-approved profit sharing scheme (subject to certain limits). (see page 159)

6.   Staff entertainment and outgoings at a reasonable cost.

7.   Pool transport to place of work.

8.   Mileage allowance for the use of the employee's car for business purposes. The rate cannot exceed the civil service mileage rate. (see page 143)

9.   Scholarship income and bursaries.

10. Lump sum payments on retirement or removal from an employment within certain limits. (see page 250)

11. Payments under the Redundancy Payment Act 1967. (see page 247)

12. Payments made on account of injury or disability.

13. Working clothes, overalls and tools provided by the employer.

14. Employer's contributions to a statutory or Revenue-approved pension scheme.

15. Cost to the employer of providing life assurance cover of up to eight times the employee's salary.

16. Employees can receive a single annual non cash benefit up to a maximum value of €500 tax free subject to the following conditions;

     ● The benefit or voucher cannot exceed €500 in value

     ● It cannot be exchanged in part or in full for cash

     ● It cannot be part of any salary sacrifice arrangement between the employee and employer.

     ● Only one benefit or voucher per employee may be given in any one year

17. Cost of providing sick pay/permanent health insurance.

18. Cost of providing contributions for medical insurance premiums paid to authorised insurers (higher rate tax payers will suffer BIK penalties)

19. Monthly/annual bus/rail travel passes provided by employers to their employees.

20. The provision of bicycles and associated safety equipment by employers to employees who agree to use their bicycle to travel to work, will be treated as a tax exempt benefit in kind, up to a limit of €1,000 per employee. This exemption may only apply once in any five year period in respect of any employee.

21. From 1 Jan 2018 to 31 Dec 2022 a 0% rate of BIK applies on employer provided electric cars or vans. This exemption does not apply to hybrid cars or vans. From 1 Jan 2019 a cap of €50,000 on the

original market value (OMV) of the car or van applies. Any amount in excess of €50,000 is taxable in the normal manner.   Electric charging points provided for use in the workplace for charging such vehicles are also exempt from BIK from 1 Jan 2018.

Employee benefits & shares

If you receive a benefit from your employer, then subject to certain exemptions PAYE, PRSI and USC will be applied by your employer on the taxable benefit (notional pay) received.

Normally any PAYE, PRSI or USC due in respect of the taxable benefit must be paid to the Collector General for the month in which the benefit is received. In the case of the benefit in kind (BIK) on a company car or van, the provision of accommodation or a preferential loan the annual notional pay amount can be spread out over the full tax year.

Best estimates

In order for the employer to calculate the PAYE/PRSI on benefits provided, they must make a "best estimate" of notional pay in respect of certain benefits.

However, in many cases e.g. on the provision of vouchers, the employer will be aware of the exact value of the benefits provided. This is called the "notional pay" amount.

Valuation rules

Except where there are specific rules e.g. company car (see page 147), the amount of the taxable benefit (i.e. the notional pay), which will be liable to PAYE/PRSI will be the higher of

- The expense incurred by the employer in connection with the provision of the benefit to the employee

    or

- The value realisable by the employee for the benefit in money or money's worth.

    Less any amount made good to the employer by the employee.

Insufficient wages/salary to cover benefit

Where the amount of salary paid to an employee is insufficient to collect the full amount of PAYE, PRSI and USC due on the "notional pay", the employer must pay any shortfall to the Collector General.

Any shortfall, paid by an employer must be recovered from the employee. Any amount not recovered by the 31 March following the end of the tax year in which the benefit is received, is treated as a taxable benefit in the following year and liable to PAYE and PRSI, resulting in a double charge to tax.

Small benefits

Where an employer provides a benefit of less than €500 per annum to employees no PAYE/PRSI will apply. If the value of the benefit exceeds €500, PAYE/PRSI will apply to the full benefit.

Company cars

Where a company car is available for the private use of an employee, the employee is liable to PAYE, PRSI and USC in respect of the car.

A car is defined as all cars and includes crew cars and jeeps.

The "notional pay" to which PAYE, PRSI and the USC applies, is on the cash equivalent of the car. This cash equivalent is normally calculated at 30% of the "original market value" (OMV) of the car supplied. This calculation is applied regardless of whether the car is acquired new or second hand. However, this 30% can be reduced for high business mileage as follows;

Annual Business Travel

Business mileage		% of original market value
Lower limit	Upper limit	
Kilometres	Kilometres	%
Up to 24,000	But not exceeding 24,000	30%
In excess of 24,000	But not exceeding 32,000	24%
In excess of 32,000	But not exceeding 40,000	18%
In excess of 40,000	But not exceeding 48,000	12%
In excess of 48,000		6%

Travel to and from work is considered private use.

If an employee wants to claim a reduction of the BIK due to high mileage a record must be kept of all business travel.

Calculation of notional pay

Step 1:   Find out the original market value of the car.

The 'OMV' of the car is usually the list price of the car including duties, VRT and VAT. If a discount was received when the vehicle was bought the list price may be reduced by the discount provided the discount would normally be available on the open market when buying a single vehicle.

Step 2:   Ascertain the business mileage for the year and calculate the cash equivalent using the chart above using the chart above.

Example

You are provided with a company car on 1 January 2017. The OMV of the car is €35,000, and your business mileage is less than 15,000 a year. You make no payments towards the running costs of the car.

Your "notional pay" in respect of the company car would be calculated as follows;

$$€35,000 \times 30\% = €10,500$$

If you are paid weekly, €201.92 "notional pay" (€10,500 / 52) will be added to your normal salary and income tax, PRSI and USC will be applied to this amount.

Step 3:   Deduct amounts paid by the employee to the employer in respect of the car. Taking the above example, but assuming you make a payment directly to your employer of €1,000 in respect of the running cost of the car, you also pay all your own private fuel. Your BIK would work out as follows:

Notional pay as per previous example	€10,500
Less: The running expenses paid directly to your employer	€1,000
Notional pay amount	€9,500

There is no deduction for the private fuel, as you did not make this payment directly to your employer.

In some cases an employee will pay a lump sum contribution towards the purchase of a company car. In this case, the lump sum is deducted from the "notional pay" in the first year the car is provided. This deduction is only allowed in the first year.

Electric cars and vans d Vans

An exemption from benefit in kind for employer provided electric cars or vans was introduced on 1 Jan 2019 and runs until 31 December 2022.

A cap of €50,000 on the original market value (OMV) of the car or van that is exempt from BIK applies from 1 January 2019. Any amount of the OMV over €50,000 is taxable in the normal manner.

This exemption is limited to cars or vans which derive their motive power solely from electricity. No exemption is available in respect of hybrid cars or vans.

Electrical charging points provided for use in the workplace for charging electric vehicles are also exempt from a BIK charge.

20% reduction in BIK for low mileage

Your BIK charge can be reduced by 20% provided all of the following conditions are met:

- You spend 70% or more of your time away from your place of work.

- Your annual business mileage exceeds 8,000 kilometres p.a. but does not exceed 24,000 kilometres p.a.

- You work an average of at least 20 hours per week.

- Maintain a log book, detailing the mileage, nature and location of business and amount of time spent away from your employer's business premises. This log must be available for inspection by Revenue, if requested, and must be certified by your employer as being correct.

End of year adjustment

The exact business mileage for an employee cannot be determined until the end of a tax year. So during the year employers should make a best estimate of the business mileage for the year, based on available information and records. However, prior to the end of the tax year this best estimate should be reviewed to ensure that it is correct. Any necessary adjustment should then be made before the end of the tax year.

Company car available for less than a full year

Adjustments will be necessary where a car is not available for the full year, e.g. where

- An employee receives a car after the start of the tax year.

- An employee gives up a car before the end of the tax year.

Equally an adjustment will be required where a car is for some other reason not available for private use for part of the tax year, for example, where an employee is working abroad for an extended period. In this case, a car provided to an employee will not be regarded as available for private use for that part of the year which the employee is outside the State for the purpose of performing the duties of the office or employment, provided the following conditions are met:

- The employee travels abroad without the car.

- The car is not available for use by the employee's family or household during the employee's period of absence outside the State.

Where a car is not available for part of a year, the business mileage thresholds and the percentage cash equivalents used should be calculated by reference to the following calculation;

$$\frac{\text{Number of days in the tax year the car is available for private use}}{365} \times 100$$

Company car or mileage allowance?

Many people now look at the option of using their own car for business and taking a mileage allowance for business travel instead of a company car.

To see which option is best for you, first work out how much your car costs.

Motoring costs

Each year the AA publishes a leaflet entitled "Motoring Costs" in which they divide motoring costs into two distinct categories:

● Standing charges.

● Operating costs.

A standing charge is any fixed annual cost which remains the same regardless of your annual mileage. An operating cost, on the other hand, is a cost which is directly related to your mileage, for example, petrol.

Of course, your overall motoring costs depend to a large extent on the type of car you drive, your age, driving experience etc., but to make everything as straightforward as possible, we have outlined below what the AA estimated were the average standing charges for the different CO_2 emission bands A - G. You can check your car CO_2 emissions on www.ratemycar.ie. Now that you can identify the standing charges, we next outline what the AA estimated were your operating costs in June 2018 expressed in cents per kilometre.

"The exact business mileage for an employee cannot be determined until the end of a year."

By referring to these two tables, you can see that if you own a car in the CO_2 emission band C, drive 16,000 kilometres per annum between standing charges and operating costs, the AA estimates it will cost you an average of €11,947.20 p.a. or €229.75 p.w.. The corresponding figure for a car win the band E emission level is €16,792 p.a. or €322.92 p.w.

Operating costs per kilometre (in cents)

Standing charges

Motor tax band	Band A €	Band B €	Band C €	Band D €	Band E €	Band F €
Motor tax	120	270	390	570	750	1,200
Insurance	999	1,210	1,348	1,456	1,685	1,945
Driving licence	5	5	5	5	5	5
Depreciation	1,451	1,690	2,432	3,074	5,420	8,098
Interest costs	111	138	189	231	281	421
Garage /parking	4,059	4,059	4,059	4,059	4,059	4,059
NCT test	21	21	21	21	21	21
Total charges	**6,766**	**7,393**	**8,444**	**9,416**	**12,221**	**15,749**

Cost per kilometre (in cent)

Motor tax band	Band A €	Band B €	Band C €	Band D €	Band E €	Band F €
8,000 km/pa	84.57	92.42	105.56	117.71	152.76	196.87
16,000 km/pa	42.28	46.21	52.78	58.85	76.38	98.44
24,000 km/pa	28.19	30.81	35.19	39.24	50.92	65.62
32,000 km/pa	21.14	23.11	26.39	29.43	38.19	49.22

Operating costs per kilometre (in cents)

Motor tax band	Band A	Band B	Band C	Band D	Band E	Band F
Petrol	9.18	10.67	11.29	13.17	14.62	15.80
Oil	0.10	0.12	0.16	0.18	0.19	0.20
Tyres	0.05	1.68	1.78	2.45	2.66	2.65
Servicing	1.52	2.00	2.18	2.54	2.64	2.65
Repairs	5.85	6.14	6.48	7.37	8.46	9.11
Total	16.70	20.61	21.89	25.71	28.57	30.41

* Petrol based on 131.90c per litre (unleaded) for each cent more, or less, add or subtract

	0.08	0.10	0.10	0.12	0.13	0.14

Total costs per km (in cent)- based on 16,000 km

Motor tax band	Band A	Band B	Band C	Band D	Band E	Band F
Standing charges	47.21	46.21	52.78	58.85	76.38	98.44
Operating costs	16.70	20.61	21.89	25.71	28.57	30.42
Cents per kilometre	63.91	66.82	74.67	84.56	104.95	128.86

Civil service mileage rates

The civil service mileage rates for cars and motor bikes are shown on page 143.

Provided your employer agrees and provided you do not charge an amount in excess of the civil service mileage rates, these charges will be tax free into your hand.

Evaluating which is best for you in your particular circumstances can be a complex exercise and we suggest that you go about it as follows:

- First estimate your annual standing charges (A).

- Estimate your operating costs per kilometre (B).

- Estimate your total annual mileage (C).

- Calculate how much of your total annual mileage is for business purposes.

From A, B and C you can calculate your total annual cost. By applying the civil service mileage rate to your annual business mileage you can calculate the value of reimbursements your employer may pay you tax-free.

Taking a salary increase instead of a company car

Another consideration is salary in lieu of a company car. For example, if you do relatively low business mileage and are considering the option of giving up the company car in favour of a salary increase coupled with the ability to claim a small mileage allowance. The question you must ask yourself is "Will I lose money"? The example below will help you to answer this question.

Example

You have a company car with an original market value of €30,000, which falls into category C for CO_2 emissions. Your total mileage is 13,000 km per year of which 8,000 km are business kilometers. Assuming you pay tax at 40%, your BIK will work out as follows with a company car.

	€
Original market value of car	€30,000
BIK @ 30%	€9,000
Your increased tax bill (€9,000@ 52%) (Income tax @ 40%, PRSI (4% & USC @ 8%)	€4,680

The estimated cost of running your car is €9,707.10 per annum.

You have the option of giving up your company car, taking a salary increase of €3,000 and a mileage allowance of €4,818. Should you take it?

Your position

The cost to you of the company car is €4,680 per annum i.e. your additional tax bill. If you provided your own car and you got an increase in salary of €3,000 and mileage allowance of €4,818, the net cost of running your car will work out at €3,449. A saving of €1,231 per annum.

	€
Running cost of car	€9,707
Salary increase of €3,000 (Net of Tax @ 40%, PRSI @ 4% & USC @ 8%)	(€1,440)
Mileage allowance	(€4,818)
Net annual cost of car	**€3,449**

Car pools

Cars included in car pools are treated as not being available for an employee's private use and no tax liability arises on the provision of a car from a car pool provided all of the following conditions are met:

- The car is made available to, and actually used by, more than one employee and in the case of each of them it is made available to them by reason of their employment, but is not normally used by any one of the employees to the exclusion of the others.

- Private use by each employee is incidental to other use.

- The car is not normally kept overnight at, or in the vicinity of, any of the employee's homes.

Company van

If an employee has the use of a company van for private use the Benefit in Kind is calculated at 5% of the OMV of the van.

No BIK will be charged on company vans where the following conditions are met:

- The van is supplied to the employee for the purposes of the employee's work.

- The employee is required by the employer to bring the van home after work.

- Apart from travelling from work to home and back to work, other private use of the van by the employee is forbidden by the employer and there is no other private use.

- In the course of their work, the employee must spend at least 80% of their time away from the premises of the employer to which they are attached.

Business mileage involving travel direct from/to home

Where an employee proceeds on a business journey directly from home to a temporary place of work (rather than commencing that business journey from their normal place of work) or returns home directly, the business mileage should be calculated by reference to the lesser of :

- The distance between home and the temporary place of work

  or

- The distance between the normal place of work and the temporary place of work.

Payment of medical insurance

Tax relief for medical insurance premiums paid to an authorised insurer is granted at source. Subscribers pay 80% of the gross premium, which is the same as giving tax relief at the standard rate of 20%. If your employer pays medical insurance on your behalf you will not have been given the tax relief at source and so you will have to reclaim this directly from the tax office.

Claiming relief

You can claim this relief.

- On www.revenue.ie through the Revenue myAccount service facility, if you have registered for this service with the Revenue.

- By phoning your local tax office

The tax relief per person covered by a policy is limited to

- Per adult - the lesser of the premium paid or €1,000

- Per child - the lesser of the premium paid in respect of that child or €500. The full adult maximum amount of €1,000 or the relevant premium paid if lower, applies to all individuals aged 21 or over regardless of whether they are availing of a child premium.

Preferential loans

A preferential loan is a loan made to an employee by their employer (directly or indirectly) on which they pay no interest or interest at a rate lower than the specified rate.

The Benefit in Kind for tax purposes is the difference between the interest paid (if any) and interest calculated at the specified rate. However, the amount of interest assessed to tax will qualify for mortgage interest relief as "deemed interest" providing it is a qualifying loan subject to the normal limits.

The specified rate for a home loan is 4%. For non-home loans the specified rate is 13.5%.

Example

You are married and joined the bank in January 2016 and were granted a preferential house purchase loan of €60,000 @ 3% p.a. You pay tax at 40%, your position is as follows for 2020:

		2020 €
	Preferential house purchase loan	€60,000
	Interest paid €60,000 @ 3%	€1,800
	Benefit-In-Kind (BIK) €60,000 @ 4%	€2,400
Less:	Interest paid	€1,800
	Taxable BIK	€600
	Interest relief for tax purposes	
	Interest paid	€1,800
	Deemed interest paid	€600
	Total	**€2,400**

Accommodation

If your employer provides you with accommodation rent free or at a reduced rate and this accommodation is not necessary for your employment, then a taxable benefit arises. This benefit is normally the market rate of the annual rent which could be obtained on a yearly letting of the accommodation.

Any amounts paid by the employee to the employer by way of rent are deductible from the taxable benefit.

Relocation costs - relating to employment

Strictly, the cost of relocating your home is a personal expense. However, if it is a requirement of your job that you move home and certain procedures are followed, your employer may compensate you for these costs in a tax free manner.

The types of expenses covered are:

- Auctioneer's fees, solicitor's fees and stamp duty arising from moving home.

- Furniture removal costs.

- Storage charges.

- Insurance of furniture and items in transit.

- Cleaning stored furniture.

- Travelling expenses on removal.

- Temporary subsistence allowance while looking for new accommodation.

Formal requirements

- The cost must be borne directly by the employer in respect of actual expenses incurred by you.

- The expenses must be reasonable.

- The payments must be properly controlled.

Receipts must be provided (apart from temporary subsistence), and your Inspector of Taxes must be satisfied that moving home is necessary for your job.

Share schemes

More and more employers are looking at share schemes as a way of rewarding their employees. Some of these schemes attract favourable tax treatment provided certain conditions are met.

Approved profit share scheme

An approved profit sharing scheme allows a full or part time employee or a full time director to receive shares tax free from their employer up to an annual limit of €12,700 provided certain conditions are met.

A Trust is set up by the company, this Trust must purchase shares in the company on behalf of the employees with funds received from the company. The Trust must hold the shares for two years before transferring them to the employee, who must then hold the shares for three years after receiving them. If the shares are disposed of by the employee before the end of the three year period income tax is charged on the lower of:

- The market value of the shares at the date they were initially apportioned to the employee

  or

- The sale proceeds from the sale of the shares

However, if the employee/director ceases employment or reaches retirement age within the three year period, income tax will be payable at 50% of the lower of the above.

Approved profit sharing schemes are tax efficient for both the employee and employer as the employee can receive shares tax free up to an annual limit of €12,700 and the employer can offset the cost of the shares against the company's profits.

Shares appropriated to employees on or after 1 January 2011 under Revenue approved profit sharing schemes will continue to be exempt from income tax but will be subject to employees PRSI and the universal social charge (USC).

Share options

A share option arises where a company grants to its employees or directors an option to subscribe for shares in the company at a preferential price. A taxable benefit arises when the predetermined share price is less than the market value.

The amount liable to tax is the difference between the market value of the shares at the exercise date and the price you actually pay. This liability arises at the date you exercise the option.

If the options are capable of being exercised more than seven years after they were granted, income tax may also arise on the date the option is granted. The amount liable to income tax is the difference between the market value of the shares at the date the option was granted and the option price. Any tax paid at this early stage can be offset against the total tax liability when the option is eventually exercised.

Capital Gains Tax may also be payable on the shares if they increase in value from the date you exercise the option. Any amounts assessable to income tax are deemed to be part of the cost for Capital Gains Tax purposes.

Example

You are granted an option in August 2017 to purchase 2,000 shares in your employer's company at a future date for €7 per share. When you exercise your options in August 2020 the share price was €9 per share.

This tax would be payable 30 days after the date of exercise of the stock options.

	The amount liable to income tax in 2020	€
	Market value of shares in August 2015	€9 x 2,000 = €18,000
Less:	Option price	€7 x 2,000 = €14,000
	Benefit liable to income tax	€4,000

Returns by employers

Employers must provide certain information to the Revenue Commissioners about the stock options granted and exercised by employees.

Stock options and self-assessment

If you receive stock options from your employer, you are liable to tax under self-assessment in respect of the profit arising from the stock options.

Income tax is payable to the Collector General 30 days from the date of exercise of any stock options. The income tax rate payable is 40% of the net cheque received i.e. 40% of the difference between the sale price of the shares less the option price. If you think that your entire income tax liability for the year will be chargeable at the standard rate of income tax (currently 20%) you must obtain prior approval from Revenue to pay tax at the standard rate.

You should complete Form RTSO1 and forward it together with a cheque for the income tax due to the Collector General. You should also submit details of the share options received on your annual tax return - Form 11.

USC and PRSI must also be paid at the same time as the income tax using form RTSO1.

Savings related share option scheme

A save a your earn (SAYE) scheme is the most common form of a Saving Related Share Option Scheme. It contains a contractual savings scheme with a share option scheme. Under an approved SAYE scheme a company grants options over shares to its employees. The share options are granted at a price which is fixed by the directors at the time of the grant. This may be at the full market price value or at a discount of up to 25% on the market value.

SAYE schemes operate by allowing the employee to save between €12 and €500 per month out of their net income over a three, five or seven year period in order to finance the purchase of the shares. The employee must save in a special savings scheme which has been set up for SAYE schemes, with a qualifying savings institution. Any interest or bonus paid on the savings contract will be exempt from tax including deposit interest retention tax.

Example

5 Years Saving Contract	€
Monthly savings	€50.00
Share price at grant	€3.33
Discounted option price (75% of market value)	€2.50
Savings on maturity	€3,000
Interest on maturity	€250
Total savings & interest	**€3,250**
Options granted for 1,300 shares	

Normally when an employee exercises a share option, a charge to income tax will arise based on the excess value of the shares over the option price regardless of whether or not the shares are retained. However, options granted through a SAYE scheme approved by the Revenue Commissioners will not be liable to income tax on either grant or exercise provided the option is not exercised before the third anniversary of the grant. After this time any disposal of the shares will trigger a charge to capital gains tax based on the excess of the net sales proceeds over the actual option price.

Example

As part of a share incentive scheme, you save €200 per month from January to June 2019. At the end of six months you have saved €1,200.

Shares in your employer's company are €10 per share at June 2020. You buy 140 shares at 30 June 2020 at €8.50, at 15% discount, total cost of €1,190. You keep the shares until November 2020 when you sell them for €2,100.

	€
Income tax liability at 30 June 2020 - (Date Shares Acquired)	
Market value of shares acquired (140 x €10)	€1,400
Price paid (140 x €8.50)	€1,190
Taxable benefit	**€210**

A liability to Capital Gains Tax may arise when the shares are sold in November 2020, if the market rate at the time of sale exceeds €1,400.

Any gain on options that were granted and/or exercised under SAYE approved share option schemes on or after 1 January 2011 will continue to be exempt from income tax but will be subject to PRSI and the universal social charge (USC).

Share incentive schemes/employee share purchase plans (ESPP)

These are schemes whereby a fixed amount is deducted from your salary every month. After the end of a fixed period, say six months, you purchase shares in your employer's company at a discounted price.

This discount is a taxable benefit for you and is liable to income tax. If you sell the shares immediately on acquiring them no further liability to tax arises. However, Capital Gains Tax may be payable if you keep the shares and sell them at a profit at a later stage.

As share incentive schemes are designed to encourage employees to invest in their employer's business, many schemes prohibit the sale of shares immediately after they are acquired. Where the employee is prohibited from disposing of the shares for a number of years, the Revenue will allow an abatement in the income tax charge depending on the number of years of the prohibition on the disposal.

The abatement is as follows:

No. of Years	Abatement
1 Year	10%
2 Years	20%
3 Years	30%
4 Years	40%
5 Years	50%
Over 5 Years	60%

Restricted stock units (RSU's)

A Restricted Stock Unit is a grant (or promise) to an employee to the effect that, on completion of a 'vesting period', they will receive a number of shares. A restricted stock unit is, generally, evidenced by way of a certificate of such entitlement.

The 'vesting period' is the period of time between the date of the grant of the shares and the date on which the vesting condition is satisfied. Vesting periods are usually satisfied by, for example, the passage of time or by the individuals' employment performance.

Tax treatment of RSU's

An RSU is not a share option but rather is a taxable emolument of the employment.

Timing of taxation of awards of RSU's

The income tax liability of the shares arises either

- On the date of vesting (rather than on the date of the grant) of a restricted stock unit; or

- Where the shares pass to the employee on a date prior to the date of vesting, on that prior date.

Payment of dividend equivalents

In some instances, employees granted an RSU may be entitled to amounts equivalent to the dividends accruing to the shares promised under an RSU. Such dividend equivalents are taxable emoluments.

Employee share ownership trusts (ESOT's)

Employee share ownership trusts (ESOT's) were first introduced in the Finance Act 1997. They were primarily used by State companies which were being privatised.

A company can place shares for a maximum of 20 years in an ESOT. They are designed to work in conjunction with profit sharing scheme as shares can be released from the ESOT each year into the company's profit sharing scheme.

The €12,700 tax free limit which applies to a profit sharing scheme can be increased to a once-off €38,100 after 10 years in respect of shares previously held in an ESOT provided;

- The shares have been transferred to the Trustees of an approved profit sharing scheme by the trustees of an ESOT;

    and

- In the first five years of the establishment of the ESOT, 50% of the shares retained by the Trustees were pledged as security on borrowings.

- No shares which were pledged as security for borrowings by Trustees of the ESOT were previously transferred to the Trustees of a profit sharing scheme.

Key employee engagement programme (KEEP)

A share based renumeration incentive was introduced with effect from 1 Jan 2018 to facilitate the use of share-based remuneration by unquoted SME companies to attract key employees. Any gains arising to employees on the exercise of KEEP share options will be subject to Capital Gains Tax, in place of the current liability to income tax, USC and PRSI on exercise. This incentive is available for qualifying share options granted between 1 January 2018 and 31 December 2023. The maximum value of KEEP options which can be granted to any employee is

- €100,000 in any one tax year
- €300,000 over the lifetime of the scheme
- Any amount equal to the employees annual salary, subject to the overall limits

9 Self-employment

If you are self-employed or a PAYE worker and have other non-PAYE income, you will be regarded as a "chargeable person" and will be liable to self assessment.

Proprietary directors are also subject to the self assessment system even if all their income is taxed under PAYE. A proprietary director is one who holds more than 15% of the share capital of a company.

Under the self-assessment system, you are required to

- Submit your completed Income Tax Return - (Form 11) to your Inspector of Taxes on/before 31 October following the year of assessment e.g. your 2019 tax return must be submitted on/before the 31 October 2020.

- Pay your preliminary tax on the due date in the year of assessment e.g. your preliminary tax for 2020 is due on 31 October 2020.

Preliminary tax

Preliminary tax is an estimate of income tax payable for the year. It is payable by 31 October in the year of assessment e.g. on 31 October 2020 you pay your Preliminary Tax for 2020.

The amount payable is the lower of

- 90% of your final liability for the current tax year,

  or

- 100% of your liability for the previous tax year

Payment by direct debit

If you choose to pay your preliminary tax by direct debit, your payments will be based on 105% of your final tax liability for non PAYE income in the pre-preceding year e.g. if your final tax liability for non PAYE income in 2018 was €8,000 - your 2020 preliminary tax liability can be paid by 12 monthly instalments of €700 (€8,000 x 105% ÷ 12).

Surcharge

If you don't submit your tax return by 31 October, a surcharge will be added to your tax bill. The amount of the surcharge will depend on when your tax return is eventually submitted.

A surcharge of 5% of the total tax due (up to a maximum of €12,695) is added where your tax return is submitted before 31 December following the year of assessment or 10% (up to a maximum of €63,485) where the return is submitted after 31 December following the year of assessment.

Local property tax (LPT) surcharge

A chargeable person may incur a Local Property Tax (LPT) generated surcharge of up to 10% of their Income Tax (IT) Corporation Tax (CT) or Capital Gains Tax (CGT) liability.

Revenue will apply this LPT surcharge when:

- The LPT return that was due has not been filed and an IT, a CT or a CGT return is filed
- There are outstanding LPT liabilities at the date of filing the IT, CT or CGT return
- Any LPT due is not being paid in accordance with an agreed payment arrangement.

An LPT generated surcharge will be imposed on whatever date the IT, CT or CGT return is filed. The surcharge is in addition to the actual LPT liability plus interest that may arise for late payment.

The LPT generated surcharge may be capped provided that the following conditions are met:

- The LPT generated surcharge is higher than the combined LPT liabilities outstanding
- The person has filed the LPT return
- The person has paid any outstanding LPT, or enters into an agreed payment arrangement.

Relevant dates

Pay preliminary tax	31 October in year of assessment e.g. 31 October 2020 pay preliminary tax for tax year 2020.
File tax return	31 October following the end of the tax year e.g. tax return for 2019 (year ended 31 December 2019) must be filed by the 31 October 2020.
Pay balance of tax	31 October following the return filing date. Balance of tax due for 2019 (year ended 31 December 2019) must be paid by 31 October 2020.

ROS

If you pay your income tax and file your tax return using Revenue Online Service (ROS) you can avail of an extension to the 31 October deadline. In 2019 ROS filers had until 12 November 2019 to file their 2018 returns and pay their tax.

Contract of service vs contract for service

If you work for an employer for more than eight hours a week you are entitled to a contract of employment and are employed under a contract of service. This contract gives you the benefit of protective legislation, including the Holidays Act 1973, the Unfair Dismissal Acts 1977 and 1993, the Minimum Notice and Terms of Employment Act 1973 and many others. As an employee you pay PAYE and PRSI.

As a contractor you have an independent business and your contract for work is a contract for services so you are not protected under the employment legislation mentioned earlier. You are regarded as "self-employed" for tax purposes.

Setting up as a contractor

There are a number of issues you must face as a contractor. These include, do you operate as a Sole Trader / Partnership or Limited Company? VAT is also another consideration.

Limited company

Limited companies prepare audited accounts annually, which may be more costly than preparing accounts as a sole trader.

Paying corporation tax

Companies must pay preliminary tax via ROS to the Collector General under self assessment.

The total amount of preliminary tax paid must be equal to or greater than 90% of the company's final tax liability for the accounting year.

Corporation tax is charged on company's profits at a rate of 12.5% for trading income and 25% on non-trading income. The taxable profit is computed in the same way as the taxable profit for a sole trader. A companies tax return form CT1 should be submitted to the Inspector of Taxes on a date nine months after the end of the company's year end but not later than 21 days after the ninth month. If returns are filed electronically the return filing and payment deadlines are extended to the 23rd day of the relevant month.

If you operate as a company, you, as a director, can decide the level of salary you will receive under the PAYE system.

From a pension point of view, a company can make more generous pension contributions to your retirement fund and have these contributions offset against its taxable profits.

If a director owns a car and pays their own car insurance, motor tax and petrol costs, they can claim a mileage allowance for any business miles they travel on behalf of the company in accordance with the civil service mileage rates (see page 144) and have this cost offset against the profits of the company.

"As a sole trader you are liable to income tax at 20% or 40% on the profits earned by the business each year."

Start up companies

A relief from corporation tax for start up companies in their first 3 years of trading, was introduced for companies who were incorporated on or after 14 October 2008 and who set up and commenced a qualifying trade between 1 January 2009 and 31 December 2018. The 2018 Finance Act extended this relief to new companies that start trading in 2019, 2020 & 2021. The relief is granted by reducing the corporation tax payable on the profit of this new trade and chargeable gains on the disposal of any assets used for the purposes of a new trade.

Prior to Finance Act 2011, full relief was granted where the total amount of corporation tax payable by a company for an accounting period did not exceed €40,000. Marginal relief was granted where the total amount of corporation tax payable by a new company for an accounting period amounted to between €40,000 and €60,000. No relief applied where corporation tax payable was €60,000 or more.

For accounting periods beginning on or after 1 January 2011 the value of the relief is based on the amount of the employer's PRSI paid by a company in an accounting period, subject to a maximum of €5,000 per employee and an overall limit of €40,000.

Sole trader

As a sole trader you are liable to income tax at 20% or 40% on the profits earned by the business each year, regardless of the actual cash you withdraw from the business. Tax is due for payment on 31 October each year. You are also liable to PRSI and the universal social charge.

Cars

As a sole trader the cost of running a car can be apportioned between your business and private use on a basis agreed with your Tax Inspector.

VAT

If you provide a service and your sales are in excess of €37,500 p.a. you must register for VAT. If you provide goods the VAT limit is €75,000 p.a.

The implications of VAT registration are as follows;

- VAT must be charged on all invoices.

- VAT on business expenses (other than entertainment and motor expenses can be reclaimed).

- Proper VAT records must be kept and VAT returns completed.

Insurance

If you are operating a business from your own home, you need to be aware your home is also now a business premises and can be treated as such for insurance purposes.

Insurance companies have become increasingly aware of the dual use of private homes and expect clients to inform them when their home is being used for business purposes. This may not necessarily result in a higher annual insurance premium, but it may affect your right to make a successful claim if equipment is stolen or damaged or if somebody is injured on your premises.

Registering for income tax

You should advise Revenue when you start a business as a self-employed / sole trader. You should use the Revenue Online Service ROS to register or if you have a tax agent they can do this for you.

Capital gains tax (CGT)

Using your house for business purposes means you can claim some of the running costs against your annual income tax bill. These can include electricity, gas, telephone, insurance, etc.   However, on the sale of your home you may face a CGT bill for the part of your home which was used as a business.

Start your own business (SYOB)

As an employment activation measure, the Start Your Own Business (SYOB) incentive provides an exemption from income tax, to individuals who set up a qualifying, un-incorporated business, having been unemployed for a period of at least 12 months prior to establishing the business. The first €40,000 of profits per annum will not be subject to income tax for the first two years. However, PRSI and USC will apply to the profits. This scheme applies to qualifying businesses set up between from 25 October 2013 to 31 December 2018.

Calculation of your profit

Income tax is charged on taxable profits. Taxable profits are your gross income less expenses which are allowed for income tax purposes.

The following expenses are specifically disallowed:

- Any expenses which are not wholly and exclusively made for the purpose of the trade.

- Entertainment expenses - this would include the provision of accommodation, food or drink or any other hospitality for clients. Entertainment provided for staff, within reason would be an allowable expense.

- Personal expenses.

- Capital expenditure incurred on improvements to the business premises.

- Any debt except bad debts and doubtful debts that are not expected to be recouped.

Capital allowances

Depreciation, as such, is not allowable for tax purposes but Capital Allowances in the form of wear and tear allowances are allowed for plant and machinery, fixtures and fittings and motor vehicles which are used for the trade or profession. The rate of wear and tear allowance for plant and machinery and motor vehicles is 12.5% p.a. for eight years. For taxis and short term hire vehicles the annual rate of wear and tear is 40% each year. Accelerated capital allowances may be claimed for expenditure incurred on certain energy efficient equipment bought for the purpose of the trade.

Capital allowances on business cars can only be claimed on an amount up to €24,000. If the business car costs in excess of this amount, the capital allowances can only be claimed on €24,000.

A revised scheme of capital allowances and leasing expenses for cars used for business purposes was introduced for cars purchased or leased on or after 1 July 2008. The revision links the availability of such allowances expenses to the CO_2 emission levels of vehicles. Cars are categorised by reference to CO_2 emissions with the emissions bands being broadly consistent with the VRT system, as follows:

Category A vehicles	Category B/C vehicles	Category D/E vehicles	Category F/G vehicles
0-120g/km	121 -155 g/km	156 - 190g/km	191 g/km [+]

Cars with CO_2 emission levels in category A/B/C above will benefit from capital allowances at the relevant specified limit (currently €24,000), regardless of the cost of the car. Cars in the category D/E will receive allowances of 50% of the €24,000 car value threshold or 50% of the cost of the car, if lower. Cars in category F/G will not qualify for capital allowances.

Keeping books and records

If you are self employed you must keep full and accurate records of your business from the start. You need to do this whether you send in a simple summary of your profit or loss, prepare the accounts yourself, or have an accountant do it for you. It is important for you to remember that the figures which are contained in your accounts, and your tax returns, must be correct. The records you keep must be sufficient to enable you to make a proper return of income for tax purposes.

You should bear in mind that you may need to keep accounts for reasons unconnected with tax. For example, your bank may want to see your accounts when considering an application for a business loan.

You must keep your books and records for a period of six years unless your Inspector of Taxes advises you otherwise.

Witholding tax on payments for professional services

Tax at the standard rate is deducted by Government departments, State bodies, HSE, etc. from payments made for professional services.

The tax deducted can be claimed in the year in which it is withheld, i.e. tax withheld in 2020 can be offset against your tax liabilities for 2020 and any excess can be reclaimed.

Basis of assessment - new business

When you commence your business you are liable to income tax on your profits as follows

First year

Actual profits from commencement to following 31 December.

Second year

(i)   If there is one set of accounts made up to a date within that tax year and these accounts are for 12 months, these accounts will form the basis period for the second year of assessment.

(ii)   If the accounts are for less than one year or if there is more than one set of accounts ending within the tax year, then the basis of assessment is the full amount of the profits for the 12 months ending on the latest of these dates.

(iii) In all other cases, the actual profits for the tax year.

If the actual profits of the second year are less than the profits for the first 12 months of trading the difference can be used to reduce the income for the third year of assessment.

Third and following years

Profits for accounts for 12 months ending in the actual tax year.

Basis of assessment - cessation of business

When you cease your business your profits are assessed to tax as follows:

Final   Actual profits from 1 January to date of cessation.

Penultimate Where the actual profits (1 January to 31 December) of the penultimate tax year exceed the profits assessed for that tax year, the assessment will be increased to the amount of the actual profits.

Partnership

A partner is assessed on their share of the partnership profits as adjusted for tax purposes, by reference to the profit sharing ratio in force during the period.

Capital allowances on plant and equipment are split between the partners according to their profit sharing ratio in the tax period.

The profits of a trade or profession carried on by a partnership are not assessed for income tax on the partnership as such, but each partner is deemed to be carrying on a separate trade and, each is assessed for tax individually.

Relevant period

For trades or professions carried on by a partnership, there is what is referred to as the "relevant period". This begins when two or more persons commence to carry on a trade or profession in partnership, continue as partners or join or leave the partnership, provided at least one person who is a partner before a change in the partnership remains on after the change. The relevant period ceases only in any of the following circumstances:

- The cessation of a trade.

- Where all the partners but one retire.

- Where a completely new group of partners replaces the old partners.

When the relevant period commences, the partners are assessed on the basis that they have set up new trades and each partner is assessed for tax under the commencement rules for Cases I and II. For the duration of the relevant periods, the partners are treated as continuing these separate trades and are assessed for tax accordingly.

Completing your income tax return

Under Pay and File you must file your 2019 Tax Return and pay your liabilities on or before 31 October 2020. On that date you must also pay your preliminary tax liability for 2020 and any balance of Income Tax due for 2019. It is your responsibility to calculate your own tax liabilities.

If your tax return is submitted after 31 October a surcharge (5% where the return is submitted within two months, otherwise 10%) may be added to your tax liability.

If you submit your tax return and also pay your tax liability online via Revenue Online Services (ROS), the 31 October deadline will be extended. In 2019 ROS filers had until 12 November 2019 to pay and file their 2018 tax return.

Revenue On-Line Service (ROS)

As an alternative to completing a paper tax return, you can file your return electronically through the Revenue On-Line Service (ROS).

ROS (Revenue Online Service) is an internet facility which provides customers with a quick and secure facility to file tax returns, pay tax liabilities and access their tax details, 24 hours a day, 7 days a week, 365 days a year.

The main features of ROS include facilities to:

- File returns online.

- Make payments by credit/debit card, debit instruction or by online banking.

- Obtain online details of personal/clients Revenue Accounts.

- Calculate your tax liability.

- Conduct business electronically.

- Claim repayments.

ROS will provide you with an instant calculation of your tax liability, letting you know how much to pay on 31 October.

You can access ROS through Revenue's website www.revenue.ie

Mandatory e-Filing

Since 2009 the categories of taxpayers obliged to pay and file electronically has been expanding. From 1 January 2015 all newly registering income tax cases became mandatory e-filers. Also if your tax affairs are dealt with by large case division or if you claim certain tax reliefs e.g. pension payments, BES, seed capital relief, you will be deemed to be a mandatory e-filer and you must submit your annual tax return online.

What information should I submit with my tax return?

You should not submit any supporting documentation with your tax return unless expressly asked to do so; for example where you have a genuine doubt about any item in the return you should make a note of this on the tax return by way of "expression of doubt". Supporting documentation, including business accounts, must be retained for six years as it may be requested by Revenue for the purpose of an audit.

Do not enter terms such as 'per attached', 'as before', etc on your tax return. You must enter the requested information.

Incomplete returns will be sent back to you for proper completion and you might incur a surcharge if the corrected return is submitted late.

Before submitting your return, ensure you sign and date the declaration on the front page of the return. If you are filing the return as an executor, guardian or administrator, or as an authorised agent, state the capacity in which you are signing the return and for whom you are acting.

Revenue audit

A revenue audit is a cross-check of the information and figures shown by you in your tax returns against those shown in your business records.

A revenue audit covers the following types of tax returns:

- Income tax, corporation tax, or capital gains tax returns and/or

- The returns submitted in respect of VAT, PAYE/PRSI, or relevant contracts tax (RCT).

How are taxpayers selected for audit?

Revenue uses three methods of selection:

Screening tax returns

The vast majority of audit cases are selected in this way. Screening involves examining the returns made by a variety of taxpayers and reviewing their compliance history. The figures are then analysed in the light of trends and patterns in the particular business or profession and evaluated against other available information.

Projects on business sectors

From time to time, projects are conducted to examine tax compliance levels in particular trades or professions. The returns for a large number of taxpayers in a particular sector are screened in detail and a proportion of these are selected for audit.

Random selection

This is in addition to the first two methods. It means that all taxpayers have a possibility of being audited. Each year, a small proportion of audit cases are selected using this method.

The self-employed and PRSI

With few exceptions, all self-employed people between the ages of 16 and 66 must pay PRSI contributions on their reckonable income if their gross income exceed €5,000 in a year. Reckonable income can be both earned and unearned and includes the following:

- Income from a trade or profession.

- Income from which tax has been deducted at source such as annuities, bank interest or building society interest and dividends.

- Irish rents and income from foreign property.

Self-employed individuals including propriety company directors pay PRSI under Class S.

PRSI is charged at 4% on all income or a minimum of €500 whichever is the greater.

However, the following are excluded for PRSI purposes:

- Any sum received by way of benefit, pension allowance or supplement from the Department of Social Protection.

- Any sums received from FÁS for training courses.

- Any payments received by way of occupational pension, also income continuance plans payable in the event of loss of employment due to ill health where the scheme has been approved by the Revenue Commissioners.

- Redundancy payments (either statutory or non-statutory), "golden handshake" type payments and early retirement gratuities. However redundancy payments with the exception of statutory redundancy are liable to the universal social charge (USC).

- Health Board payments by way of Infectious Diseases Maintenance Allowance or Mobility Allowance.

- Payments received by a person in respect of the following offices; income related to a member of the Dáil, An Seanad or the European Parliament, the judiciary, public offices under the State such as Labour Court members, the Comptroller and Auditor General, Harbour Commissioners etc.

- Prescribed relatives i.e. certain relatives who help out a self-employed person in the running of a family business, assuming they are not partners in the business.

Paying PRSI

If you pay income tax directly to the Collector General, you also pay your PRSI contributions to the Collector General.

Class "S" benefits

Self-employed people paying Class "S" PRSI will generally be entitled to the following benefits, assuming they have paid the minimum qualifying contributions:

- State Contributory Pension.
- Widow's/Widower/Surviving Civil Partner's Contributory Pension.
- Orphan's Contributory Allowance.
- Maternity, Paternity and Adoptive Benefits.

Universal social charge (USC)

The universal social charge was introduced from 1 January 2011. It is payable on gross income including notional pay, after relief for certain trading losses and capital allowances, but before pension contributions.

All individuals are liable to the USC if their gross income exceeds €13,000 per annum, (€250 per week in 2020). The rate of USC for 2019 and 2020 are as follows:

USC Thresholds 2019 and 2020			
2019		2020	
	Rate		Rate
Income up to €12,012.00	0.5%	Income up to €12,012.00	0.5%
Income from €12,012.01 to €19,874.00	2%	Income from €12,012.01 to €19,874.00	2%
Income from €19,874.01 to €70,044.00	4.5%	Income from €19,874.01 to €70,044.00	4.5%
Income above €70,044.00	8%	Income above €70,044.00	8%

Individuals whose Non-PAYE income exceeds €100,000 in a year are liable to an additional USC surcharge of 3% on any Non-PAYE income over €100,000.

A reduced rate of USC applies to the following:

- Individuals aged 70 years or over whose aggregate income for the year is €60,000 or less.

- Individuals (aged under 70) who hold a full medical card whose aggregate income for the year is €60,000 or less.

The reduced rate of USC in 2019 and 2020 is as follows:

USC Thresholds 2019 and 2020			
2019	Rate	2020	Rate.
Income up to €12,012	0.5%	Income up to €12,012	0.5%
Income above €12,012	2%	Income above €12,012	2%

Note 2:   "Aggregate" income for USC purposes does not include payments from the Dept of Social Protection.

Note 3:   A "GP only" card is not considered a full medical card for USC purposes.

Exempt categories

- Where an individual's total income for a year does not exceed €13,000.

- All Department of Social Protection payments.

- Income already subjected to DIRT.

10 Working abroad / Foreign income

Generally, your liability to Irish Income Tax on foreign income depends on

- Whether you are resident in Ireland.
- Whether you are ordinarily resident in Ireland.
- Whether you are domiciled in Ireland.

Residence

You will be regarded as being resident here for tax purposes in the current tax year

- If you spend 183 days or more here

  or

- If the combined number of days you spend here in the current tax year and the number of days you spent here in the last tax year exceeds 280. In applying this two year test, a period of less than 30 days spent in Ireland in a tax year will be ignored.

Your presence in Ireland for a day, means at any time during the day.

Electing to be resident

If you come to Ireland and are not regarded as resident here for tax purposes but you can show that you intend to remain and be resident here next year, you may elect to be treated as resident for tax purposes from the date of your arrival.

Electing to be non-resident

This is not possible in any circumstances.

Ordinarily resident

The term "ordinarily resident" as distinct from "resident", relates to your normal pattern of life and denotes residence in a country with some degree of continuity.

When does ordinarily residence begin?

If you have been resident here for three consecutive tax years, you become ordinarily resident from the beginning of the fourth tax year.

When does ordinarily residence cease?

If you have been ordinarily resident here, you will cease to be ordinarily resident at the end of the third consecutive year in which you are not resident. For example, if you are resident and ordinarily resident here in 2015 and leave the State in that year, you will remain ordinarily resident up to the end of the tax year 2018.

Domicile

Domicile is a complex legal concept. It is generally the country which you consider to be your natural home. When you are born, you obtain a domicile of origin which is normally the domicile of your father.

Resident & domicile

If you are resident and domiciled in Ireland you are liable to Irish income tax on your worldwide income. If you have foreign income on which you have paid foreign tax you are normally liable to Irish tax on the gross amount of this income. You may be able to claim a credit against your Irish tax liability for the foreign tax paid or to a refund or partial refund of the foreign tax and a credit for the balance, provided a Double Taxation Agreement is in place between Ireland and the foreign country.

Resident/not domiciled or ordinarily resident in Ireland.

If you are resident but not domiciled or ordinarily resident in Ireland, you are liable to Irish income tax in full on your income arising in Ireland and on your foreign employment income only if you perform the duties of this employment in Ireland. Any foreign non-employment income is only liable to Irish tax if it is remitted to Ireland.

Not resident but ordinarily resident and domiciled

If you are not resident but ordinarily resident and domiciled in Ireland you are liable to Irish tax on your world wide income. The only exception to this is income from a trade, profession or employment no part of which is carried out in Ireland, apart from incidental duties. If you have other foreign income it will not be taxed in Ireland provided the amount is less than €3,810.

Individual not resident and not ordinarily resident

If you are not resident and not ordinarily resident in Ireland, in general, you are liable to Irish income tax only on income arising in Ireland. In addition a non resident individual is generally not entitled to personal tax credits and reliefs. They are liable to tax at the standard rate and the higher rate.

Full personal tax credits and reliefs

- If you are a resident here, you are entitled to full personal tax credits and full tax reliefs.

- If you are not resident here but are resident in another member state of the European Union and 75% or more of your worldwide income is taxable here, you will also be entitled to full personal tax credits and full tax reliefs here.

Partial personal tax credits and reliefs

- If you are a citizen of Ireland or a citizen, subject or national of another member state of the European Union, **or**

- If you are a former resident of the State who is now resident outside of this country because of your health or because of the health of a member of your family resident with you, **or**

- If you are a resident or national of a country with which Ireland has a double taxation agreement which provides for such allowances.

If any of the above applies and you are non-resident here for tax purposes you will be entitled to a certain proportion of personal tax credits and tax reliefs. The exact proportion of these allowances is determined by the relationship between your income which is subject to Irish tax and your income from all other sources.

Tax summary

Individual	Liability To Irish Income Tax
Resident and domiciled in Ireland	On worldwide income from all sources.
Resident but not domiciled or ordinarily resident in Ireland	On all Irish income and non Irish income remitted to Ireland
Ordinarily resident but not resident here in the relevant tax year.	On worldwide income. However, employment or income from an employment trade or profession which is exercised wholly abroad or income from other sources which does not exceed €3,810 will be ignored for tax purposes. Double taxation agreements may exempt some foreign income.
Not resident or ordinarily resident	Taxed on income arising from Irish sources.

Double taxation

Generally, Irish residents are liable to Irish income tax on worldwide income and non-residents are liable to Irish income tax on income arising in Ireland. As similar provisions apply to residents of other countries, this can give rise to double taxation. The purpose of double taxation agreements is to prevent this double taxation of income. This may be achieved either by;

- Exempting certain income from tax in one country,   **or**

- By offsetting the tax paid on income in one country against the tax liability arising on that same income in another country.

Example

In 2020 a single man who is an Irish citizen but not resident here, had the following sources of income:

	€
Rental income in Ireland	€10,000
US Dividends	€3,000
Rental Income in UK	€4,000
Total Income	**€17,000**

As the individual is not resident here, they are liable to Irish tax only on income arising in Ireland and entitled to partial personal tax credits as follows;

	€
Irish Income	€10,000
Taxable €10,000 @ 20%	€2,000
Less: Tax Credits €1,650 x €10,000 / €17,000	€970
Net tax payable	**€1,030**

PAYE exclusion order

If you are employed abroad by an Irish Employer and carry out all the duties of your employment abroad your employer can apply to Revenue for a PAYE exclusion order. A PAYE exclusion order will be issued for the relevant tax provided the employee

- Is not resident in the State for tax purposes for the relevant tax year,

- Exercises the duties of the employment wholly outside the State

In general, individuals will have to be absent from the State for a complete income tax year or for a sufficient period over two income tax years to 'break' Irish residence to qualify for a PAYE Exclusion Order. In determining where the duties of the employment are exercised, incidental duties performed in the State may be ignored. 'Incidental' in this context means fewer than 30 days working here over a full tax year.

To apply for a PAYE exclusion order the employer needs to send a letter to Revenue stating the length of time the employee will spend out of state. Revenue will then provide a letter authorising the employer to operate no PAYE on payments made to that employee. The PAYE exclusion order exempts the employee from paying PAYE and USC but PRSI liability will still arise for the employee and employer.

A PAYE exclusion order is in place as long as the employee remains non-resident subject to an expiry date on the exclusion order. An application for a PAYE exclusion order cannot be backdated.

A PAYE exclusion order may also be available for non-resident pensioners such that they will receive their Irish source pension without the deduction of Irish payroll taxes.

Year of arrival / return

If you move to Ireland but are not already resident here for tax purposes and if you can show that you intend to remain here and to be resident in Ireland for tax purposes the following year, you may elect to be treated as a resident here for income tax purposes from the date of your arrival and your tax position will work out as follows:

Example

You returned to Ireland on 1 Sept 2020 after spending three years abroad. Your earnings in Ireland from 1 Sept 2020 to 31 Dec 2020 were €18,500.

	€
Irish Income	€18,500
Tax Payable €18,500 @ 20%	€ 3,700
Less: Tax Credits	
Personal	(€1,650)
PAYE	(€1,650)
	(€3,300)
Net tax payable	€ 400

You will be liable to Irish tax on any foreign income which may accrue to you after the date of your return, subject to any relevant double taxation agreement.

Year of departure / split year treatment

If you are resident in Ireland during the tax year you leave and you will be non resident for the following tax year, you will be deemed to be non resident from the date of departure. In order to avail of this arrangement (known as split year treatment) it is necessary that you satisfy your local tax office of your intention not to be resident in Ireland for the tax year following your departure.

Example

You leave Ireland on 30 September 2020 to take up a two year contract in the USA. From 1 January 2020 to the date of departure you earn €40,000 in Ireland and pay PAYE of €8,230. Your income in the USA from 1 October 2020 to 31 December 2020 will be €21,000. Your position in 2020 will be as follows:

	Split Year Treatment €
Salary - Ireland (up to Sept 2020)	€40,000
Taxable	€40,000
Tax Payable	
€ 35,300 @ 20%	€7,060
€ 4,700 @ 40%	€1,880
	€8,940
Less: Tax Credits	
Personal Credit	(€1,650)
PAYE Credit	(€1,650)
Tax Liability	€5,640
Less: PAYE Paid	(€8,230)
Refund Due	**(€2,590)**

Residence and married couples

Your spouse's resident status is not governed by your residence status. If the residence status of your spouse differs from yours, you may choose to be treated as single people for tax purposes if it is to your advantage to do so.

Renting while abroad

Many homeowners going abroad for a limited period will rent their homes while they are abroad. This income is taxable in Ireland regardless of residence status.

Example

You rent your home for €1,200 per month while you work abroad. You have a mortgage of €85,000, mortgage interest of €4,800 per annum and outgoings (agency fees, insurance, repairs etc.) of €1,600.

		€
	Gross Rental Income	€14,400
Less:	Mortgage Interest	(€ 4,800)
	Other outgoings	(€ 1,600)
	Taxable Income	**€ 8,000**

In order to claim mortgage interest relief as a rental expense it is necessary to register the tenancy with the Private Residential Tenancies Board (PRTB). From 1 Jan 2019 100% of mortgage interest paid on a loan to buy/improve or repair a rental residential property can be deducted as a rental expense against the gross rents received.

Rent paid to non-resident landlord

Where rents are paid directly to someone who lives abroad, the tenant must deduct income tax from the rent paid at the standard rate of income tax and pay this tax over to the Revenue Commissioners. At the end of the year the tenant must give the landlord a completed Form R185 (available from your local tax office or on www.revenue.ie), showing the amount of tax withheld by them from the gross rent paid, and confirming that this tax has been paid over to the Revenue Commissioners on behalf of the landlord. When the landlord completes their Irish tax return, they will get credit for this tax against their liability to tax on the rent. If they have no liability they can claim a refund of the tax deducted by the tenant.

This obligation on the tenant to deduct tax from your rental income is removed if the rent is paid to a person whose usual place of abode is in the State e.g. an Irish based estate agent acting on behalf of the landlord. The agent would then be liable as collecting agent for the landlord and must submit a tax return in relation to the rents and pay any tax due on the rent to the Collector General on behalf of the landlord.

Capital gains tax (CGT)

When you sell your main residence, it is normally exempt from CGT. However, if you have rented your main residence for a number of years, at the date of sale, the CGT exemption will be restricted on a time basis.

For CGT purposes, certain periods of absence are regarded as periods of occupation e.g.

- The last 12 months of ownership.

- Any period of absence throughout which you worked in a foreign employment or any period of absence not exceeding four years during which you were prevented from occupying the residence because of employment, provided you occupy the residence before and after the period of absence.

Example

You bought your home in January 2007 for €250,000. You rented it out from 1 January 2015 to 31 December 2018 while you worked abroad. You sold it in December 2019 for €275,000. Your CGT liability will be calculated as follows:

"If you work abroad and rent your home, your tenant is obliged to deduct tax at the standard rate from the rental income."

Period of Ownership:	
1 January 2007 - 31 December 2014	8 Years Principal Private Residence (PPR)
1 January 2015 - 31 December 2018	4 Years Rented
1 January 2019 - 31 December 2019	1 Year Deemed PPR - last 12 months of ownership
Total Period of ownership	13 years
Non Principal Private Residence	4 Years

	€
Sale Price	€275,000
Less: Selling Costs	(€5,000)
	€270,000
Purchase Price Jan 2007	€250,000
Capital Gain	€20,000
Less: Capital Gains Exemption	(€1,270)
Taxable Gain	€18,730
Tax @ 33%	**€6,180.90**

However, you may claim CGT exemption for the eight years while the property was your main private residence, together with the last 12 months of ownership which is deemed to be your Principal Private Residence. So, your CGT liability will be €1,482 (€18,730 x 4/13 - €1,270 @ 33%).

You could also claim total exemption from total CGT, provided you returned and lived in your former home for a period before you sold it.

Foreign earnings deduction (FED)

For the tax years 2012 to 2022 inclusive, relief from taxation may be claimed on a proportion of income earned by individuals who are resident in the State but who spend significant amounts of time working in a "relevant state". The relief applies to income tax for the years of assessment 2012 to 2022 but does not apply to Universal Social Charge or PRSI.

"Relevant state" means Brazil, Russia, India, China or South Africa, and

- From 1 January 2013, includes Egypt, Algeria, Senegal, Tanzania, Kenya, Nigeria, Ghana or the Democratic Republic of the Congo.

- From 1 January 2015, includes Japan, Singapore, the Republic of Korea, Saudi Arabia, the United Arab Emirates, Qatar, Bahrain, Indonesia, Vietnam, Thailand, Chile, Oman, Kuwait, Mexico and Malaysia.

- From 1 January 2017 it includes Columbia and Pakistan.

Qualifying conditions

The basic condition is that within a period of 12 months (part of which is in the tax year to which the claim relates), the employee has worked in one or more of the relevant states for a minimum period of;

- At least 60 days in 2012, 2013 and 2014
- At least 40 days in 2015 and 2016
- At least 30 days in 2017 to 2022

Exclusions

The Foreign Earnings Deduction does not apply to civil or public servants nor does it apply to income

- From an employment to which the remittance basis of taxation applies.
- To which the "key employee research and development" tax relief applies.
- To which the "split year" residence rules applies.
- To which the Transborder Worker Relief applies; **or**,
- To which relief under the Special Assignee Relief Programme (SARP) applies.

From 1 January 2015 the qualifying conditions were eased by deeming time spent travelling to a relevant state, or from a relevant state to Ireland or to another relevant state, to be time spent in a relevant state.

How much allowance can you claim?

The amount of the allowance due is less than or equal to €35,000 or the specified amount.

The specified amount is calculated using D x E / F

- D is the number of qualifying days worked in a relevant state during the tax year.
- E is all the income received from the employment in the tax year. This includes any taxable share options less any qualifying pension premium. It excludes allowable expenses payments, Benefit in Kind (BIK), and termination payments.
- F is the total number of days that the employment is held by you in the year.

The tax relief is claimed at the end of the relevant tax year.

In order to make a claim you must apply in writing to your local tax office and include a statement from your employer that includes the date of your departure and return to Ireland and your location or locations while you worked abroad.

Coming to live in Ireland

If you become resident in Ireland you will only be liable to Irish income tax from the date of your arrival provided you were non-resident here in the previous year. Even though you will only be taxed in Ireland on income for part of the year, you will receive a full year's tax credits. If you arrive in Ireland and are not resident here for tax purposes, any income arising in Ireland will be liable to Irish tax. However, you will only receive tax credits for the portion of the year that you are actually here.

Emergency tax

If your employer does not receive a Revenue Payroll Notification (RPN) for you, they will be obliged to deduct tax on an emergency basis from your salary.   The RPN will tell your employer how much income tax and universal social charge (USC) to deduct from your pay. Under emergency tax a temporary tax credit is given for the first month of employment. See page 140 for more details. In order for you to ensure that an RPN is sen to your employer you must first get a Personal Public Service (PPS) number.

Your Personal Public Service (PPS) number is a unique reference that enables you access Social Welfare benefits, public services and information in Ireland.   You also need a PPS number to register for tax in Ireland.

Obtaining a PPS number

In order to obtain a PPS number you must show that you actually require one, for example if you are taking up employment in Ireland. To get a PPS number you need to present yourself at your local social welfare office together with some form of ID e.g. your passport and complete an application form.   You will then be issued with a PPS Number. Once you have obtained your PPS number you can register for income tax through myAccount on ROS.ie and apply for a tax credit cert (TCC). Your employer will also receive a Revenue Payroll Notification (RPN) for you once your TCC issues and you will receive a refund of any tax which you may have overpaid.

You can expect to pay tax on all income, which may include:

* Gross salary.

* Bonuses and commissions.

* Cash allowances for housing, school fees, cost of living , etc.

* Benefit-In-Kind (BIK).

* Share incentives, though various rules apply depending on the scheme.

If you have earnings from other sources, such as rental income, share dividends or deposit interest, it will also be subject to tax whether it has been earned here or abroad.

Special assignee relief programme (SARP)

SARP is a relief from income tax aimed at employees who move to Ireland with their employer or an associated company.   The relief operates by allowing a 30% deduction from any employment income in excess of €75,000 The relief was first introduced in Jan 2012. It applies to those arriving to work in Ireland and runs up to the end of 2022. It can then be claimed for five consecutive years.

The relief operates by allowing a 30% deduction from any employment income in excess of €75,000. For 2019, the relief was subject to an income cap of €1,000,000 for new claimants. Existing claimants were not subject to the income cap in 2019, but instead the cap applies from 2020.

In order to qualify the individual must:

* Have a base salary of at least €75,000;

* Be a full-time employee of a company tax resident in a country with which Ireland has a Double Taxation Agreement (or Information Exchange Agreement) for 6 months immediately prior to arrival;

* Become tax resident in Ireland and arrive in Ireland to perform duties for their employer or an associated company of their employer (relief does not apply to organisational "new hires");

* Not have been tax resident in Ireland for the five years immediately preceding the year of arrival; and

* Have made an application to Revenue within 90 days of arrival.

Capital gains tax (CGT)

Once you are resident here any assets you still hold abroad but dispose of could be subject to Irish Capital Gains Tax at a rate of 33%, though this would not include your principal private residence. An annual CGT exemption of €1,270 applies in Ireland. The amount of tax you will have to pay will also be affected by whether or not you are domiciled here and how much, if any, of the gain from assets outside of Ireland is brought into Ireland.

Leaving Ireland

"The purpose of the double taxation agreement … is to prevent the same income being taxed twice"

When you leave Ireland, provided you have been resident here for tax purposes, you will be taxed on your income up to the date of your departure, though you can offset a full year's tax credits against this income. Depending on when you leave Ireland, you may be entitled to a refund upon departure.

In order to claim a refund you must complete a Form 12 for PAYE or a Form 11 if you are self employed, which can be completed and submitted online through ROS.ie for self employed and myAccount on ROS.ie for PAYE employees.

Trans border Workers Relief

This relief applies to individuals who are resident in Ireland but who work and pay tax in another country. You can claim this if you commute daily or weekly to work outside Ireland, to a country with which Ireland has a Double Taxation Agreement.

The relief means that such residents will not pay tax in Ireland on income from the foreign employment. Tax, however, may be payable in the foreign country in which the individual is working.

To qualify for this relief you must:

- Be tax resident in Ireland

- Work in a country with which Ireland has a double tax treaty.

- Have paid tax in the other country and are not due a refund of the tax.

- Be present in Ireland at least one day for every week you work abroad.

- Employment must be held for a continuous period of at least 13 weeks.

- The duties of the employment must be performed wholly outside the State.

- The employment must not be with the Government or an authority set up by the State.

You cannot claim this relief if you receive the Seafarers' Allowance, Foreign Earnings Deducation (FED) or split year treatment. You cannot claim relief if you or your spouse or civil partner are proprietary directors of the company you work for abroad. do you calculate how much relief is due?

The relief works by removing the earnings from a qualifying foreign employment from liability to Irish tax where foreign tax has been paid on these earnings. An individuals income tax liability for a particular year is reduced to the "specified amount". The "specified amount" is calculated as follows;

Total Irish tax due x (income other than foreign employment income/ total income)

You will not received any credit for foreign tax paid if you qualify for Transborder Workers Relief.

You must apply in writing to Revenue for this relief. In your application you must include a final statement of Income Tax liability from the other country.

UK double taxation agreement

The double taxation agreement between Ireland and the UK covers income tax, corporation profits tax, corporation tax, capital gains tax.

The purpose of double taxation agreements is to prevent the same income from being taxed twice. This is achieved either

- By exempting the income from tax in one of the countries; **or**

- By setting off the tax payable on the income in one country against the tax payable on the same income in the other country.

Rental income

Rents may be taxed both in the country in which the property is situated and in the country of residence of the individual in receipt of the rent. A credit is given against the tax payable in the country of residence, for the tax paid in the other country.

Dividends

Dividends are taxed both in the country in which the recipient individual is resident and in the country of payment i.e. the country in which the company paying the dividend is resident. An Irish resident individual in receipt of UK dividends is taxed on the amount of the net dividend received. They do not receive any tax credit for any tax which may have been deducted from the UK company paying the dividend.

Interest

Interest received is, in general, liable to tax only in the country of residence. Any tax deducted in the country of payment can be recovered in full.

Salaries, wages, directors fees and other similar remuneration derived by or received by a resident individual of one country from an employment exercised in the other country may be taxable in both countries. A credit is given against the tax payable in the country of residence for the tax payable in the other country.

Pensions

A pension (other than a governmental pension to which the provisions of Article 18 apply see below) or an annuity paid in one country to an individual resident in the other country in consideration of past employment is taxable only in the country of residence under the agreement.

Income from governmental functions

Remuneration paid by a government or a local authority of one country to an individual resident in the other country in respect of services rendered in the discharge of governmental functions, will be taxable only in the country of payment unless the individual is a citizen of the country of residence or did not become resident of the other country solely for the purpose of rendering the service.

For example, a UK citizen resident in Ireland who receives a pension from the UK Government is liable only to UK tax on the pension.

Payment to students

Payments to students or business apprentices who are resident in one country, but who are present in the other country solely for the purpose of education or training, will not be taxable in that other country provided that the payments:

- Are made for the purpose of maintenance, education or training; **and**

- Are made from sources outside that other country.

Average rates of exchange between Ireland and the U.K

Tax year ending	€
31/12/17	Stg. £0.87667
31/12/18	Stg. £0.8834

U.K. tax rates

	Rate	Income after allowances 2017/18	Income after allowances 2018/19	Income after allowances 2019/20
Basic rate:	20%	£0 - £33,500	£0 - £34,500	£0 - £37,500
Higher rate:	40%	£33,501 - £150,000	£34,501 - £150,000	£37,501 - £150,000
Additional rate :	45%	Over £150,001	Over £150,001	Over £150,001

UK personal income tax summary tax allowances

	2017/18 Stg.£	2018/19 Stg.£	2019/20 Stg.£
Personal allowance for people born after 5 April 1948 Note 1	£11,500	£11,850	£12,500
Income limit for personal allowances Note 1	£100,000	£100,000	£100,000
*Married couple's/civil partnership allowance minimum amount (Born before 6 April 1935) Note 1 & 2	£3,260	£3,360	£3,450
Maximum amount of married couples/civil partnership allowance (Born before 6 April 1935) Note 1 & 2	£8,445	£8,695	£8,915
Marriage allowance Note 3	£1,150	£1,190	£1,250
Blind person's allowance	£2,320	£2,390	£2,450

Notes:

1   £1 reduction for every £2 of additional income over the income threshold

2   Relief at 10% if at least one of the couple was born before 6 April 1935

3   The allowance is transferable between spouses or civil partners who were born after 5 April 1935. It can only be transferred where neither the transferor nor the transferee is liable to income tax above the basic rate.

11 Capital gains tax

Capital Gains Tax (CGT) is a tax on gains arising from the disposal of capital assets.

Persons chargeable

All persons resident or ordinarily resident in the State for tax purposes are liable to Capital Gains Tax (CGT). Individuals who are resident and domiciled in Ireland are chargeable on all gains wherever arising, while those who are resident and non-domiciled are liable in respect of all Irish gains and other gains to the extent that the gains are remitted to Ireland.

Non-Irish residents are liable only in respect of gains made on the disposal of assets related to Irish property, or mining/exploration rights.

Chargeable assets

All forms of property are assets for CGT purposes including options, debts and foreign currencies, except those specifically exempted.

Disposal

A disposal for CGT takes place whenever the ownership of an asset changes. This includes a part-disposal and also where no payment is received e.g. a gift or exchange. An exception to this latter rule is on death. In the case of death, no chargeable disposal takes place and the person who receives the asset is treated as acquiring it at the market value at the date of the death.

Married couples

Transfers between spouses do not give rise to a CGT charge - the spouse who received the asset is deemed to have acquired it on the date and at the cost at which the other spouse acquired it.

Capital gains tax rates

For disposal made on or after 6 December 2012 a rate of 33% applies to most chargeable gains including gains from the sale of development land.

"Transfers between spouses do not give rise to a CGT charge."

Capital gains tax payment dates

The due date of payments for CGT are;

- For disposals occurring between 1 January - 30 November , CGT is due to be paid by 15 December in the same year.

- For disposals occurring in December, the payment date will be the following 31 January.

Exemptions and reliefs

Annual allowance

The first €1,270 of a chargeable gain arising to an individual in each tax year is exempt. This is an individual allowance and is not transferable between spouses.

Principal private residence (PPR)

No CGT arises on the disposal of your main residence and grounds of up to one acre, provided it has been occupied by you as your principal private residence throughout the entire period of ownership. You are still deemed to occupy the residence as your principal private residence where you are absent for any period of employment abroad or during absence of less than four years imposed by conditions of your employment, provided you live in the house before and after the period(s) spent abroad. If your house was not your PPR for the entire period of ownership e.g. if you rented the house for a period, any gain arising on the sale of the house will be apportioned between the period when it was your PPR and the period when it was not. The gain when it was your PPR is exempt and the balance of the gain is liable to CGT.

Principal private residence relief is restricted where part of the PPR comprises of development land and the consideration exceeds €19,050. This would include the disposal of a garden or part of a garden of a principal private residence as development land, e.g. if sold as a site, or for access, right of way, etc. No restriction applies if the consideration (or open market value, if transferred in a non-arm's length transaction, e.g. gift) does not exceed €19,050.

Tangible moveable assets

A gain arising to an individual on the disposal of tangible moveable assets is exempt if the total consideration received does not exceed €2,540.

Life assurance policies/deferred annuities

Disposals of these contracts are exempt from CGT in the hands of the original beneficial owner. A chargeable gain can arise on the disposal of such contracts by a person who is not the original beneficial owner if they acquire them for a consideration of money or money's worth. A rate of 40% applies on disposal of certain foreign life assurance annuitised offshore funds.

Irish government securities

Exempt.

Site from parent to child

The transfer of a site from a parent to a child is exempt from CGT, provided,

- It is for the construction of the child's principal private residence,

- The market value of the site does not exceed €500,000,

- It is less than one acre in size.

A parent can transfer one site to each child for the purpose of this exemption.

"A parent can transfer one site to each child for the purpose of this CGT exemption"

However, if the child subsequently disposes of the site without having occupied a principal private residence on the site for at least three years, then the capital gains which would have accrued to the parent on the initial transfer will accrue to the child. However, the gain will not accrue to the child where they transfer an interest in the site to their spouse.

Retirement relief

Disposal of business or farm or shares in a family company.

A gain arising to an individual aged over 55 who, having owned a farm or business or shares in the family company, for more than 10 years, disposes of a farm or business for a consideration of less than €750,000, is disregarded for CGT. Marginal relief applies where the proceeds exceed €750,000 and reduces the CGT payable to the lower of, half of the difference between the proceeds and €750,000, or the CGT as computed in the normal way.

The consideration limit of €750,000 is reduced to €500,000 for individuals aged 66 or over. Marginal relief will also apply on the reduced limit of €500,000. Although this relief is commonly known as "retirement relief" a claimant does not have to retire in order to claim the relief.

Disposals within the family of business or farm or shares in family company

Prior to 1 January 2014 complete exemption could be claimed by an individual meeting the above conditions if they dispose of their farm/business to their child (or nephew/niece working in the business).

From 1 January 2014 a market value ceiling of €3 million applies for individuals aged 66 and over. A charge to CGT will arise to the extent that the market value of the assets disposed of exceeds €3 million. This exemption is lost if the recipient disposes of the farm/business within six years.

CGT entrepreneur relief

CGT relief is available for entrepreneurs who dispose of certain business assets. Under this relief gains made on the disposal of business assets made on or after 1 January 2017 are charged at a reduced rate of 10% up to an overall limit of €1 million. Only gains made on or after 1 January 2016 are counted towards the €1 million limit.

Disposal on emigration

Irish non-residents normally pay Irish CGT on disposals relating to Irish property or mineral/exploration rights only, known as "specified assets".

So, if you are emigrating and wish to dispose of "non-specified assets" before you become non-resident any chargeable gain on such disposals e.g. shares in a company will be liable to Irish CGT.

Capital Gains Tax on such disposals may be reduced if the disposal takes place after you become non-resident, for Irish tax purposes. It is also important to note that the date of disposal for CGT purposes is the date of contract.

Relief for properties bought between 7 December 2011 and 31 December 2014

An exemption from capital gains tax applies on the disposal of a property purchased under an unconditional contract dated between 7 December 2011 and 31 December 2014, provided the property is held for at least four years and up to seven continuous years. The relief applies to both residential and commercial property disposed of on or after 1 January

2018 which were situated in Ireland and all other European Economic Area (EEA) states.

Full exemption from CGT applies on the disposal of the property where it is held for at least four years and up to seven years from the date of acquisition.

You can get partial relief if you have owned the property for more than seven years. To calculate the partial relief, divide seven by the number of years you have owned the property. This will give you the proportion of the gain that is exempt. For example, if you owned the land or buildings for ten years, the gain will be reduced by seven-tenths (7/10).

Frequently asked questions

1   If I sell my house will I have to pay Capital Gains Tax (CGT)?

No, if the house (including grounds of up to one acre) has been occupied as your sole or main residence throughout your period of ownership you will be exempt from CGT on the sale.

2   What happens if my property has "development value"?

Where your property has development value i.e. if it is sold for a price higher than its normal current use value, then the relief from capital gains tax as outlined above is confined to what it would be if the property did not have development value.

3   What happens when I sell foreign assets?

If you are resident or ordinarily resident, and domiciled in the State you are liable to CGT on worldwide gains.   Therefore, if you dispose of a foreign asset, for example a property in another country or shares in a foreign company, Irish CGT will apply. Where foreign capital gains tax is paid a credit may be available against your Irish CGT for some, or all, of that amount.

4   If I sell part of my garden to a builder, who builds a house on it, am I liable to pay capital gains tax?

Yes. Normally when an individual disposes of their principal private residence and a garden or grounds of up to one acre (excluding the site of the house), then any gain on such a disposal is exempt from capital gains tax. However, where a dwelling house or garden/part of a garden, is sold for greater than its current use value, then this constitutes the sale of development land and principal private residence relief will apply only to the current use value. In general terms the difference between the consideration and the current use value is liable to capital gains tax. Development land rules do not apply to disposals where the total consideration from such disposals does not exceed €19,050.

5   What happens if I dispose of an investment property?

You will be liable to CGT on any gain you make. In circumstances where the disposal proceeds are less than market value, the market value is used to calculate any gain arising. The gain you make (ignoring indexation and purchase and sale costs) is simply the difference between the purchase price and the sale price.

6   I have an investment property and intend gifting it to my children, is this gift liable to CGT?

Disposals also include gifts and CGT may be payable. The market value at the date of the gift is used as the "deemed" sale proceeds and CGT is then calculated in the normal manner.

7   If I transfer an asset to my spouse do I have to pay CGT?

No, the asset is transferred as if no gain/no loss occurred on the transfer. The benefiting spouse inherits the base cost and period of ownership from the spouse making the disposal. In the event that the benefiting spouse subsequently disposes of the asset the original base cost and period of ownership is used to calculate any gain arising. (Transfers between spouses are taxable if the benefiting spouse is non-resident in the year the transfer takes place).

8   Can I offset CGT losses against other income?

CGT losses can only be offset against any other CGT gains which occur in the same year as the CGT loss, or they can be carried forward and used against any future capital gain.

9   An investment fund made a loss when I encashed it. Can I offset this loss against a capital gain I made when I sold some shares?

Unfortunately an investment fund gain is subject to exit tax of 41%, not CGT of 33%. If the fund makes a loss, it is not considered a capital loss and cannot be offset to reduce a CGT liability.

Computation of gains and losses

Basically, this is done by deducting from the proceeds received, the cost of the disposed asset less any allowable expenses incurred on the acquisition or disposal of the asset.

Indexation relief

When you sell an asset, the original cost and enhancement expenditure may be increased by indexation before any CGT liability is calculated.

Where an asset is acquired prior to 6 April 1974, the "cost" to be indexed is the market value at 6 April 1974, rather than the original cost. Indexation relief does not apply to development land.

Indexation relief only applies for the period of ownership up to 31 December 2002.

Example: Sale of investment property

In January 2020, a married couple sold a house for €450,000. The costs associated with selling the property amounted to €25,000. They had bought the house in January 1979 for €32,000. The couple had added an extension costing €40,000 to the house in March 1998.

The house was not their principal residence and they had no other chargeable gains in the tax year 2020.

Capital Gains Tax Computation 2020		€	€
	Sales Price	€450,000	
Less:	Selling Costs	€25,000	€425,000
Deduct:	Cost in January 1979 adjusted for inflation: i.e. €32,000 x 4.148	€132,736	
	1997/98 Expenditure adjusted for inflation: i.e. €40,000 x 1.232	€49,280	€182,016
	Capital Gain		€242,984
Less:	Exemption (house in joint names)		€2,540
	Taxable @ 33%		€240,444
	Tax Payable	**€79,346**	

Note: The Capital Gains Tax of €79,346 is payable on 15 December 2020.

Capital gains tax indexation factors

Year of purchase	Year of Disposal					
	98/99	99/00	00/01	2001	2002	2003 et seq
1974/75	6.215	6.313	6.582	6.930	7.180	7.528
1975/76	5.020	5.099	5.316	5.597	5.799	6.080
1976/77	4.325	4.393	4.580	4.822	4.996	5.238
1977/78	3.707	3.766	3.926	4.133	4.283	4.490
1978/79	3.425	3.479	3.627	3.819	3.956	4.148
1979/80	3.090	3.139	3.272	3.445	3.570	3.742
1980/81	2.675	2.718	2.833	2.983	3.091	3.240
1981/82	2.211	2.246	2.342	2.465	2.554	2.678
1982/83	1.860	1.890	1.970	2.074	2.149	2.253
1983/84	1.654	1.680	1.752	1.844	1.911	2.003
1984/85	1.502	1.525	1.590	1.674	1.735	1.819
1985/86	1.414	1.436	1.497	1.577	1.633	1.713
1986/87	1.352	1.373	1.432	1.507	1.562	1.637
1987/88	1.307	1.328	1.384	1.457	1.510	1.583
1988/89	1.282	1.303	1.358	1.430	1.481	1.553
1989/90	1.241	1.261	1.314	1.384	1.434	1.503
1990/91	1.191	1.210	1.261	1.328	1.376	1.442
1991/92	1.161	1.179	1.229	1.294	1.341	1.406
1992/93	1.120	1.138	1.186	1.249	1.294	1.356
1993/94	1.099	1.177	1.164	1.226	1.270	1.331
1994/95	1.081	1.098	1.144	1.205	1.248	1.309
1995/96	1.54	1.071	1.116	1.175	1.218	1.277
1996/97	1.033	1.050	1.094	1.152	1.194	1.251
1997/98	1.017	1.033	1.077	1.134	1.175	1.232
1998/99	-	1.016	1.059	1.115	1.156	1.212
1999/00	-	-	1.043	1.098	1.138	1.193
2000/01	-	-	-	1.053	1.091	1.144
2001	-	-	-	-	1.037	1.087
2002	-	-	-	-	-	1.049
2003 et seq	-	-	-	-	-	-

Note: The indexation rates have remained the same since 2003

12 Social welfare benefits

PRSI contributions help pay for social welfare pensions and benefits. The subject is a wide one, and in this chapter we outline:

● How much you pay.

● Your benefit entitlements.

Who pays PRSI?

With very few exceptions

● All employees whether full-time or part-time earning €38 or more per week.

● Self employed workers with an income of €5,000 a year or more who are aged 16 over and under pensionable age, are liable for PRSI contributions.

From 1 January 2013, modified rate contributors, who have earned self-employed income or self-employed income which comes within PAYE, are liable for PRSI contributions on this income and any unearned income they have.

Modified rate contributions are payable by civil and public servants recruited prior to April 1995, paying PRSI under class B, C or D. Prior to 1 January 2013 those paying a modified rate of PRSI were exempt from PRSI on income other than earnings. From 1 January 2013 that income is liable to a 4% PRSI charge. This PRSI charge will not give rise to any social insurance entitlements.

Prior to 1 January 2014 employed contributors and occupational pensioners under state pension age, whose only additional income was unearned income were exempt from PRSI on this unearned income. From 1 January 2014 this exemption was abolished if the additional income exceeded €5,000 in a year.

This means that unearned income such as rental income, investment income, dividends and interest on deposits is liable to PRSI at a rate of 4%. This additional PRSI charge will not give rise to any social insurance benefits. PRSI will not be payable after you reach 66 years of age.

Contribution years

The contribution year for PRSI purposes is the same as the tax year. Contribution years are normally referred to as tax years.

Benefit years

The benefit year begins on the first Monday in January each year. Your entitlement to short-term PRSI benefits is normally based on your paid and/or credited contributions in the relevant tax year, which is the second last complete tax year before the benefit year in which you claim.

For a claim made in	The relevant tax year is
2019	2017
2020	2018

If you cease to pay PRSI contributions, your entitlement to benefits will normally last for the remainder of that calendar year and the following calendar year.

PRSI contributions are calculated as a percentage of your gross pay, less any payments to a permanent health benefit scheme which are deducted at source by the employer and approved by the Revenue Commissioners. PRSI contribution costs are normally shared by the employee and employer. For the majority of employees, PRSI contributions are collected through the PAYE tax system.

The following charts show how the Class A1 rate, which is the PRSI Class most employees pay, is calculated in the 2019 and 2020 tax year.

Class A

This class covers employees under the age of 66 in industrial, commercial & service type employment who have reckonable pay of €38 or more per week, from all employments as well as public servants recruited after 5 April 1995.

Non Cumulative Weekly Earnings Band	PRSI Class	2019		2020	
		Employee %	Employer %	Employee %	Employer %
		All income	All income	All income	All income
Up to €38	JO	0	0.50	0	0.50
€38 - €352	AO	0	8.70	0	8.80
€352.01 - €386*	AX	4.00	8.70	4.00	8.80
€386.01 - €424*	AL	4.00	10.95	4.00	11.05
more than €424	A1	4.00	10.95	4.00	11.05

* PRSI credits were introduced from 1 January 2016 and apply to employees insured at Class A whose earnings are between €352.01 and €424 per week. The amount of PRSI credit depends on your gross weekly earnings. The maximum PRSI credit of €12 applies at gross weekly earning of €352.01. For earnings of between €352.01 and €424 the maximum weekly PRSI credit of €12 is reduced by 1/6 of the earnings in excess of €352.01. There is no PRSI credit once gross weekly earnings exceed €424.

Employees who earn €352 or less per week are exempt from PRSI however employers PRSI is still payable.

Self Employed

	Income	Rate	Minimum contribution	Exemption threshold
2020	All	4%	€500	€5,000 p.a.
2019	All	4%	€500	€5,000 p.a.

Claiming social insurance benefits

Normally, to claim a social insurance benefit it is necessary to have a minimum number of PRSI contributions. PRSI contributions are normally classified as either PRSI paid or PRSI credited.

PRSI contributions are payable each week you are working in insurable employment. There is no charge for PRSI credits, but for many benefits they can be as valuable as PRSI contributions paid.

Pre-entry credits

When you become insured for the first time under the Social Welfare Acts you are automatically given PRSI credits for the earlier part of that tax year, in addition to credits for the previous two tax years. For example, if you commenced employment for the first time on 5 October you would be entitled to credits from the 1 January to 4 October plus the two previous tax years. These credits can help you qualify for Illness and Jobseekers Benefit as soon as you have worked and paid PRSI contributions for 52 weeks.

Credits after you have become insured

If you stop paying PRSI contributions, PRSI credits are normally awarded for the weeks you receive illness benefit, jobseekers benefit, maternity benefit, paternity benefit, adoptive benefit, health & safety benefit, carer's benefit, invalidity pension, state pension transition or injury benefit. Similarly, credits may be awarded for the weeks in which you received jobseekers assistance or carer's allowance, if you are eligible for credits. If you have never worked, you would not get credits with jobseekers assistance.

A break in PRSI

If two consecutive tax years have elapsed without contributions having been paid or credited, no additional PRSI credits can be awarded until a further 26 PRSI contributions have been paid.

Voluntary contributions

A person who ceases to be insured under Pay-Related Social Insurance can, if under 66 years of age, opt to continue insurance on a voluntary basis for limited benefits, provided

- At least 520 weeks PRSI contributions have been paid

- You apply within 60 months of the end of the tax year during which you had last paid PRSI or were awarded a PRSI credit

- You agree to pay voluntary contributions from either the start of the contribution week in which you leave compulsory PRSI or the start of any contribution year of your choice within the period covered by your admittance as a voluntary contributor.

PRSI classes and benefit entitlements

	A	B	C	D	E	H	J	M	P	S	See Page
Adoptive benefit	*	-	-	-	*	*	-	-	-	*	229
Carer's benefit	*	*	*	*	*	*	-	-	-	-	238
Illness benefit	*	-	-	*	*	*	-	-	*	-	240
Health & safety benefit	*	-	-	-	*	*	-	-	-	-	232
Invalidity pension	*	-	-	-	*	*	-	*	*	-	226
Jobseekers benefit	*	-	-	-	-	*	-	-	*	-	233
Maternity benefit	*	-	-	-	*	*	-	*	*	*	227
Paternity benefit	*	-	-	-	*	*	-	*	*	*	228
Occupational injuries benefit	*	*	-	*	-	-	*	*	-	-	241
State pension contributory	*	-	-	-	*	*	-	-	-	*	215
Guardian's payment contributory	*	*	*	*	*	*	-	-	-	*	225
Treatment benefit	*	-	-	-	*	*	-	-	*	-	227
Widow(er)/surviving civil partner's contributory benefit	*	*	*	*	*	*	-	-	-	*	221
Working family payment	*	*	-	*	*	*	-	*	-	-	231
Working in the EU Jobseekers benefit, health services	*	-	-	-	-	*	-	-	-	-	243

There are three rates of voluntary contributions and the rate you pay is determined by the last rate of PRSI contribution which you paid.

- The high rate of 6.6% of your reckonable income in the previous tax year, subject to a minimum payment of €500 applies if you were compulsorily insured at the PRSI class A, E or H. Voluntary contributions at this rate normally provide pension benefits and a bereavement grant.

- The reduced rate of 2.6% of your rechargeable income in the previous tax year, subject to a minimum payment of €250, applies if you were compulsory insured at class B, C or D. Voluntary contributions at this level normally provide for widow(er)/surviving civil partner's contributory pension and orphan's contributory allowance and a bereavement grant.

- A flat rate voluntary contribution of €500 applies to self-employed people insured at Class S who cease self-employment or who are no longer obliged to pay Class S because their income falls below the insurable limit which is currently €5,000. This gives cover for State contributory pension, widow(er)/surviving civil partner's contributory pension, orphan's contributory allowance and bereavement grant.

Remember, social insurance contributions are not a tax but their effect is very similar as you pay contributions out of your gross income. However, it should also be pointed out that benefits received are not means-tested and you are entitled to them as a right once you satisfy the necessary contribution conditions.

PRSI benefit entitlements

Summarised on page 213 are:

- The main benefit entitlements applicable to the relevant PRSI classes.

- The page reference to where you will find the necessary back-up information in this guide your entitlement to a non-contributory pension.

Social welfare pension

Social welfare pensions fall under two main categories

- Contributory pensions.

- Non-contributory pensions.

Contributory pension

Your entitlement to a contributory pension is based on the amount and contribution class of PRSI you have paid during your working life.

Any other income you have, will not affect your entitlement to a contributory pension.

Non-contributory pension

If you don't qualify for a contributory pension you may be entitled to a non-contributory pension. Any income or assets you have, may affect your entitlement to a non-contributory pension.

State contributory pension

The State contributory pension is payable to insured people from the age of 66. It is paid to you even if you are still working. It is payable in respect of PRSI class A, E, F, G, H, N and S.

The main conditions which must be met in order to qualify are:

- You must have become insured before the age of 56

- You must have paid at least 520 full - rate employment contributions **and**

- You must have paid a yearly average of at least 48 paid or credited full-rate contributions from 1979 to the end of the tax year before you reach age 66, **or**

- A yearly average of at least 10 full-rate paid or credited contributions from 1953 (or the time you started insurable employment, if later) to the end of the tax year before you reach age 66.

Note: A yearly average of 10 full-rate contributions will give you the minimum State contributory pension. For a maximum pension, you need an average of 48 full rate contributions.

State pension elements

A State pension is payable in three distinct elements:

- A personal amount.
- An increase for a qualified adult.
- An increase for each dependent child.

If you qualify for a weekly social welfare payment, you will normally get extra amounts for a qualified adult and child dependents. A qualified adult is usually a spouse but can be the person you are cohabiting with. Your spouse/partner is regarded as your dependent provided they are not getting a social welfare payment in their own right or have income of less than €100 per week and are not on a full-time FÁS non-craft training course. A spouse/partner can have income of up to €310 per week and still be regarded as partially dependent.

If you are entitled to an increase for a dependent spouse/partner and have dependent children you can claim the full rate for a dependent child. If you do not qualify for a payment for a qualified adult you are entitled to half rate for a dependent child.

The following are the maximum rates

State contributory pension maximum weekly rates	From Mar. 2019 €	From Jan. 2020 €
Maximum rate (under 80)		
Personal Rate	€248.30	€248.30
Person with qualified adult under 66	€413.70	€413.70
Person with qualified adult 66 or over	€470.80	€470.80
Maximum personal rate (over 80)		
Personal Rate	€258.30	€258.30
Person with qualified adult under 66	€423.70	€423.70
Person with qualified adult 66 or over	€480.80	€480.80
Increase per child - Under 12	€34.00	€36.00
Increase per child - Over 12	€37.00	€40.00
Living Alone Allowance for people age 66 or over	€9.00	€14.00

You cannot claim an increase for a qualified child with your state pension if your spouse/civil partner/ or co-habitant has an income of over €400 per week.

State non - contributory pension

If you don't qualify for a State contributory pension you may qualify for a State non-contributory pension. To claim a State non-contributory pension you must

- Be aged 66 or over.
- Be living in the State.
- Satisfy a means test.

The following are the maximum rates.

"State contributory pension is paid to you even if you are still working."

State non-contributory pension/ blind pension maximum weekly rates	From Mar. 2019 €	From Jan. 2020 €
Under 80		
Personal rate	€237.00	€237.00
Person with qualified adult	€393.60	€393.60
Aged 80 or over		
Personal Rate	€247.00	€247.00
Person with qualified adult	€403.60	€403.60
Increase per child - Under 12	€34.00	€36.00
Increase per child - Over 12	€37.00	€40.00
Living alone allowance	€9.00	€14.00
Blind pension under 66	€203.00	€203.00
Increase for a qualified adult dependent	€134.70	€134.70

Means test

When you make a claim for a non-contributory pension, a social welfare inspector will normally investigate your entitlement to this pension in your own home and attempt to establish your weekly means.

In assessing your means, a social welfare inspector will take account of

- Cash income.

- The value of any property personally used by you, such as a farm or shop. Your home is excluded unless you are getting an income from it. Rental income received from a person living with the pensioner is not counted, provided the pensioner is living alone except for that person.

- The value of any investments or capital held.

- The means of your spouse or other person cohabiting with you as husband and wife.

- Income from employment or self employment.

The formula for assessing the means from capital for all social welfare payments (except disability allowance and supplementary welfare allowance) is as follows:

Capital	Weekly means assessed
First €20,000	Nil
Next €10,000	€1 per €1,000
Next €10,000	€2 per €1,000
Over €40,000	€4 per €1,000

State pension (non-contributory), blind pension and carer's allowance

If you are one of a couple and apply for State pension (non-contributory), blind pension or carer's allowance your combined capital is halved and this lower amount is assessed using the relevant formula (see 'rules' above). After you apply the relevant formula the resulting amount is then doubled to get your means from capital.

National pensions framework and the roadmap for pension reform 2018-23

The "National Pensions Framework" and the "Road Map for Pension Reform 2018-2023", sets out the Government's intention for radical and wide scale reform of the Irish pension system.

The age at which you will receive a state pension increased to 66 from 1 Jan 2014 and will rise to 67 in 2021 and 68 in 2028. So if you were born on or after 1 January 1955 the minimum qualifying State pension age will be 67. If you were born on or after 1 January 1961 the minimum qualifying State pension age will be 68 (see chart on page 220).

The other change which is proposed and will apply to individuals who reach State pension age on or after 1 January 2020, is the introduction of a total contributions approach (TCA) to replace the current yearly averaging system. This means that the amount of pension paid to you will be directly proportionate to the number of social insurance contributions and/or credits you have made over your working life.

If you were born after 1 January 1954, when you reach pension age, you will need a total of 40 years contributions and/or credits to get the maximum State pension. You will be able to get the minimum State pension if you have paid 520 full-rate contributions (10 years). The minimum pension will be one quarter of the maximum rate. You can then get a further 1/40th of the pension for each additional year of contributions that you have. People who have to take time out of the workforce to take up caring duties will be eligible to accumulate up to 20 years credits towards meeting the full 40 year contribution record. Similarly, unemployed people and others with an entitlement will, as now, be able to get credited contributions provided that they have a minimum number of paid contributions.

If you need additional contributions to qualify for a State pension, you will be able to continue paying full-rate contributions after you reach pension age.

If you wish to postpone claiming your pension, you will be able to defer the payment to a date of your choice. If you choose to do this, an actuarial increase in rate will be paid from the date you wish your payment to begin.

Legislation is required before the above changes comes into effect.

National Pension Framework proposed changes to pension age

Date	State Pension age	Date of birth of those reaching state pension age
January 2014	66	1949 to 1954
January 2015 to December 2020	66	
January 2021	67	
2021	67	No one will reach pension age in 2021 as anyone turning 67 during that year will have already qualified for State Pension at age 66 in 2020
January 2022 to December 2027	67	1955 to 1960
January 2028	68	
2028	68	No one will reach pension age in 2021 as anyone turning 68 during that year will have already qualified for State Pension at age 67 in 2027
January 2029 onwards	68	

Extra benefits - household benefits package

If you are aged 66 or over and you qualify for a full or reduced pension or you satisfy a means test, you may be entitled to an electricity/natural gas allowance, free television licence, under the household benefits package scheme, subject to the qualifying conditions one of which is that you live alone or with certain "excepted people". All people aged 70 or over qualify regardless of income or who lives with them. Recipients of certain other payments e.g. invalidity pension, carer's allowance may qualify regardless of their age. You must be residing permanently, on an all year round basis at the address for which you are claiming the household benefits package and no other person in the household can be in receipt of the allowances. The accounts must be in your name. The means tested fuel scheme is not part of the household benefits package.

Island allowance

This is an additional allowance of €12.70 per week for social welfare pensioners aged 66 or over who are living on certain offshore islands. It is also payable to recipients of blind pension, carer's allowance, invalidity pension, one parent family payment, widow's(ers)/surviving civil partners pension or contributory/non-contributory pension.

Widow(er)'s/surviving civil partner contributory pension

The Widow(er)'s/surviving civil partner contributory pension is payable on the death of a spouse provided

- You are widowed/surviving civil partner , **or**

- You are divorced from your late spouse and have not remarried, **or**

- You have had your civil partnership dissolved before your partners death and have not entered into a new civil partnership, **or**

- You are not cohabiting, **and**

- You satisfy the PRSI contribution conditions, **or**

- Your late spouse/partner was getting a state contributory pension which included an increase for you or would have but for the fact that you were getting a state non-contributory pension, blind person's pension or a carer's allowances in your own right.

The PRSI conditions may be based on either your own or your late spouse's PRSI record.   However, the two PRSI records cannot be combined.   Whichever PRSI record is used must have

- At least 260 weeks PRSI paid to the date pension age was reached or to the date your spouse/civil partner died, if earlier,   **and**

- Either an average of 39 weeks PRSI paid or credited over the three or five tax years whichever is more beneficial before reaching pension age (66 years) or before your spouse died, if earlier for a maximum pension, **or**

- For a minimum pension, a yearly average of at least 24 weeks PRSI paid or credited is needed since starting work up to the end of the tax year before reaching pension age (66 years) or the date your spouse dies, if earlier. For a maximum pension, a yearly average of 48 weeks PRSI paid or credited is needed.

"You may be entitled to free electricity/ natural gas, television licence ..."

With the exception of class J, K and M almost all PRSI contributions, including self-employed, civil servants and public sector workers, are included for the contributory widow(er)/surviving civil partner's pension and contributory orphan's allowance. Your entitlement to the contributory widow(er)/surviving civil partner's pension is not affected by any other income you may have.

Widow(er)'s/surviving civil partner contributory pension

The following are the maximum rates of contributory and non-contributory pensions:

Widow(er)'s/surviving civil partner contributory pension maximum weekly rates		From Mar. 2019 €	From Jan. 2020 €
Maximum personal rate - under 66		€208.50	€208.50
Maximum personal rate - aged 66 - 79		€248.30	€248.30
Maximum personal rate - aged 80 or over		€258.30	€258.30
Child dependent	Under 12	€34.00	€36.00
	Over 12	€37.00	€40.00
Living alone allowance		€9.00	€14.00

Widow(er)'s/surviving civil partner non - contributory pension

If you are a widow(er)/surviving civil partner and have no dependent children, you may be entitled to claim a non-contributory widow(er)'s pension on the death of your spouse, provided you are not already entitled to a contributory widow(er)'/civil partner's pension and you satisfy the means test.

Widow(er)'s/surviving civil partner non-contributory pension maximum weekly rates	From Mar 2019 €	From Jan 2020 €
Maximum personal rate - under 66	€203	€203

One-parent family payments

The One-Parent Family Payment is a means tested payment for both men and women who, for a variety of reasons, are bringing up a child without the support of a partner.

You qualify for a payment if you are aged under 66 with at least one qualifying child and are a qualifying parent.

A qualifying parent is

- A widow(er) or a surviving civil partner, **or**

- A separated spouse **or**

- An unmarried person **or**

- A civil partner who is not living with the other civil partner of the civil partnership or civil union.

From 2 July 2015 to get the one parent family payment you must have at least one relevant child below the age of 7.

Back to work family dividend (BTWFD)

The Back To Work Family Dividend (BTWFD) scheme aims to help families to move from social welfare into employment. It gives financial support to people with qualified children who are in or take up employment or self-employment and as a result stop claiming a jobseeker's payment or a one-parent family payment.

If you qualify for the scheme you will get a weekly payment for up to two years. You will be paid the equivalent of any increases for qualified children that were being paid on your jobseekers or one-parent family payment (up to a maximum of four children) for the first year in employment.

Guardian's payment contributory

Where both parents have died, or one parent has died and the other has abandoned the child, this allowance is payable, provided that the PRSI contribution conditions are met. These require that at least 26 weekly contributions have been paid at any time by the orphan's parent or stepparent, at the appropriate rate.

The PRSI contribution classes which cover the guardian's contributory payment are the same as those for the contributory widow(er)'s pension. The allowance is payable up to the age of 18, or 22 if the orphan is full-time education. The current rate is €186.00 per week.

Guardian's payment non - contributory

The guardian's payment non-contributory is paid for a child or children if

- Both parents are dead.

- One parent has died and the other is unknown.

- One parent is dead and the surviving parent has abandoned or failed to support the child.

- The child satisfies a means test.

- The child is living in the State.

A claim cannot be made for a child living with step parents. The allowance may be payable to the guardian of an orphan if the orphan does not already qualify for a Guardian's contributory payment. The maximum rate of allowance currently payable is €186.00 per week. Entitlement to the maximum rate of payment depends on the mean test. The allowance is payable up to the age of 18, or 22 if the orphan is in full-time education. However, the means test must be satisfied throughout the entire period.

Invalidity pension

An invalidity pension is payable instead of a illness benefit if you have been incapable of work for at least 12 months and likely to be incapable of work for a further 12 months or you are permanently incapable of work or you are over age 60 and suffering from a serious illness or incapacity.

You must have paid PRSI at class A, E or H.

In order to claim invalidity pension you must have paid the appropriate PRSI contributions for at least 260 weeks and you must have had at least 48 weeks PRSI paid or credited in the last tax year before you apply.

From December 2017 Invalidity pension was extended to self employed individuals.

The following are the maximum rates.

Invalidity pension maximum weekly rates	From Mar. 2019 €	From Jan. 2020 €
Personal rate	€208.50	€208.50
Increase for adult dependents	€148.90	€148.90
Increases for child dependents - Under 12	€34.00	€36.00
Increases for child dependents - Over 12	€37.00	€40.00
Living alone allowance	€9.00	€14.00

Note

Increases for dependent child payable with the pensions dealt with in this section are paid for children living with you and dependent on you up to the age of 18, or 22 if they are in full time education. The full rate for a dependent child is paid to you if you are entitled to an increase for an adult dependent. If you do not qualify for payment for a qualified adult, the increase for child dependents is paid at half rate.

Qualified adult dependent payment

A qualified adult payment may be payable in addition to the basic benefit in respect of your spouse/partner, if your spouse/partner is wholly or mainly maintained by you. If your spouse/partner has income of more than €310 per week or is receiving some other Social Welfare Benefit this supplement may not be paid to you.

Treatment benefits

The treatment benefit scheme is available to insured workers and retired people who have the required number of PRSI contributions. Dental and optical benefits and the medical appliances scheme (hearing aids) is extended to self employed individuals from March 2017.

Treatment benefit covers dental benefit, optical benefit, contact lenses and hearing aids.

Maternity benefits

Maternity benefit is payable to women in current employment or self employed women insured at PRSI Classes, A, E, H and S.

Maternity benefit is not payable on your spouse's insurance. It is payable only where the mother is an insured person and satisfies the PRSI conditions on her own insurance record.

Who can qualify

You will qualify for maternity benefit if you

- Are in employment which is covered by the Maternity Protection Act 1994 immediately before the first day of your maternity leave. The last day of insurable employment may be within 16 weeks of the expected date of birth of the baby, **or**

- Are or have been self-employed, **and**

- Satisfy the PRSI contribution conditions.

Contribution conditions

- You must have at least 39 weeks PRSI paid in the 12 months immediately before the first day of your maternity leave. **or**

- 39 weeks PRSI paid since you first started work and at least 39 weeks PRSI paid or credited in the relevant tax year. **or**

- 26 weeks PRSI paid in the relevant tax year and 26 weeks PRSI paid in the tax year prior to the relevant tax year.

If you are self-employed you must have 52 qualifying PRSI contributions paid:

- In the relevant tax year, **or**

- 52 qualifying PRSI contributions paid in the tax year immediately prior to the relevant tax, **or**

- 52 qualifying PRSI contributions paid in the tax year immediately following the relevant tax

PRSI paid at Class A, E, H, S are deemed as qualifying contributions. You must take a minimum of two weeks and a maximum of 16 weeks before the end of the week in which the baby is due. If your baby is born later than expected and you have less than four weeks maternity leave remaining, you may be entitled to extend your maternity leave to ensure that you have a full four weeks off following the birth.

Where maternity benefit has been in payment for a minimum period of 14 weeks, the balance of your payment may be postponed for up to six months if the child is hospitalised. The payment will resume within seven days following written notification of the discharge of the child from hospital.

Your payment will be stopped if you is work in insurable (paid) employment during your maternity leave. The current rate of maternity benefit is €245 per week.

Paternity benefit

From 1 September 2016 a new two week paternity benefit was introduced. The PRSI contribution conditions and the rate of benefit will the same as those for maternity benefit.

Parental benefit

From 1 November 2019 a new social insurance Parental benefit payment is payable for two weeks for each parent.

Insurance from employment in another country

If you were previously insurably employed in a country covered by EU Regulations or in a country with which Ireland has a Bilateral Social Security Agreement and you have paid at least one full rate PRSI contribution in Ireland, you may combine your insurance record in that country with your Irish PRSI contribution in Ireland within 16 weeks of the end of the week in which your baby is due.

Adoptive benefit

Adoptive Benefit is payable for 16 weeks from the date of placement of the child to adoptive parents paying PRSI at class A,E, H and S who satisfy the contribution conditions. The rate of payment and the PRSI contribution conditions are the same as those applying for maternity benefit (see page 227).

Taxation of Maternity/Paternity/Adoptive benefit

From 1 July 2013 maternity benefit, adoptive benefit, and health and safety benefit are liable to income tax. Paternity benefit received from 1 September 2016 is also liable to income tax. However, universal social charge (USC) and PRSI are not payable on these payments. The actual rate of tax you will pay will depend on your personal circumstances and the tax relief and tax credits you are claiming.

The Department of Social Protection (DSP) will continue to pay these benefits without any deduction of tax. However the DSP will notify Revenue of the amount of any benefits to be taken into account for income tax purposes.

If you are self-employed and pay your tax through the self-assessment system you should include details of any maternity paternity or adoptive benefit received, on your annual tax return.

If you pay tax through the PAYE system Revenue will, where possible, automatically reduce your annual tax credits and rate bands to take account of the tax payable on your social welfare benefits.

Habitual residence test

The habitual residence test means that in order to get certain payments, you will have to show that you have been habitually resident in Ireland or in the common travel areas of the UK, the Channel Islands or the Isle of Man for a substantial continuous period.

The following payments are now subject to a habitual residence condition:

- Jobseekers allowance.

- State non-contributory pension.

- Blind pension.

- Guardian payment (non contributory)

- Widow(er)'s/surviving civil parters non contributory pensions.

- One-Parent Family payment.

- Carer's allowance.

- Disability allowance.

- Supplementary welfare allowance

- Child benefit.

- Domiciliary care allowance

Child benefit

This is a benefit paid every month to the parent or guardian of children normally living with you and being supported by you. A qualified child is

- A child under age 16

    and/or

- A child age 16 or 17 who is in full time education or attending a FÁS Youthreach course or is physically or mentally disabled and dependent on you.

Child benefit ceases when the child reaches age 18.

Child benefit rate

No. of children	From Mar 2019	From Mar 2020
One child	€140.00	€140.00
Two children	€280.00	€280.00
Three children	€420.00	€420.00
Four children	€560.00	€560.00
Five children	€700.00	€700.00
Six children	€840.00	€840.00
Seven children	€980.00	€980.00
Eight children	€1,120.00	€1,120.00

Working family payment (WFP)

Working Family Payment formerly Family income supplement (FIS) is a weekly tax-free payment available to employees (not the self employed) with children. You must have at least one child who normally lives with you or is financially supported by you. Your child must be under 18 years of age or between 18 and 22 years of age and in full-time education.

To qualify for WFP, your net average weekly family income must be below a certain amount for your family size. The WFP you receive is 60% of the difference between your net family income and the income limit which applies to your family.

From March 2019 WFP recipients benefit from a maintenance disregard of €95 per week in respect of housing costs, with the remainder to be assessed at 50%

Conditions

In order to qualify for WFP you must satisfy the following conditions

- Work 19 hours or more per week (or 38 or more hours per fortnight). You can combine your weekly hours worked with your spouse/civil partner/co-habitant's to meet this condition.

- Be in employment which is likely to last at least three months.

- Look after one or more children.

- Earn less than a set amount which varies according to family size.

Generally the payment continues for one year and is not affected by, for example, an increase in earnings or other income in the family.

You cannot get WFP if you are taking part in a community employment scheme, or any FÁS schemes except Job Initiative. You cannot get WFP is you are getting one of the following social welfare payments: jobseekers benefit, jobseekers allowance State pension transition or pre-retirement allowance.

Rates

WFP is calculated on the basis of 60% of the difference between the income limit for the family size and the assessable income of the person(s) raising the child(ren). The combined income of a couple (married, in a civil partnership or cohabiting) is taken into account.

WFP income limits

If you have	Weekly family income is less than	
	2019	2020
One child	€521.00	€531.00
Two children	€622.00	€632.00
Three children	€723.00	€733.00
Four children	€834.00	€834.00
Five children	€960.00	€960.00
Six children	€1,076.00	€1,076.00
Seven children	€1,212.00	€1,212.00
Eight children	€1,308.00	€1,308.00

It is important to be aware, that no matter how little you may qualify for, you will still get a minimum payment of €20 per week.

Health and safety benefit

This is a weekly payment for women insured at Class A, E or H, who are pregnant or have recently had a baby or are breastfeeding (up to 26 weeks) and who have been awarded health and safety leave under the Maternity Protection Act, 1994.

Health and safety leave is granted to an employee by her employer when the employer cannot remove a risk to the employee's health or safety or her pregnancy or breastfeeding, or assign her alternative "risk free" duties.

Jobseekers benefit

Jobseeker's Benefit is a weekly payment to people who are out of work and covered by PRSI. From 1 November 2019 self-employed individuals are eligible for jobseeker's benefit.

To qualify for jobseeker's benefit you must

- Be unemployed (you must be fully unemployed or unemployed for at least four days in seven).
- Be under 66 years of age.
- Have enough PRSI contributions.
- Be capable of work.
- Be available for and genuinely seeking work.
- Have a substantial loss of employment and as a result be unemployed for at least four days in seven.

PRSI contributions

In order to qualify for jobseeker's benefit, you must pay Class A, H or P PRSI contributions. Class A is the one paid by most private sector employees and

- Have at least 104 weeks PRSI paid since you first started work, **and**
- Have 39 weeks PRSI paid or credited in the relevant tax year (a minimum of 13 weeks must be paid contributions*), **or**
- Have 26 weeks PRSI paid in the relevant tax year and 26 weeks PRSI paid in the tax year immediately before the relevant tax year.

* If you do not have 13 paid contributions in the relevant tax year, you must have the 13 contributions paid in any one of the following years:

- The two tax years before the relevant tax year.

- The last complete tax year.

- The current tax year.

The relevant tax year is the second last complete tax year before the year in which your claim is made. So, for claims made in 2020, the relevant tax year is 2018.

There are a number of circumstances in which you will be awarded credited contributions. For example, pre-entry credits are given when you start employment for the first time in your working life. However, you will only qualify for jobseeker's benefit when you have 104 contributions actually paid. Credits are also normally awarded while you are getting certain social welfare payments, including jobseeker's benefit (provided it is for six days), jobseeker's allowance or illness benefit.

Contributions you have paid in other member states of the EU/EEA will be added to your Irish contributions. If you are applying for jobseeker's benefit and need the contributions paid in another EU/EEA country to help you qualify, then your last contribution must have been in Ireland.

You may be disqualified from getting jobseeker's benefit for up to 9 weeks if you:

- Left work voluntarily and without a reasonable cause.

- Lost your job through misconduct.

- Refused an offer of suitable alternative employment or suitable training.

- Are aged under 55 and get a redundancy payment of more than €50,000. The exact length of your disqualification (up to nine weeks) will in practice, depend on the precise amount of redundancy payment you received - see page 235.

How long is jobseeker's benefit paid for

Jobseeker's benefit is paid for a maximum of nine months to new claimants who have at least 260 paid contributions.

Jobseeker's benefit is paid for a maximum of six months to new claimants who have less than 260 paid contributions.

If you are under 18 you will only get jobseekers benefit for a maximum of 26 weeks.

If you are aged between 65 and 66 when your jobseekers benefits claim would end you can continue to claim it until you reach 66 provided you have at least 156 PRSI contributions.

Work and jobseeker's benefit

To get jobseeker's benefit you must be unemployed or have lost at least one day's employment and as a result be unemployed for at least four days out of seven days. You may continue to get jobseeker's benefit if you can only find part-time or casual work.

Redundancy

If you are under 55 and get a redundancy payment of more than €50,000 you will be disqualified from claiming Jobseeker's Benefit for the following length of time

Amount of redundancy payment	Period of disqualification
€50,000 - €55,000	1 Week
€55,001 - €60,000	2 Weeks
€60,001 - €65,000	3 Weeks
€65,001 - €70,000	4 Weeks
€70,001 - €75,000	5 Weeks
€75,001 - €80,000	6 Weeks
€80,001 - €85,000	7 Weeks
€85,001 - €90,000	8 Weeks
€90,001 and over	9 Weeks

On strike

If you are on strike, you are not considered unemployed and not entitled to jobseeker's benefit. However, your family may get supplementary welfare allowance.

Maximum weekly jobseeker's benefit payment for those over the age of 26

Jobseekers benefit maximum payments (over 26's)	From March 2019 €	From Jan 2020 €
Personal rate (over 26)	€203.00	€203.00
Increase for Qualified adult	€134.70	€134.70
Each qualified child - under 12	€34.00	€36.00
over 12	€37.00	€40.00

Jobseekers benefit for self-employed

In order for a self employed individual to qualify for Jobseeker's Benefit they must:

- Be aged between 18 and 66

- No longer be self-employed. You must have lost your self-employment involuntarily and not because of a temporary shutdown or seasonal closure.

- Be unemployed (you can work as an employee for up to 3 days each week) but be capable of work

- Be available for and genuinely seeking full-time work

- Have enough PRSI contributions either at Class S A or H

To qualify for Jobseeker's Benefit (Self-Employed) you need:

- At least 156 weeks of Class S contributions or at least 104 weeks of paid Class A or H PRSI since first starting work

- 52 weeks of Class S contributions paid in the relevant tax year. So, for claims made in 2020 the relevant tax year is 2018.

Qualifying adult (IQA)

An adult dependant cannot have gross weekly earning or income of more than €310. If an adult dependant earns less than €100 you will get a full increase for a Qualified Adult (IQA). If an adult dependant earns between €100 and €310 you will get a reduced rate of IQA (as per chart page 237). If they earn more than €310 you will not get an IQA.

Increase for qualified adult (IQA)

Qualified adult gross weekly income or earnings	Rate per week €
Up to €100.00	€131.40
€100.01 to €110.00	€126.40
€110.01 to €120.00	€121.40
€120.01 to €130.00	€115.70
€130.01 to €140.00	€109.80
€140.01 to €150.00	€104.10
€150.01 to €160.00	€98.30
€160.01 to €170.00	€92.50
€170.01 to €180.00	€86.70
€180.01 to €190.00	€80.80
€190.01 to €200.00	€75.10
€200.01 to €210.00	€69.20
€210.01 to €220.00	€63.50
€220.01 to €230.00	€57.60
€230.01 to €240.00	€51.90
€240.01 to €250.00	€46.10
€250.01 to €260.00	€40.30
€260.01 to €270.00	€34.50
€270.01 to €280.00	€28.70
€280.01 to €290.00	€22.90
€290.01 to €300.00	€17.10
€300.01 to €310.00	€11.30
Over €310.00	Nil

Extra benefits

If you are getting jobseeker's benefit, you may be entitled to

- Fuel scheme

- Back to school clothing and footwear allowance - an allowance designed to help towards the cost of uniforms and footwear for children who are attending school. The scheme is payable between June and September each year.

- Medical card - if your income is below a certain level, you may get a medical card. It covers you for free doctor's care, approved prescriptions etc. Contact your local health office for more information.

- School book scheme - each year the Department of Education and Skills provides grants to primary and secondary schools towards the cost of school books for students in financial need. You should contact the school principal for more information. The school principal will also advise you whether the school runs a book loan scheme, whereby your children's books are provided for a nominal rental charge each year.

Taxation of jobseeker's benefit

Jobseeker's benefit is taxable. However, if you are getting jobseeker's benefit because your normal working week has been reduced (systematic short-time work) your jobseeker's benefit is not taxed.

How to apply

You should apply for jobseeker's benefit the first day you become unemployed.

It is important to apply on the first day you become unemployed because you will not get paid for the first three days of your claim.

Jobseeker's benefit application forms are available online on www.welfare. ie. You can also get an application form at your local social welfare office.

Carer's benefit

Carer's benefit is payable to PRSI classes A,B,C,D,E and H. It is payable to people who leave work in order to care for a person(s) in need of full-time care and attention.

Who can qualify

You will qualify if you - the carer:

- Are age 16 or over and under age 65/66.

- Live with the person(s) you are looking after or in close proximity.

- Have been employed for eight weeks during the previous 26 weeks.

- Satisfy the PRSI contribution conditions.

- Give up employment to care for a person(s) on a full-time basis. This employment must have been for a minimum of 16 hours per week or 32 hours per fortnight.

- Are not employed or self-employed outside the home. You may however work up to 15 hours per week provided the net amount you receive is less than €332.50 p.w.

- Are living in the State.

- Are not living in a hospital, convalescent home or other similar institution

and

- The person(s) you are caring for is/are

  - So disabled as to need full-time care and attention (medical certification is required)

  - Not normally living in a hospital, home or other similar institution.

The rate of carer's benefit is currentyly €220.00 per week.

PRSI conditions

For a first claim you must have

- 156 contributions paid since entry into insurable employment. **and**

- 39 contributions paid in the relevant tax year. **or**

- 39 contributions paid in the 12 month period before the commencement of the carer's benefit. **or**

- 26 contributions paid in the relevant tax year and 26 contributions paid in the relevant tax year prior to that.

Carers support grant

An annual respite care grant is paid in June each year and is extended to all carers providing full-time care to an older person or a person with disability, regardless of means, who are not in receipt of an unemployment payment or working outside the home for more than 10 hours per week. This grant is worth €1,700 and is paid in respect of each person being cared for.

Illness benefit

Illness benefit is available to PRSI classes A, E, H and P.

It is payable if

- You are under 66.

- Are unfit to work due to illness.

- Satisfy the PRSI conditions.

The weekly rate of Illness benefit from March 2019 is €203.

PRSI conditions:

- At least 104 weeks PRSI paid since you started work, **and**

- 39 weeks PRSI paid or credited in the relevant tax year, of which 13 must be paid contributions, **or**

- 26 weeks PRSI paid in the relevant tax year, **and**

- 26 weeks PRSI paid in the tax year immediately before the relevant tax year.

If you do not have 13 paid contributions in the relevant tax year, the following years may be used to satisfy this condition:

- Either of the two most previous tax years.

- The most recent complete tax year, **or**

- The current tax year.

The relevant tax year is the second last complete tax year before the benefit year in which the illness benefit claim is made. For claims made in 2020 the relevant year is 2018.

Tax

Illness benefit is taxable, but it will be paid directly to you without income tax deductions. If you are employed, your employer will take your illness benefit into account for PAYE purposes. If you are unemployed, the Revenue will take account of the amount paid to you when adjusting your tax credits or reviewing the tax affairs of your spouse.

Occupational injuries benefit

Occupational injuries benefit is a weekly payment if you are unfit for work due to

- An accident at work.

- An accident while travelling directly to or from work.

- An occupational disease.

There are a number of benefits available and there are different conditions attached to each benefit which include

- Injury benefit.

- Disablement benefit.

- Incapacity supplement.

- Constant attendance allowance.

- Medical care scheme.

There are also death benefits under this scheme that include

- Widow(er)/surviving civil partner's pension that is paid at a higher rate than ordinary contributory widow(er)/surviving civil partner's pension.

- Orphan's pension.

- Dependent parent's pension.

- Funeral grant.

Occupational injuries benefits are available to people covered by PRSI Class A, D, J and M - most workers in Ireland. Injury benefit is not paid for the first three days of your illness or incapacity and payment can be made for up to 26 weeks starting from the date of your injury or the start of your illness.

If you are still unable to work after 26 weeks, you may be entitled to illness benefit, disability allowance or supplementary welfare allowance. You may be entitled to disability benefit if you suffer a loss of physical or mental faculty as a result of the accident or disease. If you don't qualify for illness benefit or another social welfare payment and you are getting disablement benefit, you may be eligible for incapacity supplement.

To check rates and to apply for benefits contact

"Special grant of €6,000 is paid to widows or widowers with dependent children following the death of the spouse."

> Occupational Injuries Benefit Section,
> Department of Social Protection,
> Áras Mhic Dhiarmada
> Store Street
> Dublin 1
> Tel (01) 704 3018

Or contact your local Social Welfare office for more information.

Early retirement due to ill health

This scheme applies if you are a public servant paying PRSI at classes B,C and D and have to give up work because of ill health. It basically gives you PRSI credits to keep your insurance record up-to-date and protects your contributory widow's/widower's pension, orphan's contributory allowance and bereavement grant.

To apply for these credited contributions, you should complete the application form CR35.

Widowed parent's grant

A special grant of €6,000 is paid to widows or widowers with dependent children following the death of their spouse. It is payable to widows or widowers who qualify for the widow/widower's contributory pension or a one-parent family payment.

Funeral grant

If the death was due to an accident at work or occupational disease, a funeral grant under the occupational injuries scheme may be payable.

Working in the EU

As Ireland is a member of the EU, you are legally entitled to look for work in any member state without a work permit. Each member state has a national placement service, similar to Solas. If you wish to seek work in any of the EU countries, you can apply through a Solas employment services office for a job in the country of your choice. Details of your application will be circulated abroad through the SEDOC system free of charge and if any suitable vacancies arise, you will be notified.

If you qualify for jobseekers benefit here and have been registered and in receipt of benefit for at least four weeks, you may have your jobseekers benefit transferred to another EU country for up to 13 weeks, provided you look for and register for work in that country within seven days. You must register for work within seven days from the date you last claimed jobseekers benefit in Ireland for your unemployment payments to be continuous.

Form U2

This is required to claim jobseekers benefit. It gives details of your social insurance and employment record. If you are leaving Ireland to move to Northern Ireland or Britain your Social Welfare Local Office will issue you with the Form U2 which you take to the UK social services. If you are moving to another EU country the Department of Social Protection will send the U2 form to your new address in that EU country.

Health services

EU Regulations also apply to your health service entitlements. In the UK you are entitled to UK health services, as soon as you have an address in the UK and register with a doctor. If you are on a temporary stay in any other EU country you will be entitled to the same health services as the nationals of that country. The European Health Insurance Card (EHIC) is normally required to claim these health benefits in all EU countries, excluding the UK.

PRSI/EU documents

Form E104 is required if you are claiming illness or maternity benefit.

Form U2 is required if you are claiming jobseekers benefit.

The European Health Insurance Card (EHIC) is required to claim health service benefits in EU countries excluding the UK.

Taxation of social welfare payments

Non-taxable

The following payments are not liable to Income Tax-

- Jobseekers allowance
- Family income supplement
- Back to work allowance
- Health & safety benefits
- Supplementary welfare allowance

Taxable

The following payments are taxable -

- State pension transition
- State Contributory pension
- Illness benefit
- Widow's/widower's contributory pension
- Jobseekers benefit
- Maternity/paternity/adoptive benefit
- Orphan's contributory allowances
- Occupational injuries benefit
- Invalidity pension
- One parent family payment

- Carer's allowance

- Deserted wife's benefit

- Carer's benefit

Taxable social welfare payments are not taxed when you receive them, they are paid to you gross. You should contact your tax office when you receive a social welfare payment to ensure that any tax due on that payment will be paid by you.

Taxation of jobseekers benefit

Jobseekers benefit, is a taxable source of income. However additional payments for child dependents paid with jobseekers benefit, is exempt from tax. Systematic short-term working, which is short-term working for a limited time period normally 6-8 weeks is exempt from tax. Casual short-term working is liable to income tax. Casual short-term working differs from systematic short-term working in that casual working if for an unlimited period.

Social welfare payments are paid gross. Therefore you should ensure if you are self-employed and are also in receipt of a taxable social welfare benefit e.g. State pension you should include details of this pension on your annual tax return.

If you are an employee paying your tax through PAYE, and are in receipt of a taxable payment from social welfare you should contact your tax office to ensure that your tax credits and rate bands are reduced to account for the tax payable on your social welfare payment.

"Fair deal" - nursing home support scheme

Also known as the 'Fair Deal' scheme, the Nursing Home Support Scheme provides support to people who require long term nursing care. Under the "Fair Deal" scheme you make a contribution towards the cost of your care and the State pays the balance. The amount of your contribution depends on your financial position.

Fair Deal begins by arranging a care needs assessment by a health care professional from your local nursing home support group and then a financial assessment looks at your income and assets to determine your contribution to care and the corresponding level of "State support".

Under Fair Deal you are obliged to contribute 80% of your income and 7.5% of the value of any assets you own per annum. (5% if the application was made before 25 July 2013.) Your principal residence is only included in the financial assessment for a maximum of three years.

The first €36,000 of assets for an individual or €72,000 for a couple are excluded in the financial assessment

Where assets include land and property, the contribution may be deferred during the person's lifetime and it will be collected by the HSE after death. This is an optional benefit of the scheme called the "Nursing Home Loan" which requires written consent to a charging order that is then registered against your house or other assets.

If you opt for the Nursing Home Loan your remaining spouse/partner can also apply to have repayment deferred during their lifetime.

In the case of a couple, where one spouse/partner avails of long-term nursing care and the other remains in their home, only 50% of their qualifying income will be assessed under the 80% contribution rule and the contribution based on the value of their principal residence, will be capped at 11.25%. (The latter had been capped at 7.5% for applications before 25 July 2013.)

Once the amount to be contributed has been assessed, the HSE will then pay the balance of the cost of care. Nobody will pay more than the actual cost of care.

More details of the Fair Deal scheme can be found here: www2.hse.ie/

eng/services/list/4/olderpeople

13 Redundancy

If you lose your job you may be entitled to receive a redundancy payment. The Redundancy Payments Acts, 1967-2014 legally obliges employers to pay redundant employees what is known as a "statutory redundancy entitlement".

Statutory redundancy payment

The amount of statutory redundancy is related to an employee's length of service and normal weekly earnings (gross weekly wage, average regular overtime and payment-in-kind), all added together, up to a maximum amount of €600 per week or €31,200 per annum.

When does redundancy arise?

A redundancy situation arises where an employee's job ceases to exist, because of rationalisation/ reorganisation, not enough work available, the financial state of the firm, company closures etc, and the employee is not replaced.

Which employees are covered?

Employees are covered under these Acts if they meet the following requirements:

- Are age 16 or over.

- Have at least two years continuous service (104 weeks).

- Are in employment which is insurable for all Social Welfare Benefits. This condition does not apply to part time employees.

- Have been made redundant as a result of a genuine redundancy situation i.e. their job no longer exists and they are not replaced.

Notice of redundancy

An employer who, because of redundancy, intends to dismiss an employee who has at least 104 weeks continuous service with the firm, must give a minimum of 2 weeks written notice to the employee of the proposed dismissal.

This notice period required depends on the employee's period of service.

Period of Service	Notice required
Between 2 - 5 years	2 weeks
Between 5 - 10 years	4 weeks
Between 10 - 15 years	6 weeks
Over 15 years	8 weeks

"For the purpose of calculating statutory redundancy, a weeks pay is limited to a maximum of €600."

Calculation of statutory redundancy lump sum payments.

The amount of statutory redundancy payments which an employee is entitled to receive from their employer is calculated as follows:

- Two weeks pay for each year of employment continuous and reckonable over the age of 16.

- In addition, a bonus week.

Reckonable service is service excluding ordinary sick leave over and above 26 weeks and an occupational injury over and above 52 weeks.

Reckonable service also excludes absence from work because of lay-offs or strikes. However, short-time work is reckonable.

When calculating statutory redundancy a weeks pay is capped at €600.

Statutory redundancy payments are exempt from tax.

All excess days are calculated as a portion of 365 days. i.e 4 years 190 days = 4.52 years

Example

You started working for your current employer on 1 January 2009. Your employer decided to reduce staff numbers and you are made redundant with effect from 31 December 2019. Your current salary is €45,000 per annum.

As you have 11 full years of services you will be entitled to

11 x 2 weeks + 1 bonus week = 23 weeks

Your weekly salary is €865.38, however the maximum you can receive by way of statutory redundancy is limited to €600 per week. Therefore your statutory redundancy payment will work out as;

$$23 \text{ weeks} \times €600 = €13,800$$

This payment is tax free.

Employment appeals tribunal

Disputes concerning redundancy payments can be submitted to the Employment Appeals Tribunal which can provide a speedy, fair, inexpensive and informal means for individuals to seek remedies for alleged infringements of their statutory redundancy rights. The Tribunal also deals with disputes under other labour law areas including the Minimum Notice and Terms of Employment Acts, 1973 to 2005. These cover the right of workers to a minimum period of notice before dismissal, provided they are in continuous service with the same employer for at least 13 weeks and are normally expected to work at least eight hours per week.

The Tribunal also deals with the Unfair Dismissals Acts, 1977 to 2015 and the Protection of Employees (Employers' Insolvency) Acts, 1984 to 2007 (dealing with such areas, amongst others, as arrears of pay due to an employee, holiday and sick pay etc.) where the employer is insolvent.

Effects of change of ownership of a business on a redundancy lump sum payment

Where there is a change in the ownership of a business and you continue, by arrangement to work for the new owner with no break in your employment, you are not entitled to any redundancy payments at the time of the change of ownership. Your continuity of employment is also preserved for the purpose of the redundancy payments in the event of your dismissal or redundancy by the new employer at any future date. You are not entitled to a redundancy payment if an offer of employment by the new owner is unreasonably refused by you.

If the new owner merely buys the premises in which you were employed, this does not constitute a change of ownership of the business and your former employer will be liable to pay any redundancy payment which may be due to you.

What happens if an employer fails to pay a redundancy lump sum?

In situations where the employer is unable to pay the employees their entitlements, the Department of Social Protection can pay the full amount direct to the employees from the Social Insurance Fund (S.I.F.). In no circumstances should the employer pay part of the statutory entitlement to the employee.

The employer will then be liable for the payment and will become a preferential creditor of the Department of Social Protection. The employee fills in Form RP50 including the original employer signature and sends it into the Department of Social Protection. Before this claim can be processed an employer must provide a letter from their accountant/ solicitor confirming their inability to pay. This confirmation must be based on their own professional view of the company's finances rather than a view based on information provided by the employer and they must be able to support this confirmation should an audit be carried out at any time.

For further information or relevant forms, contact the Redundancy Payments Section, Floor 2, Department of Social Protection, Block C, The Earlsfort Centre, Lower Hatch Street, Dublin 2.

Ex-gratia payments

Legally your employer is only obliged to pay you statutory redundancy in the event of a redundancy. However many employers also pay an additional ex-gratia payment to employees. Ex-gratia payments or compensation payments over and above the statutory redundancy payment are taxable.

However, there are a number of exemptions available which reduce the amount charged to tax.

Basic exemption

The basic exemption is €10,160 together with an additional €765 for each complete year of service.

Increased exemption

The basic exemption may be increased by €10,000 to a maximum of €20,160 plus €765 for each complete year of service provided:

- You have not made any claims in respect of a lump sum in the previous 10 tax years.

    and

- If you are in an occupational pension scheme the increased exemption of €10,000 is reduced by the amount of;

    - Any tax-free lump sum from the pension scheme to which you may be immediately entitled   **or**

    - The present day value at the date of leaving employment of any tax-free lump sum, which is received or may be received from the pension scheme in the future.

If the lump sum from the pension is more than €10,000 you are not due the increased exemption. If it is less than €10,000 you are due the increased exemption of €10,000 less the amount of the pension scheme entitlement.

Standard capital superannuation benefit (S.C.S.B.)

The third exemption is the Standard Capital Superannuation Benefit. This is arrived at using the following formula:

$$\frac{A \times B}{15} - C$$

A   =   Average yearly remuneration from the employment for the last 36 months ending on the date of termination.

B   =   Number of complete years of service.

C   =   Any tax-free lump sum from the occupational pension scheme to which you may be entitled

or

The present day value at the date of leaving employment of any tax-free lump sum which is received or may be received from the occupational pension scheme in the future.

From 1 January 2011 the maximum lump sum which can be received tax free from an approved pension fund is restricted to €200,000. Therefore

"C" cannot exceed €200,000 in the S.C.S.B. calculation for 2011 and subsequent years.

For the purpose of calculating the increased exemption and the S.C.S.B. amount, the tax-free lump sum receivable from an occupational pension scheme is the present day value of any deferred tax-free lump sum receivable at retirement from the existing occupational pension scheme. A refund of pension contributions which were subject to tax at 20% are excluded.

If you sign a waiver letter i.e. a letter confirming you will not avail of any tax-free lump sum from your current occupational pension scheme now or at retirement, the value of any deferred tax-free lump sum receivable will be Nil. (See C above).

Ex gratia payments will be subject to a maximum exemption limit of €200,000 taking into consideration any prior tax-free payments (including SCSB deduction) which have been received.

When calculating your years of service for either the basic, increased exemption or the S.C.S.B. calculation the following can be counted towards a full years service;

- Time worked before and after a career break.
- Period of job-sharing or part-time work.
- For group companies, all work carried out in Ireland.

If you have taken a career break this cannot be counted as service.

If you work part-time there is no apportionment to take account of the part-time nature of your employment. Your years of service are calculated as if you worked full-time.

Example

You commenced employment with company XYZ Ltd. on 28 February 1998.

You opted for early retirement on 31 January 2020 and you received a lump sum of €60,000 (excluding statutory redundancy).

You received a tax free lump sum of €25,000 from your pension scheme.

The tax-free amount of this €60,000 is the highest of the following:

Basic exemption

$$€10,160 + (€765 \times 21) = €26,225$$

Only complete years count for the purpose of the additional €765. So even though you had 21 years 11 months service, you only receive €765 x 21.

Increased exemption

As you received a tax-free lump sum from the pension scheme in excess of €10,000, the increased exemption would not apply to you.

Standard capital superannuation benefit (SCSB)

Assuming your salary for the last 36 months was as follows:

	€	
01/01/20 - 31/01/20	€4,167	(1 months)
01/01/19 - 31/12/19	€50,000	(12 months)
01/01/18 - 31/12/18	€50,000	(12 months)
01/02/17 - 31/12/17	€41,250	(11 months)
Total salary for 36 months	€145,417	
Average salary for 12 months	€48,472	

Calculation of SCSB

$\underline{A \times B}$ less C = $\underline{€48,472 \times 21}$ less €25,000 = €42,861
15   15

The highest of the above three exemptions is the SCSB amount of €42,861. This is the amount which you can receive tax-free.

A summary of your position, assuming you pay tax at 40%, is as follows:

		€
	Gross lump sum	€65,000
Less:	SCSB Amount	€42,861
	Taxable	€22,139
	Tax @ 40%	€ 8,856
	USC @ 4.5%	€996
	Total tax and levies	€9,852
	Net Lump Sum	**€55,148**

Subsequent claim

The basic exemption and the SCSB are generally available against any subsequent lump sum payment. However, they can only be given once against a lump sum from the same employer or an associate employer.

The increased exemption of €10,000 may be claimed provided the individual has not in the previous ten years, claimed relief in excess of the basic tax-free exemption in respect of a lump sum received.

Lifetime limit on tax-free payments

A lifetime restriction on the reliefs available was introduced in 2011. From 1 January 2011, the total of all exemptions and reliefs granted to an individual in respect of all ex-gratia lump sums received cannot exceed €200,000. This maximum figure of €200,000 includes the total value of any amounts of relief previously granted to the claimant in respect of any previous ex-gratia payments

Tax exemptions for retraining on redundancy

Where an employer pays the cost of retraining an employee as part of a redundancy package, the cost of the retraining, up to maximum of €5,000, will be exempt from tax, provided:

- The employee has more than two years' continuous full-time service;

- The retraining is part of a redundancy package and is designed to improve skills or knowledge used either in obtaining employment or setting up a business; and

- The retraining is completed within six months of the termination of employment.

How is the lump sum taxed?

Your employer is obliged to deduct PAYE and the Universal Social Charge (USC) but not PRSI, on all of the lump sum less the basis exemption or SCSB, as previously outlined.

Redundancy and jobseekers benefit

Employees who are made redundant are entitled to claim Jobseeker's Benefit provided they satisfy the PRSI and other qualifying conditions. Where an employee, who is under 55 years of age, is made redundant and the total gross amount of statutory redundancy and/or a termination payment received by them exceeds €50,000, they will lose their entitlement to claim Jobseeker's Benefit of up to 9 weeks as follows;

Termination Payment	Period of loss of Jobseeker's Benefit
€50,000 to €55,000	1 week
€50,000.01 to €60,000	2 weeks
€60,000.01 to €65,000	3 weeks
€65,000.01 to €70,000	4 weeks
€70,000.01 to €75,000	5 weeks
€75,000.01 to €80,000	6 weeks
€80,000.01 to €85,000	7 weeks
€85,000.01 to €90,000	8 weeks
€90,000.01 and over	9 weeks

However, employees who are aged 55 years or over who are made redundant do not have any waiting period for Jobseeker's Benefit.

14 Pensions - financial planning for retirement

Individually, we all need to make financial provision for when we no longer want to work, or are no longer able to work, or indeed when we want to cut back on the amount of time we spend in work – that is, our retirement years.

Financial provision for retirement is made by accumulating a fund of money, or accumulating other assets such as property, stocks and shares, or bonds, that can be used to provide an income when we stop or cut back on work. One important point regarding the provision of an income in retirement is that we need to make sure our retirement income will be adequate for our needs at that time. Even if we are fortunate enough to have employers that make contributions on our behalf, constant monitoring of that provision to ensure it will be adequate is of paramount importance. In other words, we need to take control of our own financial future.

So, whether you are a self-employed sole trader, a proprietary director, or an employee, **you need to take control of your financial planning for retirement**. Taking this control on your own can be done, but unless you understand financial matters very well, it could be very difficult. This is where taking advice is important, but not just any advice. Your advice should come from a qualified, professional adviser that you can trust to give you the correct advice, and who, when it comes to arranging products for you, should be able to give you the choice of a number of different financial institutions.

One important piece of advice that any good financial adviser will give you is that **making provision for retirement should be done as tax-efficiently as possible**.

In this chapter we will look at

* Why we all need to plan for retirement;
* Why, because of their tax-efficiency, contributing to pension plans can make more sense than other forms of savings for most people;

- What sorts of investment funds are available under pension plans;

- The products available for retirement capital accumulation; and

- The products available to provide income following retirement.

Why plan for retirement?

Ask yourself the question **"If I don't make financial provision for my retirement who will?"** Firstly, the State is unlikely to be able to provide you with an adequate income in your retirement. If you are an employee your employer is unlikely to be able to provide you with adequate income in your retirement either and, your children will have enough to do to look after themselves and their families.

State pension

Currently the maximum weekly pension from the State for an individual is €248.30 per week. This is around 28% of the average industrial wage of €45,600 or so per year. This may not be a very attractive prospect for anyone earning more than €45,600 per year.

Meanwhile the State pension retirement age has been moved out to age 66 for all in 2014, 67 in 2021 and 68 in 2028 and qualifying for the maximum benefit is being made more difficult.

Social welfare pensions are paid by the State from incoming revenue on a "pay as you go" basis. This is fine while there are enough people working and making PRSI contributions to pay the pensions of retired people. But this situation is changing fast. It is estimated that by 2050 there will be only two people working for every person aged over 65. At present there are almost five people working for every person aged over 65. In 2013 the cost to the State of social welfare pensions was 6.8% of GDP and it is estimated that this will have risen to 15% of GDP by 2050.

In the boom times the Government set up the National Pension Reserve Fund to help fund pensions for public sector workers and social welfare pensions into the future. Unfortunately, this has now been decimated by "investing" in the failed banks.

So, depending solely on the State to provide an adequate income in retirement is not a good idea.

Employer pension schemes

The vast majority of employers are unlikely to be able to provide adequate income in retirement for their employees, and that includes the State and its employees. Already many employers that once provided Defined Benefit (DB) pension schemes have had to restructure their schemes. Not only in this country but worldwide a huge number of Defined Benefit schemes have closed down.

Defined Benefit schemes promise a certain level of benefits at retirement. These benefits are usually related to earnings and service with the employer. Unfortunately, in recent years employers have found that Defined Benefit schemes are just too expensive for them to maintain. This is due mainly to the fact that people are living longer and the schemes have to pay out pensions for longer. Also, the investment returns achieved by the funds have been poor, due to the state of the world economy.

In Ireland Defined Benefit schemes are largely being replaced by Defined Contribution (DC) schemes and by PRSA arrangements. The contribution levels being made to these types of pension schemes are generally totally inadequate to provide worthwhile retirement benefits. While the average contributions to DB schemes are often likely to be 25% to 30% of salary in total between employer and employee contributions, the average total contribution rate to DC schemes is only 10% of salary. Remember, the 25% to 30% of salary contributions to DB schemes have not been enough to keep many of these schemes going. So, 10% of salary is unlikely to produce adequate retirement income.

When will I retire?

Another very good question to ask yourself is **"When do I see myself stopping work or cutting back on my workload?"**

Life expectancy rates are increasing. On average people are living now to age 80. Women live five or six years longer than men, on average. So, if you see yourself wanting to retire at age 60, for example, what are you going to live off for the following two decades?

As stated earlier the State pension retirement age has been moved out to age 66 in 2014, to 67 in 2021 and to 68 in 2028. So if you are going to depend on the State for retirement income you are going to have to work longer before you can start collecting a retirement income.   That is assuming the State will be able to afford to pay you a reasonable income.

Women and retirement planning

There is a special need for women to plan their retirements as women live five or six years longer than men on average and assuming that they retire at the same age as men, they can expect to be retired longer.

Adequate retirement income

Another very important question to ask yourself is **"What level of income will be adequate for my needs in retirement?"**

Once you decide what level of yearly income you will need in retirement – bearing in mind that your mortgage will most likely be paid off, and your children are not likely to be dependant on you any longer – you should multiply this figure by 25 to 30 times to calculate the retirement capital you will need. **So, an income of €30,000 a year is likely to need retirement capital in the region of €750,000 to €900,000.** If you are going to have a dependant spouse/partner to provide for in retirement it is important that you take this into account in your calculations. Of course, if your spouse/partner has independent income then they too should be planning for retirement.

The cost of delay

It is very important to start planning for retirement early. Every year can make a big difference as can be seen from the table on page 261. Based upon the assumed investment growth rate and charges shown, an individual who starts contributing to a pension plan 10 years before retirement age will have to contribute more than five times as much as a person starting 30 years before retirement age in order to accumulate the same amount of money.

Example

€5,000 p.a. (level) pension contribution, 6% pa investment growth, 95% allocation & 1% annual management charge.

Term	Illustrative capital	Factor
10 years	€62,732	5.28
15 years	€107,623	3.78
20 years	€164,916	2.62
25 years	€238,039	1.71
30 years	€331,364	1.00

Source: Zurich Life Assurance plc

Why pension plans?

When it comes to putting money aside for the future there are many choices available to you. You could use personal investments, such as property, stocks and shares, works of art, etc. Personal savings accounts with banks or credit unions, or through life assurance policies, are another method of accumulating capital for retirement. However, saving through pension plans is for most people the most attractive option. This is due to the tax relief available.

Although the tax reliefs are not as attractive for higher earners as they were in the past, pension plans are still, for the vast majority of individuals, very tax-efficient. Basically a pension plan is a savings plan, with special tax incentives, used to build up a capital sum that will be used to provide an income in retirement for you (and your dependents). The tax incentives are

● Tax relief on personal contributions.

● Tax-exempt investment growth within the pension investment fund(s).

● Tax-free cash at retirement.

● No tax liability on employer contributions to pensions.

Because of the special tax incentives there are certain rules/criteria that must be observed. Also, income draw-down from the different types of pension plans following retirement is taxable. We will look at both of these issues in greater depth later in this chapter.

The rules/criteria and the taxation of income from pension plans are the areas that complicate pensions, but it is important to remember the basic concept is very simple. You, and maybe your employer, pay in money while you are working and at retirement you draw an income out of the fund you have accumulated.

Tax Relief on personal contributions

● Subject to certain limits (see below), for every €100 that you contribute you will pay €40 less in income tax if you are a 40% tax-payer and €20 less if you are 20% tax-payer. This is equivalent to a 66.6% subsidy from the State if you are a higher rate tax-payer and a 25% subsidy if you are a standard rate tax-payer.

● The maximum amount of pension contribution on which you can claim tax relief is based on a percentage of your net relevant earnings and depends on your age as outlined below. For the purpose of tax relief on pension contributions net relevant earnings are capped at €115,000 p.a.

Age	Percentage of net relevant earnings/remuneration
Up to 29 Years	15%
30 to 39 Years	20%
40 to 49 Years	25%
50 to 54 Years	30%
55 to 59 Years	35%
60 and over	40%

Notes

● Net relevant earnings consist of income from self-employment. A husband and wife have separate relevant earnings, which cannot be aggregated for retirement saving purposes. Investment earnings or rental income are not treated as relevant earnings and cannot be taken into consideration in calculating your maximum allowable pension contributions. Net relevant earnings consist of relevant earning less capital allowances, trading losses and certain other charges e.g. covenants and mortgage interest, for which you can claim tax relief.

- Remuneration relates to the earnings of employees and directors who pay tax under the PAYE system. It can include basic pay, bonus payments, over-time payments and any other payments that are subject to PAYE including the value of any benefit-in-kind.

- For some specific occupations the 30% limit applies irrespective of age (e.g. certain professional sports people)

- For the self-employed and individuals in non-pensionable employment, the limits on page 262, relate to the total of personal contributions, and any employer contributions, made to personal pension plans or PRSA contracts.

- For employees who are members of occupational pension schemes the limits shown on page 262 apply to the total of personal contributions, Additional Voluntary Contributions (AVCs), and/or PRSA AVCs made. Employer contributions to occupational pension schemes are not taken into account in calculating the maximum contributions for personal tax relief.

- Where an individual has more than one source of income the total figure of €115,000 applies to the aggregated income. Where one of the incomes is pensionable through an occupational pension scheme, they must use up all the relief available in respect of that pensionable income if they wish to maximise their full tax relief entitlement, and claim relief on contributions relating to their non-pensionable income after that, if there is scope to do so.

Individuals who make personal contributions to pension plans by 31 October in any given tax year can back-date the tax relief to the previous tax year, provided they advise the Revenue of their intention to back-date the relief by 31 October . This does not apply where contributions are made by salary deduction as the tax relief is given at source.

For those who are registered to file their tax returns and pay their tax bills on-line through the Revenue Online System (ROS) the Revenue allow an extension on the 31 October deadline to mid-November. These individuals have until this date to make their pension contributions and notify the Revenue of their intention to back-date the relief.

Tax-exempt investment growth

- The fact that pension funds can grow without any liability to Income Tax on investment income and without any Capital Gains Tax on investment growth means that there is the potential to accumulate larger amounts of capital than under personal savings and investments where investment returns are taxable (e.g. DIRT on deposit accounts).

Tax-free cash at retirement

- Every individual who funds for retirement through a pension plan is entitled to take a lump sum benefit at retirement. The maximum lump sum will depend on the type of pension plan that the individual has.

- For personal pensions and PRSAs the maximum lump sum is 25% of the accumulated fund. For Defined Benefit occupational pension schemes up to 150% of "final remuneration" can be taken, depending on their length of service with their employer. Members of Defined Contribution occupational schemes have a choice between the 25% of fund and the earnings and service related bases.

- The maximum lump sum that can be taken is €500,000, the first €200,000 of which can be taken tax-free, with the next €300,000 taxed at only 20%. The €200,000 is a lifetime figure and all retirement lump sums taken since 5 December 2005 are taken into account.

No tax liability on employer contributions

- For employees, there is no liability to income tax, PRSI or USC on the contributions their employers make to occupational pension schemes on their behalf. If an employers' contribution to a PRSA or personal pensions cause the total contributions to exceed the maximum allowable personal contribution limits as detailed on page 262, there is a liability to income tax and PRSI on the amount by which the limits are exceeded.

- Being a member of an occupational pension scheme makes a great deal of sense for an employee even if they are obliged to make contributions to the scheme. For example, if the employer is contributing 5% of salary and the employee is obliged to contribute a further 5%, the employee is getting the value of 10% of salary being contributed, all for a net outlay of 3% of salary if they are a 40% tax-payer, and 4% of salary if they are a 20% tax-payer.

- For individuals who own their own companies (i.e. proprietary directors) having the company contribute to an occupational pension scheme is an excellent way for them to take profits from the company and put them away for the future without any immediate liability to tax. Their spouses may also be employees/directors of the company and their retirement capital can be funded separately through an occupational pension plan.

- Self-employed individuals can also employ their spouses and other family members, and accumulate retirement capital for them through occupational pension schemes. The employer contributions are invested for the spouses / family members without any liability to benefit-in-kind taxation on the employer contributions. The self-employed individual can also receive tax relief on their contributions to the schemes.

Standard fund threshold

- In order to deter the abuse of the rules regarding the tax incentives offered to those contributing to pension plans there is a maximum limit on the value of the accumulated pension fund (or, the capital equivalent of the benefits accrued under a Defined Benefit occupational pension scheme). This limit is known as the Standard Fund Threshold (SFT), and is €2 million from 1 January 2014. From 7 December 2010 to 1 January 2014 the SFT was €2.3 million.

- Those whose accrued pension was valued at between €2 million and €2.3 million at 1 January 2014 were allowed to apply to the Revenue for a higher threshold (A Personal Fund Threshold PFT).

- At retirement those whose fund value exceeds the Standard Fund Threshold / Personal Fund Threshold must pay a once-off additional tax of 40% on the excess over their respective threshold amount. This is in addition to the normal taxation of income from pension plans which will be covered later in this chapter.

Want some good advice?
Get some good advice!

Pensions, savings, investments, life insurance - all vitally important for you and your family's financial well-being. The good news is there's a huge range of options out there - the hard part is figuring out which one is right for you.

Your local **Financial Broker** is an expert adviser who will assess your needs and is then legally obliged to recommend the most suitable product for your circumstances. At Aviva we know how complex this can be so we strongly recommend you get professional advice before making any decision.

To find an accredited broker in your area go www.brokersireland.ie

For financial advice, you're safe in the hands of your local broker!

Pension investment funds

Taking control of how and where your pension contributions are invested is very important. The services of a qualified financial adviser who can explain how investment funds work and can offer you lots of choices, may be a good idea.

You need to understand what caveats such as "Past performance is not a reliable guide to future performance" or "The value of your pension fund may go down as well as up" actually mean. You need to think about how you would feel if your retirement investments dropped significantly. Would you panic or would you understand that in all likelihood, you would recover your losses over time? This is what is known as your level of "risk tolerance".

A good financial adviser should be able to help you establish your level of risk tolerance and decide what sort of funds suit you best.

It is important that you are comfortable with the funds you choose. After all it is your money that is being invested and your retirement that is being funded. However, investment theory tells us that the greater the level of risk taken, the greater the chances of making more profits in the long term.

Pension fund investment managers are unlikely to offer you funds that are so risky that you could lose all your investment. Usually a pension fund will hold a wide range of assets, and even a fund that is invested in one asset class, such as equities, will usually hold a large number of different equities.

Unit-linked funds

There are the four main asset classes into which pension fund managers will invest

- Equities – i.e. stocks and shares in companies.

- Property.

- Fixed Income Securities (Bonds) – i.e. loans issued by governments and larger companies.

- Cash.

There are other asset classes, such as commodities, but these are not used as much as these four main classes.

Investment returns are achieved by investment income from these assets and by growth in the value of the assets.

Examples of investment income include dividends paid to the shareholders; rental income from property; dividends paid by governments and companies on bonds; and, interest earned by cash on deposit. This income is usually re-invested back into the fund by purchasing further assets.

Investment growth is achieved by the assets increasing in value, although the opposite can also happen from time to time, as a result of less favourable economic conditions. However, over the years it would be expected that most assets and the funds invested in them would grow in value, particularly over the longer term.

- Most pension funds in Ireland are operated on a unit-linked basis. That is, the contributions into the pension plan buy "units" in the fund. These units reflect the value of the assets held by the fund. If the value of the assets increases either by their sale value increasing or as a result of investment income being used to purchase more assets, the value ("price") of the units owned by the fund will increase. Depending on investment conditions unit prices can also fall in value.

- The unit-linked funds in the Irish market would mainly invest in established markets in one or more of the asset classes mentioned above, although alternative markets or assets may also be used. Where assets are owned outside the Eurozone there can be an exposure to currency fluctuations, but the effect of this may be offset through "hedging".

- A long term historical view of the returns achieved on the different asset classes shows that, equities produce the highest average returns in real terms (i.e. when compared to inflation). When it comes to pensions or any other savings or investments inflation beating returns are what count. Maintaining the purchasing power of the money you invest is very important.

- However, investing in equities can be risky as again historically statistics show that equities can be more volatile than other assets. That is, they are likely to rise and fall in value more often and the ups and downs are likely to be of a greater magnitude.

- The most popular funds in terms of money's invested are managed or mixed funds that would use a mix of the different asset classes, but with more of an emphasis on equities than on the other asset classes – with 70% or more invested in equities.

- "With-profit" funds, which are more traditional type funds, also invest in a mix of asset classes, but try to give a more systematic distribution of investment profits than managed funds, through yearly bonus declarations, and maturity bonuses. In good investment years they hold profits in reserve in order to be able to pay yearly bonuses to be added to policyholders' investments in poor years for investment returns. The maturity bonuses which may be paid when the policy is being matured or surrendered will reflect the underlying assets in the fund at the time the policy is being matured or surrendered. With-profit funds may also have a certain level of guarantee built into the contract. In recent years a number of the with-profit funds available on the Irish market have been closed to new business. Many of the funds also had "Market Level Adjustments (MLAs)" imposed. This means that on surrender of the fund the value payable to the contract owner has been reduced due to the fact that the total underlying value of the assets in the fund is less than the total value as shown in the clients' investment accounts.

- Absolute Return Funds seek to make positive returns in either a rising or falling stock-market cycle by employing investment management techniques that differ from traditional unit-linked funds. They will hold a diverse range of asset classes and use a range of investment techniques that will try to make a profit from both ups and downs in the markets and in individual stocks. Investment techniques include using short selling, futures, options, derivatives, arbitrage, leverage and unconventional assets. There are no guarantees that these techniques will work and only time will tell how well they will do in the future.

- It is important to note that the returns on the different funds will depend on the skills of those managing the funds. This is why investment return figures can vary from investment manager to investment manager even where the investments are broadly within the same sectors. The managers may be investing in similar assets but the specific assets, such as specific company shares, that they buy and the time at which they buy and/or sell these assets will make a difference to the returns achieved.

- Passive investment strategies, where the investment managers attempt to achieve the returns on a specific sector (e.g. Eurozone equities) through buying assets that track the assets held within an index of that sector (Euro Stoxx 50) have also grown in popularity in recent years. Consensus Funds are a similar idea in that the managers try to mirror the average of the assets held by other fund managers operating within a sector in order to achieve the average returns earned in that sector.

- With certain pension products a self-directed option is available, whereby the individual can decide on the individual stocks and shares, or bonds etc that they wish to invest in. Currencies other than the Euro can also be accessed through this option. In the past self-investment in property has been popular, but returns collapsed as a result of the massive fall in property values after 2008.

Since retirement planning is a long term exercise, pension investors may be better off risking higher volatility to achieve better long term returns. But not everyone will want to take that risk. It is important, therefore, to ensure that you understand fully the risks involved.

Another important point is that as retirement age approaches, you may want to reduce your exposure to more volatile equity based investments, depending on how the funds are to be used to provide an income in retirement.

Retirement capital accumulation products

This brings us to the types of specific pension products that can be used for the accumulation of retirement capital. There are a number of different types of pension contracts available.

Firstly though, it is important to understand the difference between Defined Contribution plans and Defined Benefit plans.

Defined contribution plans

- Defined Contribution plans also known as "Money Purchase" plans are the more common type of pension plan being arranged now.

- Holders of individual Defined Contribution pension plans have their own retirement account into which contributions are invested. Group occupational pension schemes can also be Defined Contribution, arranged under a group trust. Under these schemes the member also has an individual investment account.

- The investment will purchase units in the chosen fund or funds and as further contributions are added, should mean that the individual's investment account grows over the years.

- The size of the retirement account will depend on the total contributions made, the investment growth achieved and the charges deducted.

- Obviously, the earlier the pension contributions start, the more contributions are likely to be made by retirement age and the more time the money has to accumulate.

Defined benefit schemes

Defined Benefit plans are schemes where the employer promises a certain level of pension income to employees at retirement. This promise to pay benefits is funded through contributions made by the employer and the employee members of the scheme. The promised pension is normally based on a proportion of salary at retirement multiplied by the number of years service with the employer at retirement age – for example, 1/60th of final earnings for each year of service. Part of the pension income can normally be given up ("commuted") in lieu of a lump sum benefit at retirement.

The superannuation scheme for public sector employees is a Defined Benefit pension scheme. However, there is no pre-funding of benefits and the benefits are paid from the exchequer on a "pay as you go basis". The pension benefit is normally based on 1/80th of pensionable salary at retirement for each year of service, together with a gratuity (i.e. lump sum) payment based on 3/80ths of pensionable salary for each year of service, payable when the individual reaches normal retirement age. New employees joining the public sector from 1 January 2012 will have their retirement benefits based on the average of their earnings over their careers rather than on earnings at retirement age.

Personal retirement savings accounts (PRSAs)

First introduced in 2003, PRSAs are intended to be low-cost, simple to understand, accessible, portable retirement savings plans. They are Defined Contribution arrangements.

- Any resident of Ireland can contribute to a PRSA but only those with income from self-employment or from non-pensionable employment

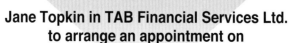

(i.e. are not members of an occupational pension scheme) will get tax relief on their contributions. However, where an individual intends returning to the workforce at sometime in the future they can make contributions to a PRSA and carry the tax relief entitlement forward to future years. An individual can have more than one PRSA but the contribution limits apply to the total contributions being made.

- Members of occupational pension schemes may make additional voluntary contributions (AVCs) to enhance the benefits provided by their occupational schemes through PRSAs.

- PRSAs may also be used to accept in transfers of occupational pension scheme members' pension fund values when a member leaves the scheme or the scheme is being wound-up. Conditions and criteria apply, the main one being that a transfer to a PRSA may only take place if the individual has been a member of the scheme or of any other scheme related to that individual's employment with, or any person connected with, the employer for less than 15 years.

- PRSAs are personally owned contracts. An employer may make contributions to an employee's PRSA, but once contributions are made by the employer they become the property of the individual employee through their PRSA.

- Employers that do not provide membership of an occupational pension scheme for employees within six months of joining employment must provide a facility whereby the employees involved can have their PRSA contributions deducted from salary at source. This applies to temporary or permanent, full-time or part-time employees.

- Tax relief on contributions to PRSAs is subject to age-related limits as outlined on page 262. Employer contributions are counted in calculating the maximum contributions and if limits are exceeded the excess amount is subject to benefit-in-kind.

- Employers receive tax relief on their contributions to employees' PRSAs, and are not liable for employers' PRSI on their contributions. Employers do not receive any relief against employers' PRSI on the employees' contributions deducted from salaries at source.

- Back-dating of tax relief on contributions made by an individual plan-holder to the previous tax year is allowed, subject to the age-related limits and earnings cap as detailed on page 262.

- The legislation governing PRSAs allows for two different types of PRSAs – standard and non-standard. For standard PRSAs, charges are restricted to a maximum of 5% of contributions and 1% p.a. of the accumulated fund, and "pooled investment" funds must be used. There are no maximum charge restrictions on non-standard PRSAs, but they can have a wider fund choice than standard PRSAs.

- All PRSA contracts must have a default investment strategy, which must be designed to fulfil the reasonable expectations of a typical PRSA investor who does not possess an in-depth knowledge of investment matters.

- The cost of risk benefits (i.e. life assurance cover, serious illness cover, or permanent health insurance cover) cannot be deducted from PRSA contributions or investment accounts.

- No costs can be charged on transfers to PRSAs from other retirement contracts or on transfers from PRSAs to other retirement contracts.

- Normally, you can mature a PRSA contract any time after you reach age 60. Benefits must be taken before age 75 and it is not necessary to stop working to draw benefits after age 60. Employees who are retiring from employment can draw benefits after age 50.

- On maturing your PRSA you will entitled to take 25% of your fund as a lump sum benefit, subject to a maximum of €500,000. Under current legislation the first €200,000 of the lump sum will be tax-free with the excess over €200,000 being taxed at 20%. For PRSA AVCs the accumulated fund will be aggregated with the main scheme benefits and the maximum lump sum that can be taken will be subject to the rules governing occupational pension schemes.

- A PRSA from which retirement benefits have not commenced on or before the date of the owner's 75th birthday is treated as becoming a vested PRSA, on that date. A consequence of a PRSA vesting in these circumstances is that, the individual cannot access the PRSA assets in any form from the date of his or her 75th birthday. So you should ensure you mature your PRSA before your 75th birthday.

Personal pensions / Retirement annuity contracts (RACs)

Personal pensions have been available in Ireland since 1968. Personal pensions are very similar to PRSAs, but there are some differences.

- As with PRSAs, personal pension plans are personally owned by the individual. An employer may make contributions to an employee's personal pension plan, but once contributions are made by the employer they become the property of the individual employee through their personal pension plan.

- One area of difference between personal pensions and PRSAs is that only those with income from self-employment or from non-pensionable employment (i.e. not members of an occupational pension scheme) can contribute to personal pension plans.

- Tax relief on contributions to personal pension plans is subject to the same age-related limits that apply to PRSAs or any personal contributions to pension arrangements. These limits are outlined on page 262. As with PRSAs, employer contributions are counted in calculating the maximum contributions and if limits are exceeded the excess amount is subject to benefit-in-kind. An individual can have more than one personal pension but the contribution limits apply to the total contributions being made.

- As with PRSAs, employers receive tax relief on their contributions to employees' plans, and are not liable for Employers' PRSI on their contributions. Employers do not receive any relief against Employers' PRSI on the employees' contributions deducted from salaries at source.

- Back-dating of tax relief on contributions made by an individual plan-holder to the previous tax year is allowed, subject to the age-related limits and earnings cap as detailed on page 262.

- The cost of life assurance cover can be deducted from personal pension contributions or investment accounts. Also, personal pension plan legislation allows plans that solely provide a benefit on death before retirement to be put in place. This can be a very tax-efficient method of providing life assurance protection.

- Normally, you can mature a personal pension plan contract any time after you reach age 60. Benefits must be taken before age 75 and it is not necessary to stop working to draw benefits after age 60.

- On maturing your personal pension plan you will entitled to take 25% of your fund as a lump sum benefit, subject to a maximum of €500,000. Under current legislation the first €200,000 of the lump sum will be tax-free with the excess between €200,000 and €500,000 being taxed at 20%.

- A wider fund choice can be available under personal pension plans than under PRSAs, particularly Standard PRSAs.

Occupational pension schemes

Otherwise known as employer-sponsored pension schemes, company-paid pensions, or employee pensions, occupational pension schemes are the most attractive retirement funding product from a tax-efficiency perspective. This is because the individual employee or director is not liable for tax on the employer contributions to the scheme.

Employers will often establish an occupational scheme for their employees out of a sense of duty to those employees; to reward their employees for their hard work and loyalty; to attract better quality employees to their employment; and, to retain better quality employees.

- Employers receive tax relief on their contributions to occupational pension schemes and are not liable for Employers' PRSI on their contributions. Employers do not receive any relief against employers' PRSI on the employees' contributions deducted from salaries at source.

- Employees receive income tax relief on their contributions subject to the age-related limits (see page 262).

- In order to qualify for the pension tax incentives, occupational pension schemes must be established under trust for the benefit of the sponsoring employer's employees and their dependents, and they must be approved by the Revenue Commissioners.

- Only employees and directors who are taxed under the PAYE system may become members of occupational pension schemes.

- An administrator must be appointed to the scheme. This can be a life assurance company or a specialist pension administration firm.

Occupational pension schemes can be arranged on Defined Contribution basis or a Defined Benefit basis.

- Defined Contribution schemes can be arranged on an individual basis ("Executive Pensions") using individual trusts or on a group basis ("Group Defined Contribution Pension Schemes") using a group trust. The members of the scheme will each have their own individual investment account into which contributions are placed, and the account is then invested in pension funds. Benefits at retirement are provided for the individual members from their accounts.

- Defined Benefit schemes are normally arranged on a group basis using a group trust. The scheme will normally have one pooled fund, into which contributions are placed, and the pooled fund is then invested. The retirement benefits will very often be paid to the individual scheme members out of this fund. However, as an alternative, the trustees of Defined Benefit schemes may purchase annuities to provide the retirement income for the scheme members.

- Occupational pension schemes are subject to a set of rules laid out by the Revenue Commissioners under the Revenue practice notes. These rules lay down a set of maximum benefits that can be paid to scheme beneficiaries on retirement at the scheme's normal retirement age, on the early retirement of the scheme member, and on the death of the scheme member. These limits are detailed later in this chapter.

- The maximum contributions that can be paid on behalf of an employee by the employer and employee to a Defined Contribution scheme are much greater than those allowed to PRSAs or personal pension plans. Samples of the maximum allowable rates are shown on the table on page 278, and the earnings ceiling of €115,000 does not apply to the employer contributions. However, the Standard Fund Threshold (€2 million) – or, Personal Fund Threshold – does apply to each individual member.

Maximum allowable contributions to defined contribution schemes as a percentage of salary per annum

Years to NRA	NRA 60		NRA 65	
	Male	Female	Male	Female
30	72%	67%	54%	49%
35	86%	80%	63%	58%
40	108%	100%	76%	69%
45	144%	133%	95%	86%
50	216%	200%	126%	115%

*   *assuming individual has a spouse/civil partner and no pre existing retirement benefits*

NRA = Normal Retirement Age

- As all contributions are pooled there are no limits on the total contributions that can be made to a Defined Benefit pension scheme but the eventual retirement benefits are limited by the Revenue rules. For Defined Benefit scheme members the Standard Fund Threshold (SFT) is calculated by applying the benefit formula applying to the scheme.

Prior to 1 January 2014 a single valuation factor of 20 was used to place a capital value on Defined Benefit (DB) pension entitlements at retirement for the purpose of SFT. From 1 January 2014 this was replaced with a range of higher factors varying with the age at which the pension is drawn down.

Where part of a DB pension has been accrued at 1 January 2014 and part after that date, transitional arrangements apply to allow at retirement for the part accrued up to 1 January 2014 to be valued at a factor of 20 and for the remaining pension to be valued at the higher age-related factor.

- In recent years many self-employed individuals have established companies in order to avail of the more attractive tax regime that applies to occupational schemes. They become proprietary directors of the companies and draw income from the companies. They then put executive pension plans in place in respect of their company incomes.

- The spouses and family of proprietary directors can also be made employees or directors of the companies and paid an income by the company provided they are genuine employees. This income can also be pensioned under occupational pension plans. This means that the spouse then has their own separate Standard Fund Threshold and can draw a separate lump sum benefit at retirement, the first €200,000 of which will be tax free under current legislation.

Employees of the State are usually provided with pensions on a Defined Benefit basis. However, these pensions are not funded in advance. Instead benefits are paid from revenue collected by the State through taxes.

Small Self-Administered Pension Schemes (SSAPS) are occupational pension schemes established by an employer where the company directors wish to have more choice and more control over the investments made by the scheme. There are Revenue rules regarding the types of investment that a SSAPS can make and the pensioner trustee, that must be appointed to SSAPS, must ensure that these are adhered to.

Additional Voluntary Contributions (AVCs)

Employees and directors who are members of occupational pension schemes may enhance the benefits (i.e. lump sum and/or pension) provided by their schemes by making additional voluntary contributions (AVCs) to the scheme itself, or by making traditional AVCs to a separate group AVC arrangement established under trust, or by making AVCs through PRSA contracts (i.e. PRSA AVCs). Scheme benefits cannot be enhanced to a level whereby they exceed the maximum benefits allowed by the Revenue.

Although put in place to enhance occupational scheme benefits at normal retirement age, AVCs are very often used to help employees retire early from employment, where it is possible to retire early.

- Traditional AVCs must be arranged under trust on a group basis – either the main scheme trust or a separate trust.

- PRSA AVCs need not be arranged under trust. They are owned by the individual scheme member. They give more control over the investment of the contributions to the scheme member. As they can be arranged with a different provider to the provider of the main scheme, they can give the scheme member more choice.

- Traditional AVCs can be arranged on a Defined Contribution basis or a Defined Benefit basis. PRSA AVCs are arranged on a Defined Contribution basis only.

- The majority of traditional AVCs are now arranged on a Defined Contribution basis.

- Defined Benefit AVCs are often referred to as "added years" AVCs. At this point in time the added years option applies mainly to the schemes for public sector employees. They will provide additional lump sum and additional pension benefits. It is not possible to fund solely for additional lump sum benefits through the added years option.

- Defined Contribution AVCs and PRSA AVCs can be used to fund solely for additional lump sum benefit, subject to the overall maximum lump sum benefit allowed by Revenue.

- AVCs / PRSA AVCs are subject to the rules of the main occupational scheme in that benefits must be taken at the same time, either on retirement at the schemes normal retirement age or on early retirement.

- The overall total benefits provided by the main scheme and the AVCs / PRSA AVCs are subject to the Revenue rules regarding maximum benefits.

- The normal rules regarding tax relief apply, and the scheme member's total contributions, including AVCs / PRSA AVCs, are subject to the age-related limits. (Page 262).

- When putting an AVC / PRSA AVC in place the scheme member needs to consider carefully how tax-efficient the exercise will be. In simple terms, unless some of the accumulated AVC fund can be taken back on a tax-free or reduced tax lump sum basis, making AVCs into an AVC PRSA may not be tax efficient.

- AVCs and PRSA AVCs can be made either by salary deduction at source, where the employer transfers them on to the AVC provider, or by direct debit from the individual's bank account.

- Back-dating of tax relief on lump sum contributions not made by salary deduction to the previous tax year is allowed.

Long term savings plans

For certain individuals for whom further retirement funding through pension plans is not tax-efficient, using long-term savings plans to fund for their retirement may be an option. Examples of where contributing to pension plans may not be tax-efficient for certain individuals are as follows

- They are higher earning self-employed individuals who are already maximising the tax relief limits on pension contributions to PRSAs or personal pensions, and forming companies is not practical for them.

- They are higher paid employees in non-pensionable employment who are already maximising the tax relief limits on pension contributions to PRSAs or personal pensions.

- Their accumulated retirement fund is likely to exceed the Standard Fund Threshold of €2 million (€2.3 million prior to 1 January 2014).

- None of their AVC fund will be available to them on a tax-free or reduced tax basis.

- If they have more than one source of income, and one of these sources is a pensionable employment for which they are paid more than €115,000 per annum, they must use up their contribution tax relief allowances by way of AVCs in respect of that employment. If they wish to make retirement provision in respect of their non-pensioned income they cannot do this tax-efficiently through pension plans as they are not entitled to tax relief on the contributions.

While there is no tax relief available on contributions to savings plans and while the investment growth or interest accumulated is subject to tax (at 41% on life assurance policies and 33% on deposit accounts) the proceeds of the savings plan can be taken on a tax-free basis as a lump sum. For life assurance policies, investment fund options similar to those available under pension plans are available.

Income in retirement products

Over the coming pages we will look at the products that are used to provide an income from the retirement capital accumulated through pension plans and long term savings plans. We will also look at the tax treatment of the income drawn from these products.

However, we will first look at the options available to pension plan holders when they get to retirement.

As already noted those with personal pension plans and PRSAs can take up to 25% of their accumulated retirement capital as a lump sum benefit up to a maximum of €500,000, with the first €200,000 of this paid tax-free, and the balance taxed at 20%. The balance of their capital can then be used to provide an income in line with the flexible retirement options outlined below.

Members of Defined Contribution occupational pension schemes, individual or group, have a choice of options. One is to take up to 25% of their accumulated retirement capital as a lump sum benefit up to a maximum of €500,000, with the first €200,000 of this being payable tax-free, and the balance taxed at 20%, provided the rules of their scheme allows this. If they choose this option the balance of their capital can then be used to provide an income in line with the flexible retirement options outlined below.

The other option available to them is to base their lump sum benefit on a formula based on their service with the employer and their "final remuneration". If they choose this option then they must opt for an annuity to provide the retirement income.

Members of Defined Benefit occupational pension schemes must base their lump sum benefit on the formula based on their service with the employer and their "final remuneration". The retirement income must be taken from the scheme's overall fund, unless the trustees buy an annuity using capital from the scheme's overall fund. This applies also to Defined Benefit AVCs.

From 22 June 2016, ARF options were extended to all Pension Retirement Bond holders including members of Defined Benefit (DB) schemes who had transferred their DB entitlements to Personal Retirement Bonds (PRB). Therefore it may be possible for a member of a DB pension scheme to avail of ARF options by transferring their DB pension to a Personal Retirement Bond.

Flexible retirement options

If your retirement fund is in a Defined Contribution (DC) arrangement (i.e. a DC pension scheme, a PRSA, a personal pension or a personal retirement bond etc.) you have a choice of using the balance of accumulated retirement capital, after taking your tax-free cash, to provide you with an income through any combination of the following

1. Buying an annuity.

2. Investing in an Approved Retirement Fund (ARF) and gradually drawing down an income.

3. Taking your money in cash form, subject to an immediate tax liability.

Those with PRSAs, have an option to leave the retirement capital in the PRSA up to age 75, rather than investing it in an ARF or buying an annuity. From January 2017 a PRSA will automatically become a vested PRSA once the policy holder reaches the age of 75. Prior to January 2017 you could leave a PRSA unvested in a pre-retirement account indefinitely. Once the retirement lump sum is taken from a PRSA the PRSA becomes known as a "vested PRSA".

To avail of options 2 and 3 above there are requirements, one of which you are obliged to fulfil at retirement

● Have reached age 75.

● Have a guaranteed pension income of €12,700 per year ("Specified Income").

● Have €63,500 invested in an Approved Minimum Retirement Fund (AMRF), or have used €63,500 to purchase an annuity.

The pension income of €12,700 can include any ordinary pension annuity or social welfare pensions (single rate) and foreign pensions.

For employees and directors, who make AVCs / PRSA AVCs, when it comes to the tax-free cash element of their pensions at retirement they are subject to the Revenue rules relating to the overall maximum benefits that can be provided by their occupational schemes. They cannot take 25% of the AVC / PRSA AVC fund in addition to the maximum allowable benefit under those rules.

Annuities

An annuity operates on the basis of you paying all or part of your retirement fund (i.e. the annuity purchase amount) to the life assurance company and, in return, the life assurance company guarantees to pay you a pension income (annuity) for the rest of your lifetime. Depending on the type of annuity you purchase, income may also be payable for the lifetime of your financial dependents after your death.

- The amount of your income will be expressed in terms of a percentage of the capital used to buy the pension - the annuity rate. For example, if your pension plan had a value of €500,000 and the annuity rate quoted was 5% then your pension income would be €25,000 p.a.

- The factors that usually decide the annuity rate are age, the return on the government bonds purchased by the life assurance company prevailing at the time the annuity is purchased, the type of annuity (i.e. single life or joint life annuity) and additional benefits purchased such as annual increases on the annuity income and a guaranteed minimum payment period, should you die early in retirement.

- Annuity income is made up of both the bond yield on the investment of your money and a return of part of the original capital invested. With annuities, those who live well into old age benefit to a greater degree than those who die earlier in retirement, and the total of all the years' income they receive back from the annuity before they die is likely to be much larger than their original investment.

- Annuity income is subject to income tax and the universal social charge (USC) but is not subject to PRSI. The normal credits and exemption limits apply. Pension income paid directly from the fund of a Defined Benefit occupational pension scheme is subject to tax in a similar manner.

Approved retirement funds (ARFs) & approved minimum retirement funds (AMRFs)

An Approved Retirement Fund (ARF) is an investment contract, owned by the individual retiree, from which the individual can draw down income as required.

- The investment is in tax-exempt pension funds, including a self-directed fund option from some ARF providers.

- An Approved Minimum Retirement Fund (AMRF) is similar to an ARF, except that only investment growth can be drawn down before age 75, unless the AMRF becomes an ARF at an earlier date. An AMRF becomes an ARF once the Specified Income requirement is fulfilled, or on the death of the AMRF owner.

- The ARF option was designed to give the individual involved more control over the use of their accumulated retirement fund; to address the problem of lower annuity rates; and to address the needs of those who wish to pass on the value of their pension funds to their dependents on death. The purpose of AMRFs is to address the criticism that a spendthrift could dissipate their retirement benefits too quickly.

- Any withdrawal from an Approved Retirement Fund or Approved Minimum Retirement Fund is liable to Income Tax under the PAYE system. Withdrawals from ARFs and AMRFs are also subject to PRSI up to age 66 and to USC.

- From the year when an individual turns age 61, income tax, PRSI and USC are payable on "imputed distributions" from ARFs, but not AMRFs. The imputed distribution is an assumed withdrawal from the ARF. From 1 January 2015 the amount of the imputed distribution is 4% of the value of the ARF, if you are between the ages of 61 and 70 and 5% if over 71. If an ARF-holder withdraws this amount or more from the ARF during the year ending on 30 November then there is no imputed distribution and the tax is payable only on the amount withdrawn. Where withdrawals are less than 4% in the year the actual withdrawals made from both ARFs and AMRFs during the year can be deducted from the 4% value. The annual imputed distribution rate on ARFs is 6% for ARFs with asset values in excess of €2 million (or, where an individual owns more than one

ARF or vested PRSA, where the combined value of the assets in those ARFs and/or vested PRSAs exceeds €2 million). Where the combined value exceeds €2 million the 6% rate applies to the total value and not just the excess over €2 million.

The imputed distribution rates applying from 1 January 2015 are

Age	Total ARF & vested PRSA funds is €2m or less	Total ARF & vested PRSA funds greater than €2m
<61	Nil	Nil
61 to 70	4%	6%
71 and over	5%	6%

- From 1 January 2015 AMRF holders are able to withdraw up to 4% p.a. of the value of their AMRF at 1 February each year; any withdrawal will be subject to PAYE. AMRF holders are not obliged to make a withdrawals; they will have an option or choice to make withdrawal up to 4% p.a., max.

- You are not restricted to one ARF, you can spread your retirement fund amongst a number of qualifying fund managers that provide ARFs and AMRFs, but you can have only one AMRF.

- A disadvantage of ARF investment is that if the investment funds do not provide sufficient investment returns to cover withdrawals or imputed distributions the ARF may potentially dissipate before the individual ARF holder dies.

Death

Any payment or imputed payment from the ARF is a distribution and is taxable as such. The amount of the distribution is treated as income of the ARF owner for the year of assessment in which that individual dies. There are some exceptions

- A transfer to an ARF in the name of the deceased's spouse or civil partner is not a distribution.

- A transfer to a child of the individual under 21 is not a distribution.

However, a distribution made to a child aged 21 or over from

● The ARF of the deceased, **or**

● An ARF in the name of a surviving spouse or surviving civil partner funded by the ARF of the deceased spouse or civil partner

is subject to an income tax charge under Case IV of Schedule D at the rate of 30% (which is a ring fenced final liability tax).

The position regarding income tax and capital acquisitions tax on the death of the ARF holder and on the subsequent death of the spouse/civil partner into whose ARF the original ARF was transferred is summarised below.   The usual CAT thresholds apply.

Beneficiary	Death of holder		Death of Spouse/Civil partner	
	Income tax	CAT	Income tax	CAT
Spouse / civil partner	No	No	n/a	n/a
Child under 21	No	Yes	No	Yes
Child over 21	Yes	No	Yes	No
Others	Yes	Yes	Yes	Yes

Note If you intend leaving the money in your ARF to an ARF in your spouse's name on your death you are probably best advised to make provision for this in your Will. This will have the effect of ensuring that the proceeds will not be treated as a transfer of capital directly to your spouse.

Vested PRSAs

As stated earlier, those with PRSAs, but not PRSA AVCs, have an option to leave the retirement capital in the PRSA up to age 75, but not after age 75, rather than investing it in an ARF or buying an annuity. Once the retirement lump sum or any income is taken from a PRSA the PRSA becomes known as a "vested PRSA".

- If the individual does not have a guaranteed pension income of €12,700 per year which is payable for their lifetime, or does not have €63,500 invested in an Approved Minimum Retirement (AMRF), or has not used €63,500 to purchase an annuity they must leave €63,500 invested in the PRSA until age 75.

- As with ARFs income tax, PRSI and USC are payable on "imputed distributions" from vested PRSA's and in effect the vested PRSA is treated as if it were an ARF, with the 6% rate applying where the combined asset value of an individual's ARFs and vested PRSAs exceeds €2 million. Where an individual is required to keep €63,500 in the PRSA until age 75, the imputed distribution tax does not apply to the €63,500.

- If an individual wishes to avail of the vested PRSA option, and if they have a fund accumulated in another pension product, they must firstly transfer the fund to the PRSA before taking the lump sum benefit. Not all pension product funds can be transferred to vested PRSAs. The funds from personal pensions plans can be transferred. However, the funds from occupational pension schemes can only be transferred if the individual has been in the scheme, or any other scheme connected to the same employment, for less than 15 years. And, unless the scheme has been wound-up a "Certificate of Benefit Comparison" from a qualified actuary is required – and, there will be an expense involved in producing this comparison.

- Income drawn from a vested PRSA is liable to income tax, USC and PRSI in the same way as income from an ARF.

- It is possible to make further contributions to a vested PRSA, but as future withdrawals are liable to taxation it is unlikely to be tax-efficient to make such contributions. It is possible to put another PRSA contract in place to receive in further contributions. This PRSA can be matured at a later date and a lump sum benefit of up to 25%

of the fund value to be taken as a lump sum, with the €200,000 tax-free rule applying.

- A disadvantage of investment in a vested PRSA is that if the investment funds do not provide sufficient investment returns to cover withdrawals the vested PRSA fund may potentially dissipate before the individual dies.

- In the event of the death of a vested PRSA holder the fund within it is treated similar to the way the fund within an ARF is treated on the death of the ARF holder. See page 287.

Long term savings plans

As mentioned earlier the proceeds of long term savings plans are available as a lump sum payment and are not subject to tax as income.

- The proceeds of the plan can be used to provide an income in retirement in a number of different ways, such as investing it in a life assurance bond or putting it on deposit, and drawing an income from the bond without liability to tax.

- The proceeds can also be used to purchase an annuity (known as a "Purchased Life Annuity"). These are similar to pension annuities except with regard to how they are taxed. The part of the income drawn from the purchased life annuity that is seen to be a return of the capital is tax-free, and the part that is seen to be interest is taxed as income.

Maximum allowable benefits under occupational pension schemes

The benefits payable by an occupational pension scheme at retirement or on earlier death may not exceed the maximum limits set down by the Revenue Commissioners. The calculation of some of the maximum benefits can be very complicated indeed for the ordinary individual to understand, particularly with regard to early retirement. Normally your pension provider or financial adviser will be able to explain the calculations to you, if the need arises.

Maximum pension at normal retirement age

● In general, a maximum pension of at least 1/60th of final remuneration for each year of service with the employer up to a maximum of 40 years may be provided for an employee at normal retirement age. This is referred to as the n/60ths scale where "n" is the number of years service the employee will have had with the employer at retirement.

● If the employee has more than five years service with the employer an "uplifted 60ths" scale may be used, as follows;

Years of service at normal retirement age	Maximum pension as a fraction of your final remuneration
1	4/60ths
2	8/60ths
3	12/60ths
4	16/60ths
5	20/60ths
6	24/60ths
7	28/60ths
8	32/60ths
9	36/60ths
10 or more years	40/60ths (i.e. 2/3rds)

- The overall maximum pension that can be provided for an individual retiring at normal retirement age from his employer's pension scheme is the lower of

    - A pension based on the up-lifted scale shown on the previous page,

    and

    - 2/3rds of final remuneration less any retained pension benefits, if the resultant amount is greater than that calculated under the n/60ths scale.

Retained pension benefits are pension benefits arising from a previous occupational pension scheme, including buy-out bonds, or from any paid-up benefits under a personal pension plan or PRSA. Benefits accumulated through AVCs and PRSA AVCs in respect of the same employment are treated as benefits arising from the main scheme and not as retained benefits.

- The maximum pension figure must include the pension equivalent, based on current annuity rates, of the value of any retirement lump sum taken at retirement.

- Where an individual is retiring from a Defined Contribution scheme and opts for 25% of the accumulated fund as a retirement lump sum and the flexible retirement options for the balance, the accumulated fund must first be tested to ensure that the maximum allowable pension, based on the current rates, is not exceeded.

Final remuneration

Final remuneration may be defined as any one of the following

A   Remuneration for any one of the five years before the retirement date. "Remuneration" means basic pay for the year in question plus the average of any fluctuating emoluments (e.g. bonuses, over-time payments etc.) over a suitable period, usually three years or more

    or

B   The average of the total emoluments (i.e. salary plus bonuses etc) of any three or more consecutive years ending not earlier than 10 years before your normal retirement age.

or

C   The rate of basic pay at the date of retirement, or on any date within the year ending on that date, plus the average of fluctuating emoluments over three or more consecutive years, ending with the date of retirement.

Notes

- "Remuneration" includes all income and benefits that are assessable to income tax under PAYE in the relevant employment e.g. BIK on a company car can be included as part of your final remuneration.

- In the case of the first two definitions each year's remuneration may be increased in line with the Consumer Price Index from the end of the relevant year up to your retirement date. This is referred to as 'dynamising' final remuneration.

- If you own or control more than 20% of the voting rights in your company (i.e. "a proprietary director") you can only use definition B above when calculating your final remuneration. This is to stop controlling directors substantially inflating their earnings in the last years before retirement in order to increase the tax-free lump sum they can take from their pension.

Maximum tax free cash lump sum at normal retirement age

- Where a member of a Defined Contribution pension scheme is retiring from employment they have the option of taking 25% of the value of their pension fund as a lump sum benefit and availing of the flexible retirement options as outlined earlier, provided the scheme rules allow them to do this. Defined Contribution scheme members who do not avail of these options, and Defined Benefit scheme members are generally entitled to a maximum lump sum amount of at least 3/80ths of final remuneration for each year of service up to a maximum 40 years, or 1.5 times final remuneration on retirement at normal retirement age.

- For those using the remuneration and service basis of calculating the maximum lump sum benefit if the individual has more than eight years service with the employer, an "uplifted 80ths" scale may be used as follows

Years of Service at normal retirement age	Maximum tax free lump sum as a fraction of your final remuneration
1 -8	3/80ths for each year
9	30/80ths
10	36/80ths
11	42/80ths
12	48/80ths
13	54/80ths
14	63/80ths
15	72/80ths
16	81/80ths
17	90/80ths
18	99/80ths
19	108/80ths
20 or more year	120/80ths

- The overall maximum tax-free lump sum that can be provided for an individual with more than eight years service in the employment from which they are retiring is the lower of

  - A lump sum based on the up-lifted scale shown on the previous page,

    and

  - 1½ times final remuneration less any retained lump sum benefits, if the resultant amount is greater than that calculated under the 3n/80ths scale.

Retained lump sum benefits are benefits arising from a previous occupational pension scheme, including buy-out bonds, or from any paid-up benefits under a personal pension plan or PRSA. Benefits accumulated through AVCs and PRSA AVCs in respect of the same employment are treated as benefits arising from the main scheme and not as retained benefits.

Maximum pension on ill health early retirement

- Whereas there is no specific definition of ill health in the Revenue pension guidelines, incapacity is defined as follows:

  "Physical or mental deterioration which is bad enough to prevent the individual from following their normal employment, or which very seriously impairs their earning capacity. It does not mean simply a decline in energy or ability."

- If an individual retires early due to ill health, the maximum pension they can receive is the equivalent of the one they could have expected to receive had they worked until normal retirement age.

Example

John commenced employment with his current employer at age 35. The normal retirement age under the scheme rules is 65 years.

Five years later, John aged 40 retired on grounds of ill health, after suffering a serious illness. He has no retained pension benefits. His final remuneration prior to ill health was €50,000 per annum.

John would have had 30 years of service to normal retirement age, entitling him to a maximum pension on the "up-lifted 60ths" scale of 40/60ths of final remuneration.

His maximum ill health retirement pension is

40/60ths x €50,000 = €33,333 per annum

- In the case of early retirement due to ill health, "final remuneration" is calculated by a reference to the period preceding actual retirement.

- If John were a member of a Defined Contribution scheme he is very unlikely to have accumulated enough capital to be able to provide that level of benefit. This is where his PHI cover is likely to be called on to provide him with an income until normal retirement age, when the pension benefits would become payable. It would be important to have contribution protection cover in place to ensure the continuation of John's pension contributions up to retirement age.

- In the case of a Defined Benefit scheme, only the very large schemes may be able to afford to pay him this level of benefit at such an early age. PHI cover is often provided with these schemes also, and the pension would become payable at retirement age.

- If an individual is retiring in 'exceptional circumstances of serious ill health' (i.e. the expectation of life is less than 12 months) the Revenue will allow them to take the pension entitlement in cash form. The non tax-free part of the full lump sum taken in these circumstances is liable to income tax at 10%.

Maximum pension on voluntary early retirement

- Where early retirement is taking place after age 50 other than due to ill health, then the maximum immediate pension allowed is the greater of

- 1/60th of final salary remuneration for each year of actual service completed, or

- The pension worked out by the following formula - N/NS x P

    N = The actual number of years service to early retirement,

    NS = The number of years of potential service to normal retirement age.

    P = The maximum pension allowable if the scheme member had remained in service to normal retirement age.

Example

John joined his employer at age 35. The normal retirement age under the scheme rules is 65. John is now aged 50 with a final remuneration figure of €40,000 and he elects to take voluntary early retirement with his employer's consent. He has no retained pension or lump sum entitlements from previous employments or self-employment.

N is 15, actual years service completed to age 50.

NS is 30, potential service to normal retirement age.

P is 2/3rds of final remuneration – Revenue maximum pension.

So, John's maximum early retirement pension is to be the greater of

    15/60ths x €40,000 = €10,000 per annum. **and**

    15/30 x 2/3rds x €40,000 = €13,333 per annum.

- If the individual has less than 10 years service completed by the date of early retirement the maximum immediate pension is the lowest of

    - N/NS x P, as calculated above,

    - The maximum pension as calculated on the uplifted scale shown earlier, taking account of actual service to date, **and**

    - 2/3rds of final remuneration less retained pension benefits.

- While the above outlines the maximum pension benefits that may be allowed by Revenue on early retirement, it would be rare for most employers to provide this level of benefits on early retirement. Typically, the rules of a Defined Benefit scheme would provide for the calculation of benefits based on the n/60ths scale, related to service to the date of retirement, with penalties for early retirement. For example, these penalties could mean a reduction of 0.5% per month for each month between the date of early retirement and the normal retirement age (i.e. a 60% reduction if you are retiring 10 years early).

- For Defined Contribution schemes the early retirement benefits would be dependent on the fund accumulated at that stage and, in reality it is very unlikely that this would be sufficiently large to exceed the Revenue maximum allowable figures.

- Also, Defined Contribution scheme members have the right to take 25% of their accumulated fund as a lump sum benefit and avail of the flexible retirement options for the balance.

Maximum tax free lump sum on early retirement

- In the case of ill health early retirement, the maximum tax-free lump sum is similar to that available had the individual remained in the employer's service up to normal retirement age. This would give up to a maximum of $1\frac{1}{2}$ times final remuneration at the date of retirement, if the individual were to have had 20 years service at normal retirement age.

- In the case of voluntary early retirement the maximum tax-free lump sum is normally calculated by taking the greater of

  - 3/80ths of remuneration for each year of actual service, **or**

  - The sum calculated in accordance with the following formula - N/NS x LS

    - N = Number of years service completed up to early retirement.

    - NS = The potential number of years that could have been completed by normal retirement.

    - LS = The maximum allowable tax-free lump sum which could have to be provided at normal retirement age, after the restriction for any retained lump sum benefits where relevant.

Example

Mary has 25 years service with her employer when she retires voluntarily at age 50 with the approval of her employer. She has no retained lump sum benefits from previous employment or self-employment. Her final remuneration figure is €50,000 and her scheme's NRA is 60.

     N =   25   Mary's actual service

     NS =   35   Potential service

     LS =   150% of final remuneration

So, Mary's maximum retirement lump sum is the greater of

     75/80ths of €50,000 = €46,875

     and

     25/35 x €75,000 = €53,571

Also, if Mary is a member of a Defined Contribution Scheme she also has the option of taking 25% of her accumulated retirement fund by way of a tax free lump sum.

- If the individual has less than 20 years service completed by the date of early retirement the maximum immediate lump sum benefit is the lowest of

  - N/NS x LS, as calculated above;

  - The maximum lump sum on the uplifted scale as shown earlier, taking account of actual service completed to the date of early retirement;

  - **and**

  - 150% of final remuneration less retained lump sum benefits.

Example

Robert has 17 years actual service, 25 years potential service, final remuneration of €40,000 and no retained lump sum benefits. He is restricted to the lowest of

- N/NS x LS, i.e. 17/25 x €60,000 = €40,800;

- 90/80ths (i.e. figure applicable to 15 years service from the uplifted scale above) x €40,000 = €45,000; **and**

- 150% x €40,000 = €60,000

Overall in this example, Robert is limited to a lump sum benefit of €40,800.

- If a retirement lump sum is taken on voluntary early retirement the early retirement pension benefit has to be reduced by the pension equivalent of the lump sum.

- In the case of Defined Benefit schemes, the lump sum on voluntary early retirement may be restricted by the scheme rules; in the case of Defined Contribution schemes taking the maximum lump sum benefit, based on the remuneration and service formula, could potentially deplete the retirement fund completely, leaving no capital to provide an income.

- If Robert is a member of a Defined Contribution scheme he has the option of taking 25% of the accumulated fund as a retirement lump sum and using the balance of the fund in accordance with the flexible retirement options .

Maximum death-in-service benefits

- A pension scheme may provide two benefits if a member dies in service before normal retirement age.

- The maximum allowable lump sum benefit is four times remuneration at the date of death, together with a refund of any personal contributions to the scheme with "reasonable interest". This benefit would be payable to the trustees who, under the rules of the scheme, would have some discretion as to which of your dependents should receive the proceeds.

- The maximum allowable death-in-service pension, which could be paid to your spouse or to any one or all of your dependents, is 100% of the maximum pension that you could have received if you had retired on grounds of ill health at the date of your death.

Maximum death-in-retirement benefit

- Many pension schemes provide a guaranteed period of pension payments after retirement in the event of early death. This guaranteed period may be up to 10 years. If the guaranteed period is five years or less the remaining instalments may be paid at the trustees' discretion in a lump sum to your dependents. If the guarantee is more than five years, the outstanding instalments will be paid in pension form to the beneficiaries.

- Spouses' and dependents' pensions may be provided in addition to this guarantee. The maximum pension that may be provided for the spouse, or for any one or all of the dependents, is 100% of the maximum pension that could have been provided for you at retirement.

- The term "maximum pension" is defined as the maximum pension at normal retirement age, increased in line with the Consumer Price Index from the date of retirement up to the date of death.

Maximum pension increases

- Generally speaking, a pension may be increased in line with the rise in the Consumer Price Index each year. Alternatively, increases at a rate of 3% per annum may be promised and paid, regardless of the Consumer Price Index. However, if the pension at retirement was less than the maximum Revenue allowable pension at retirement age, this pension may be increased at a faster rate than the increase in the Consumer Price Index until it reaches the level of the maximum allowable pension.

15 Marriage, separation and divorce

Tax and financial issues arising from marriage are spread throughout our tax and financial system. To make everything as simple and as straight forward as possible, we will look at marriage under a number of different headings:

- Legal Impact.

- Income Tax.

- Capital Gains Tax.

- Capital Acquisition Tax.

- Social Welfare.

Legal impact

Marriage or civil partnership changes the legal status of two people from a couple to spouses or civil partners, with many consequential and financial implications. For example, a surviving spouse/civil partner's legal entitlements under the 1965 Succession Act are as follows:

If there is a Will

Irrespective of what is indicated in the Will, the minimum legal requirements of a surviving spouse/civil partner are:

Spouse/civil partner and No Issue	One-half of estate to the surviving spouse/civil partner.
Spouse/civil partner and Issue	One-third of estate to the surviving spouse/civil partner.

No Will in existence

Spouse/civil partner and No Issue	Whole estate to the surviving spouse/civil partner.
Spouse/civil partner and Issue	Two-thirds to the surviving spouse/ civil partner, one-third to issue in equal shares.

Income tax

A marriage/civil partnership ceremony in itself does not give rise to any income tax advantage. To obtain these benefits, a couple must be married and "living together".

Under the income tax rules, a couple who are married or in a civil partnership are deemed to be "living together" unless

- They are separated under an order of a Court of competent jurisdiction or by Deed of Separation,

   or

- They are in fact separated in such circumstances that the separation is likely to be permanent.

A couple who are married or in a civil partnership may choose to be taxed jointly, separately or as single people.

A couple who are married or in a civil partnership and claiming joint assessment under Income Tax rules are entitled to the following:

- A married/civil partner's tax credit which is double the single person tax credit.

- Home carer's tax credit.

- Double a single person's mortgage interest relief on their principal private residence.

- Trading losses incurred by one spouse/civil partner can be set against income of the other spouse/civil partner.

- Double the age tax credit even though only one spouse/civil partner may be over the age of 65 years.

- Tax relief can be obtained by one spouse/partner in respect of a person employed to take care of the incapacitated other spouse/civil partner.

Individualisation

For the tax year 2020 the standard rate tax band for a couple who are married or in a civil partnership is €44,300. Where both spouses/civil partners have income this can be increased by the lower of ;

- €26,300

  or

- The income of the lower earning spouse.

To gain the maximum benefit from the 'individual' band increases for a two income couple, the lower earning spouse/civil partner must have a minimum 'individual' income of €26,300 in the year 2020

For example, a two income couple where one spouse/partner earns €50,000 in the tax year 2020 and the other earns €8,000, the maximum standard rate band for couples who are married or in a civil partnership of €44,300 can be utilised by the higher earning spouse/civil partner but only €8,000 of the 20% band can be utilised by the lower earning spouse/ civil partner. The balance of €18,300 is left unused.

Once you get married or enter into a civil partnership you should inform the tax office of the date of your marriage or civil partnership, quoting your PPS Number and that of your spouse/civil partner.

Year of marriage/civil partnership

In the year of marriage/civil partnership, you and your spouse/civil partner are treated as two single people for income tax purposes for the entire tax year. However, if you pay more tax than that which you would have paid as a couple who are married or in a civil partnership, you can claim a refund. This refund will be the excess of the tax paid as two single people over the tax payable as a jointly assessed couple who are married or in a civil partnership, reduced in proportion to the part of the tax year in which you were not married or in a civil partnership.

"In the year of marriage or civil partnership, you and your spouse or civil partner are treated as two single people for income tax purposes for the entire year."

Example

A married couple have income of €60,000 and €30,000 respectively. Their date of marriage was 1 June 2020. Their tax liability for 2020 will be as follows:

	2020 €		**2020** €
Salary	€60,000		€30,000
Tax payable			
€35,300 @ 20%	€7,060	€30,000 @ 20%	€6,000
€24,700 @ 40%	€9,880		€0
	€16,940		€6,000
Less: Tax credits			
Personal	(€1,650)		(€1,650)
PAYE	(€1,650)		(€1,650)
Net tax	**€13,640**		**€2,700**
Total tax as single people			**€16,340**

At the end of the year, they may apply for a reduction in their tax liability on the basis of joint assessment as illustrated:

		2020 €
	Total salaries	€90,000
	Tax payable	
	€70,600 @ 20%	€14,120
	€19,400 @ 40%	€7,760
		€21,880
Less:	**Tax credits**	
	Personal	(€3,300)
	PAYE	(€3,300)
	Net tax	**€15,280**
Less:	Tax paid (See above)	(€16,340)
	Excess of single over joint basis of assessment	€1,060
	Restriction for pre married period €1,060 x 5/12	€442
	Tax refund due	**€618**

The tax refund due to each spouse/civil partner will be in proportion to the amount of tax each has paid.

Couples who are married or in a civil partnership / income tax options

After the year of marriage/civil partnership, you have three options as to how you are taxed.

Joint assessment

Joint assessment is automatic, unless either spouse/partner gives notice of election for separate or single assessment to the Revenue Commissioners.

The assessable spouse is normally the spouse/civil partner with the higher income and will continue to be so unless you jointly elect to change it.

Repayments made are allocated between each spouse/civil partner according to the amount of tax they have paid in the year.

Separate assessment

A claim may be made for separate assessment of income tax liability where the joint assessment basis applies. The claim must be made in the period beginning three months before and ending three months after the start of the tax year i.e. between 1 October and 31 March. A claim for separate assessment cannot be backdated and lasts until it is withdrawn. An application for a withdrawal of separate assessment must be made in writing by whichever spouse/civil partner made the initial claim. Where separate assessment is claimed the tax credits are divided between the spouses/civil partners. If at the end of the tax year, the total tax payable under separate assessments is greater than the amount payable if an application for separate assessment had not been made, you can apply for a tax refund.

Single assessment/(separate treatment)

As a couple who are married or in a civil partnership, you may each elect for single assessment. Each spouse/civil partner is treated as a single person with no right of transfer of allowances or relief's between spouses/ civil partners. Single assessment is normally only beneficial where one spouse/civil partner has foreign employment income.

Assessable spouse/nominated civil partner

If you are jointly assessed one spouse/civil partner is nominated to be the assessable spouse/civil partner. They are taxable on the total income of both spouses/civil partners and are responsible for making a return of income for both parties.

Both spouses/civil partners nominate the assessable spouse/civil partner jointly by completing the assessable spouse/civil partnership form available from www.revenue.ie or your local tax office. This should be submitted to the tax office before 31 March in the relevant tax year. You can also send a letter into your local tax office, signed by both parties nominating the assessable spouse. If you do not nominate an assessable spouse/civil partner, the tax office will treat the spouse/civil partner with the highest income in the last tax year as the assessable spouse/civil partner.

Example: 2020 income tax options

A couple are married with two children, with salaries of €50,000 and €30,000 respectively. The higher earning spouse pays pension contributions of €5,400 in the 2020 tax year. Their tax options are illustrated on page 308.

Capital gains tax (CGT)

A couple must be married/ in a civil partnership and "living together" in order to maximise their benefits under Capital Gains Tax which include:

- Entitlement to dispose of assets to each other without being subject to CGT.

- Capital losses available to one spouse/civil partner can be used by the other spouse/civil partner.

Capital acquisitions tax (CAT)

The "living together" rules do not apply to CAT and all gifts and inheritance given by one legally married spouse / couple in a registered civil partnership to the other are exempt from CAT regardless of their "living together" status.

Pension benefits

Any pension benefit taken by a person, other than the pension member, is treated as a gift or inheritance for tax purposes.

However, the spouse/civil partner exemption from CAT means any lump sum death benefit or dependent's pension benefit received by your spouse/civil partner from a pension scheme of which you were a member is exempt from tax.

Life assurance policies

An interest in possession in life assurance policies is only deemed to occur when a benefit becomes payable under the policy. So if you effect a life assurance policy on your own life for the benefit of someone else, no gift or inheritance tax will arise until the benefit becomes payable under that policy. Any sums received by you or your spouse/civil partner from a life assurance policy, of which you or your spouse/civil partner were the original beneficial owners, are exempt from tax.

Stamp duty

Transfer of all assets between spouses/civil partners is exempt from stamp duty. This exemption includes a direct transfer of assets from one spouse/civil partner to another or a transfer from one spouse/civil partner into joint names.

Social welfare

Social welfare widow(er)/surviving civil partner's contributory pension is payable to the widow(er)/surviving civil partner following the death of their spouse/civil partner, for as long as the widow(er)/surviving civil partner does not remarry or cohabit with someone else. A spouse/civil partner may qualify for this pension either on their own PRSI contribution record, or on that of the other spouse/civil partner.

If the widow(er)/surviving civil partner does not have the required PRSI contributions either on their own PRSI record or on their spouses/civil partners, then non-contributory social welfare widow(er)/surviving civil partner's pension may be payable as long as they do not remarry or cohabit with someone else and satisfy a means test.

Method of assessment	Joint Assessment (€) Amount	Joint Assessment (€) Tax	Separate – Person 1 (€) Amount	Separate – Person 1 (€) Tax	Separate – Person 2 (€) Amount	Separate – Person 2 (€) Tax	Single – Person 1 (€) Amount	Single – Person 1 (€) Tax	Single – Person 2 (€) Amount	Single – Person 2 (€) Tax
Salary	€80,000		€50,000		€30,000		€50,000		€30,000	
Less: Pension	(€5,400)		(€5,400)		(€0)		(€5,400)		(€0)	
Taxable Income	€74,600		€44,600		€30,000		€44,600		€30,000	
Tax Payable										
20%	€70,600	€14,120	€35,300	€7,060	€30,000	€6,000	€35,300	€7,060	€30,000	€6,000
40%	€4,000	€1,600	€9,300	€3,720			€9,300	€3,720		
Total		€15,720		€10,780		€6,000		€10,780		€6,000
Less: Tax Credits										
Personal		(€3,300)		(€1,650)		(€1,650)		(€1,650)		(€1,650)
PAYE		(€3,300)		(€1,650)		(€1,650)		(€1,650)		(€1,650)
		€9,120		€7,480		€2,700		€7,480		€2,700
Total Payable		€9,120		€10,180				€10,180		

Note: Separate assessment results in an additional tax bill of €1,060 which can be reclaimed at the end of the tax year. Single assessments result in the same additional bill. However under single assessment this amount could not be reclaimed back at the end of the year.

Marriage breakdown

Marriage breakdown is a major and traumatic event for couples and it is best approached in a logical and non-confrontational manner.

When a married couple decide to separate, they will normally go about it in one of the following ways:

- They decide to live apart.

- They seek a Legal Separation.

- They seek a Judicial Separation.

- They divorce.

Living apart

Legal impact

Living apart does not change the legal status of your marriage.

Succession rights

There is no automatic loss of your Succession Act entitlements if you live apart from your spouse. However,

- A spouse who is guilty of desertion, which continues for two years or more up to the death of the other spouse, is precluded under the Succession Act from taking any share in the estate of the deceased, either as a legal right or on intestacy.

- If a surviving spouse is deemed to be "guilty of conduct which justified the deceased separating and living apart", then the surviving spouse could be deemed to be guilty of desertion and precluded under the Succession Act from taking a share in the deceased spouse's estate. For example where a wife leaves home because of violent behaviour on the part of her husband, he could be found guilty of desertion and lose his Succession Act rights to her estate while, conversely, she could in fact, retain her rights to his estate.

- Any spouse who has been found guilty of a serious offence against the deceased spouse or against a child of the deceased spouse, is also precluded, under the Succession Act, from taking any legal right under the estate of the deceased.

Income tax

A couple's Income Tax position following separation is determined by three main factors:

- Whether the separation is likely to be permanent.

- Whether maintenance payments are being made by one spouse to the other.

- If maintenance payments are being made, whether these payments are *legally enforceable*.

If the separation is not likely to be permanent, there is no change in the Income Tax position and they can elect for Joint, Separate or Single Assessment.

If the separation is likely to be permanent and if there are no legally enforceable maintenance payments, the spouses are assessed for Income Tax under Single Assessment. Any voluntary maintenance payments are ignored for income tax purposes.

If the separation is likely to be permanent and if there are legally enforceable maintenance payments being made, then the couple may opt for either Single Assessment or if both spouses remain resident in Ireland, Separate Assessment. If Single Assessment applies, maintenance payments made for the benefit of the spouse (but not the children) are tax-deductible for the payer and are taxable in the hands of the recipient. Under Separate Assessment, maintenance payments are ignored for income tax purposes.

Maintenance payments made for the benefit of a child or children are ignored for tax purposes.

- The payments are made without deduction of tax.

- The payer is not entitled to a deduction for these payments.

- The payments are not taxable.

- The payments are not regarded as income of the child.

Capital gains tax (CGT)

If the separation is not likely to be permanent, there is no change in the spouse's status for CGT purposes.

If the separation is likely to be permanent, the spouses are treated as two unconnected persons for CGT purposes and

- Transfers between spouses are no longer exempt from CGT. However, any transfer by virtue of, or in consequence of, the separation will not trigger a CGT liability.

- No transfer of unused CGT losses is permitted between spouses. However unused losses may be transferred between spouses in the year of separation.

Capital acquisition tax (CAT)

Spouse's exemption from Capital Acquisitions Tax will continue to apply.

Pensions/death-in-service benefit

If a member of a pension scheme dies while still working for an employer, Death in Service Benefits may be paid to the member's dependants. Many pension schemes give discretion to the pension trustees as to how these death-in-service benefits may be paid e.g. the pension rules may require a spouse to be living with, or ordinarily residing with, their spouse at the date of death.

Life assurance

The proceeds are normally exempt from tax, provided you or your spouse were the original beneficial owners of the relevant policy.

Stamp duty

Exemption from Stamp Duty will continue to apply on relevant property transactions.

Social welfare

The contributory widow(er)/surviving civil partner's pension is payable to the widow(er)/surviving civil partner, following the death of their spouse/civil partner, for as long as the widow(er)/surviving civil partner does not remarry and does not cohabit with someone else. A widow(er)/surviving civil partner may qualify for this pension either on their own PRSI contribution record or that of their late spouse/civil partner.

Qualifying adult dependent payment

A qualifying adult dependent payment is generally payable to a claimant who is separated, provided their spouse/civil partner is wholly or mainly maintained by the claimant.

Separation

Legal separation

Under a Legal Separation, both spouses voluntarily enter into a legal agreement. This legal agreement is often referred to as a "Deed of Separation".

A Deed of Separation will usually include

- An agreement to permanently live apart.

- Arrangements for custody of, and access to, children.

- Provision for maintenance to be paid by one spouse for the benefit of the other spouse and/or children.

- Succession Act rights: one spouse may voluntarily renounce rights to the other's estate, etc.

Judicial separation

A decree of judicial separation can be obtained by a spouse applying to the courts under the Family Law Act 2019. The application may be made on one of the following grounds:

- The other spouse has committed adultery.

- That the other spouse has behaved in such a way that the applicant spouse cannot reasonably be expected to live with the other spouse.

- That the other spouse has deserted the applicant spouse for a continuous period of at least one year immediately preceding the application

- That the spouses have "lived apart" from one another for a continuous period of at least one year immediately preceding the application.

- That the marriage has broken down to the extent that the court is satisfied in all circumstances that a normal marital relationship has not existed between the spouses for at least one year immediately preceding the application.

Living apart

The Family Law Act 2019 provides a definition of 'living apart' to give certainty to the interpretation of the term in the Irish courts. It clarifies that spouses who live in the same home as one another are considered to be living apart if the spouses are not living together as a couple in an intimate and committed relationship. The Act also sets out that a relationship does not cease to be an intimate relationship merely because the relationship is no longer sexual in nature.

Ancillary orders

On the granting of, or following, a decree of Judicial Separation, the Circuit or High Court can make a number of orders relating to maintenance or specific assets. These orders are known as Ancillary Orders.

Under a Judicial Separation either spouse, or, in some cases, a person acting on behalf of a dependent child, can apply to the courts to have one or more Ancillary Orders made in relation to

- Maintenance.
- The family home.
- Property.
- Pension benefits.
- Life assurance policies.
- Succession rights etc.

While the Courts retain the discretion to grant an Ancillary Order sought by a spouse, or a person acting on behalf of a dependent child, the Family Law Act 1995 does provide specific factors which the Court is obliged to take into account before making a decision.

- The income, earning capacity, property and other financial resources which each of the spouses has, or is likely to have in the foreseeable future. The financial needs, obligations and responsibilities which each of the spouses has or is likely to have in the foreseeable future (whether in the case of remarriage of the spouse or otherwise).

- The standard of living enjoyed by the family concerned before the proceedings were instituted or before the spouses separated, as the case may be.

- The age of each of the spouses and the length of time during which the spouses lived together.

- Any physical or mental disability of either of the spouses.

- The contributions which each of the spouses has made or is likely in the foreseeable future to make to the welfare of the family, including any contribution made by each of them to the income, earning capacity, property and financial resources of the other spouse and any contribution made by either of them by looking after the home or caring for the family.

- The effect on the earning capacity of each of the spouses of the marital responsibilities assumed by each during the period when they lived together and, in particular, the degree to which the future earning capacity of a spouse is impaired by reason of that spouse having relinquished or foregone the opportunity of remunerative activity in order to look after the home or care for the family.

- The conduct of each of the spouses, if that conduct is such that in the opinion of the court it would in all the circumstances of the case be unjust to disregard it.

- The accommodation needs of either of the spouses.

- The value to each of the spouses of any benefit (for example, a benefit under a pension scheme) which by reason of the decree of judicial separation that spouse would forfeit the opportunity or possibility of acquiring.

- The rights of any other person, other than the spouses but including a person to whom either spouse is remarried.

Enforcing maintenance orders

Experience has shown a relatively high rate of defaulting on regular maintenance payments; a court can enforce these payments in one of two ways:

- *Secured Payments*. Here the periodic payments are secured on some capital asset or investment. For example, the court could order the sale of an investment property to generate the necessary funds.

- *Attachment of Earnings Order* where the court may order an employer to deduct the periodic payments from the earnings of one spouse and pay it to the other spouse.

Payments orders will normally specify the period, or periods, during which the payments are to be made, which can be a fixed number of years, or for the lifetime of either spouse. However, payment orders will generally cease on

- The death of either spouse.
- The date of remarriage of the applicant spouse.

Legal impact

A Deed of Separation will not change the legal status of your marriage.

Succession rights

- There is no automatic loss of your entitlements under the Succession Act.
- Your entitlements under the Succession Act may be voluntarily renounced under a Deed of Separation.
- Any specific bequest in your Will to your spouse will stand until you make a new Will or change your existing Will.

Income tax

A couple's Income Tax position following separation is determined by three main factors:

- Whether the separation is likely to be permanent.
- Whether maintenance payments are being made by one spouse/civil partner to the other.
- If maintenance payments are being made, whether these payments are *legally enforceable*.

If the separation is not likely to be permanent, there is no change in the income tax position and you can elect for joint, separate or single assessment.

If the separation is likely to be permanent and if there are no legally enforceable maintenance payments, the spouses are assessed for income tax under single assessment. Any voluntary maintenance payments are ignored for income tax purposes.

If the separation is likely to be permanent and if there are legally enforceable maintenance payments being made, then the couple may generally opt for either single assessment or if both spouses remain resident in Ireland, separate assessment. If single assessment applies, maintenance payments made for the benefit of the spouse (but not the children) are tax deductible for the payer and taxable in the hands of the recipient. Under separate assessment, maintenance payments are ignored for income tax purposes.

If there are no legally enforceable maintenance payments being made, the spouses are assessed for income tax under single assessment. Any voluntary maintenance payments are not tax-deductible for the paying spouse and are not taxable in the hands of the receiving spouse.

If there are legally enforceable maintenance payments being made, then the couple can generally either opt for single assessment or if both spouses remain resident in Ireland, separate assessment. If single assessment applies, maintenance payments made for the benefit of the spouse are tax deductible for the payer and taxable in the hands of the recipient. Under separate assessment, maintenance payments are ignored for tax purposes.

If you have a judicial separation, your income tax position is the same as under a legal separation.

Assessable spouse

The spouse with the greater income in the year of marriage will generally be deemed to be the assessable spouse.

The assessable spouse may be changed provided both spouses elect jointly for it to be changed. The assessable spouse is generally responsible for submitting the annual return and paying any tax due.

Year of separation

The married tax credit and double rate tax band can be claimed for the year of separation by the assessable spouse providing:

- Separation does not occur on the first day of that tax year.   **or**

- The non-assessable spouse has not submitted a claim for single assessment prior to separation.

The assessable spouse is liable to income tax for the tax year of separation on their own income under joint assessment if they were previously taxed jointly for the full year, and on the other spouse's income up to the date of separation. A tax deduction will be available for legally enforceable maintenance payments made for the benefit of the spouse (but not the children).

Year of separation/Single assessment

If a couple were paying tax under single assessment before the separation, each spouse would have been responsible for submitting their own tax returns and paying their own tax. No change in their status for income tax purposes would have occurred on separation.

Subsequent tax years

How you will be taxed in subsequent tax years will depend on a number of factors e.g.

- Voluntary maintenance payments.

- Legally enforceable maintenance payments.

- Single parent credits.

- Mortgage repayments etc.

Maintenance payments

Tax is not deducted at source from legally enforceable maintenance payments from one spouse to the other. Such payments may be allowed for tax purposes as a deduction against the income of the payer and may be chargeable to income tax, in the hands of the recipient. A spouse will not be entitled to the marriage credit where they claim a deduction for maintenance payments made.

Where maintenance is received for the benefit of a child

- The payment is made without deduction of income tax.

- The amount continues to be treated as the income of the payer, **and**

- The payer's income tax liability is calculated without any allowance for the payments made.

PRSI

If you are legally separated and you receive maintenance payments from your spouse, PRSI will be payable on the maintenance received if you are taxed as a single person. If you have opted for separate assessment, maintenance payments are ignored for income tax purposes and PRSI is not payable on the maintenance.

The PRSI payable would be the Class S1 rate, which is 4% of the gross income.

Universal social charge (USC) on voluntary maintenance payments

The universal social charge (USC) may apply to maintenance depending on whether they are voluntary payments or legally inforceable payments.

If the payment is paid under an informal arrangement

- The spouse making the payments does not receive exemption from the universal social charge (USC) on the portion of their income which they pay as maintenance.

- The spouse who receives the payments is not subject to the USC on the maintenance payments they receive.

If the payment is payable under legal obligation

- The spouse making the payments is entitled to receive an exemption from the USC on the portion of their income which they pay as maintenance either directly or indirectly to their spouse. There is no USC exemption due in respect of any portion of the maintenance payments paid towards the maintenance of children.

- The spouse who receives the payments is subject to the USC on the portion of the maintenance payments they receive in respect of themselves. Any portion of the maintenance payments paid towards the maintenance of children is not subject to the USC.

- In the case of a legally enforceable maintenance arrangement, where a separated couple have jointly elected to be treated as a married couple for income tax purposes, the spouse making the payments does not receive exemption from the USC on the portion of their income which they pay as maintenance. The spouse who receives the payments is not subject to the USC on the maintenance payments they receive.

Example

You and your spouse agree to separate.

- Your income is €50,000 p.a. for the tax year 2020. Your spouse has no income.

- You agree to pay your spouse €200 per week.

The arrangement is informal and nothing is legally enforceable.

Your tax position

	2020	
	Joint assessment married €	Single assessment separated €
Salary	€50,000	€50,000
Tax payable		
€44,300 @ 20%	€8,860	
€35,300 @ 20%		€7,060
€5,700 @ 40%	€2,280	
€14,700 @ 40%		€5,880
	€11,140	€12,940
Less: Tax credits		
Personal	(€3,300)	(€3,300)
PAYE	(€1,650)	(€1,650)
	€6,190	€7,990

The €200 p.w. maintenance which you pay is not tax deductible. Your additional tax payable as a separated person under single assessment is €1,800

Notes:

- The marriage tax credit is granted to you under single assessment because your spouse is wholly or mainly maintained by you. You are not entitled to deduct the maintenance payments as these are voluntary and not legally enforceable.

- Your spouse is not living with you and you are not entitled to the benefit of the double tax bands because the maintenance payments are not enforceable.

Example

You and your spouse agree to separate. Your spouse works in the home.

- Your salary is €56,000 p.a. in the 2020 tax year.

- You agree to pay your spouse €200 per week and the arrangement is legally enforceable.

Your tax position

As legally enforceable maintenance payments are tax-deductible, the reduction in tax payable under single assessment is €2,360.

	2020	
	Joint assessment married €	Single assessment separated €
Salary	€56,000	€56,000
Maintenance paid	€0	€10,400
Taxable	€56,000	€45,600
Tax payable		
€44,300/€35,300 @ 20%	€8,860	€7,060
€11,700/€10,300 @ 40%	€4,680	€4,120
	€13,540	€11,180
Less: Tax credits		
Personal	(€3,300)	(€3,300)
PAYE	(€1,650)	(€1,650)
	€8,590	€6,230

Capital gains tax (CGT)

Normally, under a legal or judicial separation the spouses are treated as two unconnected persons for CGT purposes:

- Transfers between spouses are no longer exempt from CGT. However, any transfer by virtue of, or in consequence of, the Deed of Separation will not trigger a CGT liability.

- No transfer is permitted between spouses of unused CGT losses.

However unused allowable losses may be transferred between spouses in the year of separation.

Capital acquisition tax (CAT)

Spouse's exemption from Capital Acquisitions Tax will continue to apply.

Pension benefits

Pension rights negotiated under a legal Deed of Separation may not be enforceable, unless the agreement is backed up by a formal court order.

The Family Law Act 1995 envisages a number of ways in which a spouse's pension benefits might be taken into account in the event of a judicial separation:

Earmarking	A charge is set against a spouse's pension benefits, so that when they become payable a designated part of these benefits are payable to the other spouse.
Pension Splitting	The relevant pension benefits are split on an agreed basis between both spouses.
Offsetting	If proper financial provision can be made by other orders (e.g. a financial compensation order), or a property adjustment order the court may decide to offset these benefits against any relevant pension rights rather than "splitting everything down the middle".

Life assurance

Specific rights obtained under a Deed of Separation in relation to life assurance policies may not be legally enforceable - to avoid problems make sure that your interest in a life assurance policy is backed up by a relevant court order e.g. Financial Compensation Order, under the Family Law Act 1995.

Once a decree of Judicial Separation is granted, a spouse or a person acting on behalf of a dependent child may seek a Financial Compensation Order which can compel either or both spouses to:

- Effect a policy of life insurance for the benefit of the applicant or the dependent child.

- Assign the whole or a specified part of the interest in a life insurance policy effected by either, or both, spouses to the applicant or for the benefit of a dependent child.

- Make or continue to make the payments which either, or both, of the spouses is, or are, required to make under the terms of the policy.

A Financial Compensation Order will generally cease on the death or remarriage of an applicant spouse.

Stamp duty

Exemption from Stamp Duty will continue to apply on relevant property transactions.

Social welfare

The contributory widow(er)/surviving civil partner's pension is payable to the widow(er)/surviving civil partner following the death of their spouse/civil partner, as long as the widow(er)/surviving civil partner does not remarry or cohabit with someone else . The surviving spouse/civil partner may qualify for a widow(er)/surviving civil partner's pension either on their own PRSI contribution record, or that of their late spouse/civil partner.

A qualified adult dependent supplement may not be payable to a claimant if that claimant's spouse/civil partner is no longer wholly or mainly maintained by the claimant.

Divorce

The grounds on which a court may grant an application for a decree of divorce are those set out in Article 41.3.2 of the Constitution:

The Family Law Act 2019 which commenced on 1 December 2019 made some important changes to the rules for getting a divorce decree in

Ireland. The Act amends the Family Law (Divorce) Act 1996 to change the number of years the couple must be living apart from one another from 4 years to 2 years before the application for a divorce can be made.

Before a court can grant a divorce, the following conditions must be met:

- The couple must have been "living apart" from one another for at least 2 out of the previous 3 years before the application is made. Before 1 December 2019, this was 4 out of the previous 5 years. The Family Law Act 2019 also provides a new definition of the term 'living apart' see page 312.

- There must be no reasonable prospect of reconciliation.

- Proper arrangements must have been made or will be made for the spouse and any dependent members of the family such as children and other relatives.

Ancillary orders

The courts, on application by either spouse or by someone acting on behalf of a dependent child, can issue one or more of a number of Ancillary Orders including the following:

- Periodical payments and secured periodical payments order.

- Lump sum payments order.

- Property adjustment order.

- Order regarding occupation or sale of family home.

- Order regarding title of property.

- Variation of benefit of either spouse, or any dependent family member, of any pre or post nuptial agreement.

- Order regarding partition of property.

- Financial compensation orders.

- Pension adjustment orders.

- Order extinguishing succession rights.

- Order for sale of property, except the family home where a remarried spouse ordinarily resides with their spouse.

- Maintenance pending relief order.

- Order for provision for one spouse out of the estate of the other spouse.

Legal impact

Divorce legally dissolves the marriage and each spouse may legally remarry after the decree.

Succession rights

Each spouse's succession rights are automatically extinguished by the decree of divorce. Any specific bequest in a Will to a former spouse will stand until a new Will is made or an existing Will is changed.

Income tax

If there are legally enforceable maintenance payments being made then the couple can generally either opt for single assessment or if both spouses remain resident in Ireland, they can apply for separate assessment provided neither spouse has remarried or entered into a civil partnership. If single assessment applies, maintenance payments for the benefit of the spouse are tax-deductible for the payer and are taxable in the hands of the recipient. Under separate assessment, maintenance payments are ignored for income tax purposes.

Capital gains tax

Divorced spouses are treated as two unconnected persons for CGT purposes:

- Transfers between spouses are no longer exempt from CGT. However, transfers by virtues of, or in consequence of, the divorce will not trigger a CGT liability.

- No transfer of unused losses between spouses.

Capital acquisitions tax

After divorce, you are no longer legal spouses and the spouse exemption ceases to apply in respect of any future gifts or inheritances for CAT purposes. The "stranger threshold" will apply for CAT purposes after the divorce. However, property transfers between former spouses on foot of a court order governing a decree of divorce will be exempt from Capital Acquisitions Tax.

> "Divorce legally dissolves the marriage and each spouse may legally remarry after the decree."

Pensions

The Family Law (Divorce) Act 1996 envisages a number of ways in which a spouse's pension scheme benefits might be taken into account in the event of a decree of divorce:

Earmarking	A charge is set against a spouse's pension benefits, so that when they become payable a designated part of these benefits is payable to the other spouse.
Pension Splitting	The relevant pension benefits are split on an agreed basis between both spouses.
Offsetting	If proper financial provision can be made by other orders, e.g. financial compensation order or property adjustment order, the court may decide to offset these benefits against the relevant pension rights rather than "splitting everything down the middle".

Life assurance

After the granting of the decree of divorce, a spouse, or a person acting on behalf of a dependent child, may seek a financial compensation order which can compel either or both spouses to:

- Effect a policy of life insurance for the benefit of the applicant or the dependant child.

- Assign the whole or a specified part of the interest in a life insurance policy, effected by either or both spouses, to the applicant or for the benefit of a dependent child.

- Make or continue to make the payments which either, or both, of the spouses is, or are, required to make under the terms of the policy.

Such an order will cease on the death or remarriage of an applicant's spouse.

Social welfare

There is no change in either spouse's entitlement to a Social Welfare widow(e) pension following a decree of divorce provided that the other spouse has not remarried or is not cohabiting with someone else.

If the deceased spouse had remarried both their current spouse and their ex-spouse are entitled to claim a widow(er) pension if they meet the normal qualifying conditions.

Cohabitants

On the break-up of a cohabiting arrangement, an individual who has been in such a relationship for a period of five years or more (known as a qualified cohabitant), or for a reduced period of two years where they are the parents of dependent children, can apply to the court for a maintenance order.

The following rules apply to payments made for the benefit of a former cohabitant

- The payments are made without deduction of tax,

- The cohabitant who makes the payments is entitled to a deduction from the income chargeable to tax and USC in respect of the maintenance payments made for the other cohabitant,

- The cohabitant who receives the maintenance is taxable on the payments.

Both cohabitants continue to be taxed as single people.

Maintenance for dependents

No tax relief is available for maintenance payments made in respect of dependent children.

Property transfers

A charge to CGT does not arise where a person disposes of an asset to a former cohabitant as a consequence of a court order under the Civil Partnership and Certain Rights and Obligations of Cohabitants Act 2010.

Each asset is treated as being disposed of for an amount that gives rise to neither a gain or a loss in the hands of the disponer. The former cohabitant acquiring the asset is deemed to acquire the asset on the same day and at the same cost as the cohabitant who originally acquired it.

Transfers between former cohabitants made on foot of a court order are also exempt from CAT and Stamp Duty.

16 Death - and taxes

Where there's a Will there's a relative!

This old proverb is never out of date. It has also been said that nothing is more inevitable than death and taxes. While good financial planning cannot lessen your sense of loss on the death of a loved one, it can reduce your tax bill.

Issues that need to be considered when you have assets to pass on, include:

- Making a Will.

- Testate and Intestacy.

- The Succession Acts.

- Capital Acquisition Tax.

- Probate.

Anyone who owns property or other assets such as a life assurance policy, savings plan or even a simple deposit account, should make a Will. A Will not only ensures that you can distribute your wealth as you wish, but it also means that your family and beneficiaries are spared the expense and distress of a complicated and drawn-out administration of your estate, as set out under the Succession Act 1965.

Wills should be drawn up with the assistance of a solicitor. The simpler the terms of the Will, the less work involved and the lower the fee. However, it will be money well spent.

Many people do not realise that a Will is revoked on marriage unless it is clearly made with the marriage in mind. An important time to make a Will, if you haven't done so already, or to review an existing one, is when you have children. This is in order that you name a legal guardian for the child(ren) in the unlikely event that both you and your spouse should die together, or soon after each other.

When you make a Will you have to name an executor, someone who has the responsibility of seeing that your wishes are carried out and your assets distributed. Married couples often name each other, or an adult child or a family advisor - a solicitor or accountant - to act as executor. Others choose a business partner, bank manager or friend. Even if you, as a spouse, are named as Executor, your family advisor can assist with the various procedures involved.

Planning ahead

Before you meet your solicitor, gather up a list of your assets and the names and addresses of the people whom you wish to be beneficiaries and make sure your Executor consents to being named in your Will.

- A Will must be in writing - verbal ones are not valid.

- A Will must be witnessed by two people, neither of whom can be beneficiaries.

- You cannot disinherit your spouse.

- Your Will will remain in force until death or marriage unless it is clearly made with the marriage in mind. If a new Will is made, it automatically revokes any previous Wills you may have made.

- You should always keep a copy of your Will in a safe place - a strongbox or safe deposit facility. Let your Executor and family know where it is and where your other valuable papers are kept.

"You cannot disinherit your spouse."

Dying "intestate"

If you die without making a Will, this is known as dying "intestate" and all your property will be distributed according to the 1965 Succession Act. (See page 329).

Since there is no official Executor, the Personal Representative of the deceased - who can be a spouse, relative or even friend, will need to obtain what is known as a grant of Letters of Administration, in order to distribute the proceeds of your estate to your beneficiaries.

SUCCESSION ACT 1965	
Relatives surviving	**Distribution of estate where the deceased dies intestate**
Spouse / civil partner and issue	2/3rds to spouse/civil partner, 1/3rd to issue in equal shares. Children of a deceased son or daughter take their parent's share.
Spouse / civil partner and no issue	Whole estate to spouse / civil partner.
Issue and no spouse/civil partner	Whole estate to issue in equal shares Children of a deceased son or daughter take their parent's share.
Father, mother, brothers and sisters	1/2 to each parent.
Parent, brothers and sisters	Whole estate to parent.
Brothers and sisters	All take equal shares. Children of a deceased brother or sister take their parent's share.
Nephews and nieces	All take equal shares.
Remoter next-of-kin	All take equal shares.

Legal rights of a spouse under a Will

Irrespective of what the deceased leaves to their spouse/civil partner, the spouse/civil partner has a legal entitlement as follows:

Relatives surviving	Spouse/civil partner's share by legal right
Spouse/civil partner and issue	One-third of estate
Spouse/civil partner and no issue	One-half of estate

While tax and financial matters are not the foremost consideration when somebody dies, they are nevertheless areas that must be sorted out before a deceased person's estate can be finalised.

What is an "estate"?

A deceased's estate consists of whatever assets (e.g. bank accounts, stocks and shares, house, land, livestock, jewellery, car, etc.) which can be passed on to beneficiaries following the deceased's death.

How does the estate pass on to the beneficiaries?

The assets, which make up the deceased's estate, can be passed on in a number of ways. Assets left by Will pass to the beneficiaries in accordance with the terms of the Will. If there is no Will (a situation known as intestacy), assets that would otherwise have passed by Will pass instead under special rules laid down by the 1965 Succession Act. In addition, assets can also pass outside of the Will or intestacy.

Examples of assets which pass under the Will or intestacy

- Assets owned in the deceased's sole name.

- Assets owned by the deceased but placed in the name of another person for convenience or some similar reason.

- Assets placed by the deceased in the joint names of the deceased and another person without the intention of benefiting that other person.

Examples of assets which pass outside of the Will or intestacy

- Assets passing by nomination, e.g. the deceased may have instructed An Post to pay Saving Certificates on their death to a particular person, called the nominee.

- Death benefits passing under a life insurance policy or pension scheme where the beneficiaries are particular family members named in the policy or scheme.

- Assets passing in which the deceased had an interest for their life only.

- Assets placed by the deceased in the joint names of the deceased and another person with the intention of benefiting that other person on the deceased's death.

The personal representative

The personal representative is the person who is responsible for finalising the deceased's affairs. He or she must, within a reasonable time, collect the assets passing under the Will or intestacy, pay any debts and distribute the surplus assets to the beneficiaries entitled to them.

If there is a Will, it is likely that the Personal Representative has been appointed by being named in the Will as its executor and has taken on the responsibility for that reason. If there is no Will (intestacy) the Personal Representative will probably have taken on the responsibility because he or she is the deceased's spouse/civil partner or one of the next-of-kin. A Personal Representative not appointed by a Will is known as an administrator.

Beneficiary

A beneficiary is a person who inherits either the whole or part of the deceased's estate whether passing under a Will or intestacy or outside of a Will or intestacy.

Trustee

Instead of providing for property to be given directly to the beneficiary, the deceased's Will may provide that, for a specified period, the property is to be held in trust on behalf of the beneficiary by trustees named in the Will. Such trusts may arise because the beneficiary concerned is very young, or because the deceased wishes the property to be held for the benefit of one person for life and, on the death of that person, to be transferred to another beneficiary. The trustees will take over the management of the trust property only after the estate has been administered by the personal representative. The trust will then continue

"A beneficiary is a person who inherits either the whole or part of the deceased's estate …"

until the time specified in the Will for the ultimate handing over of the property.

The same person can have more than one role; for example, a personal representative can also be a beneficiary.

Before assets are handed over to the beneficiaries certain procedures must be gone through. Broadly, these are as follows:

Assets passing outside of the Will or intestacy

In the case of an asset passing outside of the Will or intestacy, production of a death certificate by the beneficiary is often all that is required to establish the beneficiary's entitlement to receive the asset in question.

Assets passing under the Will or intestacy

In order to get legal confirmation of their appointment, the personal representative must apply to the Probate Office of the High Court for a document known as a Grant of Representation. The Grant of Representation acts as an assurance to financial institutions (e.g. banks, building societies, credit union, etc.) and others that they can safely place the deceased's assets in the hands of the person named as personal representative in the grant. The Grant of Representation is also known as a Grant of Probate (where there is a Will) or Letters of Administration (where there is no Will).

The application for the Grant of Representation will normally be made by a solicitor acting on behalf of the Personal Representative. In straightforward cases, it may be possible to make a personal application for the grant through the Personal Application Section of the Probate Office.

Special additional procedure relating to money in joint names

In the absence of a letter of clearance from the Revenue Commissioners, banks, building societies and other financial institutions are prohibited by law from releasing monies (other than current accounts) lodged or deposited in the joint names of the deceased and another person or persons. This applies if, at the date of death, the total of all the amounts standing with the institution in the joint names of the deceased and that other person or persons exceeds €50,000. It does not apply, however, to monies which have only been held in the joint names of the deceased and their surviving spouse/civil partner.

Applications for letters of clearance for production to financial institutions should be made to the deceased persons tax office using Form CA4 which is available on revenue.ie.

If you are a personal representative

Below is a list of actions you should take if you are a Personal Representative of a deceased person.

1.   Notify the tax office

The deceased's tax office should be advised as soon as possible of the date of death and the name and address of the Personal Representative. This will ensure that correspondence will be addressed to the Personal Representative until such time as the administration of the estate is finalised.

The address of the deceased's tax office can be found on any correspondence from that office to the deceased or you can check using the contact locator on www.revenue.ie.

Remember that:

- If a personal representative distributes the estate without paying any outstanding tax liabilities, they themselves may be liable to any outstanding tax liabilities.

- If a personal representative fails to claim a tax rebate due to the estate, they may have to make good the loss to the estate.

If the deceased was *self-employed*, the deceased's accountant should file any outstanding Income Tax returns and business accounts with the deceased's tax office. As well as Income Tax, the personal representative will also need to ensure that any outstanding VAT, employer's PAYE/PRSI, or other taxes in respect of the period up to the date of death are fully paid.

If the deceased was an employee, there may be a PAYE tax rebate due, as the deceased's tax credits for the year of death may not have been fully used up.   Any tax rebate will form part of the deceased's estate. It is the responsibility of the personal representative to file any outstanding tax returns on behalf of the deceased.

2.   Sort out the deceased's pre-death tax affairs

A Personal Representative is responsible for settling any outstanding tax matters for the period up to the date of death. Depending on the circumstances, they may need to pay additional tax or claim a repayment of tax.

3. Income and capital gains arising during the administration period

It may take the Personal Representative some time to administer the estate during which time income may be earned or capital gains may be made. Broadly the position is as follows:

"Death does not give rise to a Capital Gains Tax liability."

Income tax

- The Personal Representative is liable to pay income tax at the standard rate on income earned during the administration period. There is no entitlement to personal tax credits or to any of the reliefs otherwise available to individual taxpayers.

- In certain circumstances, the tax office may concessionally agree to treat the beneficiary as succeeding to the inheritance from the date of death. In such circumstances, the beneficiary will take full responsibility for paying income tax on the post-death income as if they had been entitled to the asset - and the income - from the date of death.

Capital gains tax (CGT)

- Death does not give rise to a Capital Gains Tax liability. For example, if the deceased bought shares for €10,000 and they were worth €15,000 at the date of death, the €5,000 capital gain is not taxable.

If the Personal Representative sells any property during the administration period, there may be a liability to Capital Gains Tax but only to the extent that the value of the property in question has increased between the date of death and the date of sale. Following on from the example above, if the Personal Representative sells the shares during the administration period for €16,000, the relevant capital gain is €1,000 and is taxable. The distribution of property by the personal representative to the beneficiaries does not give rise to a Capital Gains Tax liability.

Death and taxes

Inheritance tax

If after your death the beneficiaries of your estate receive sums in excess of the Thresholds for Capital Acquisitions Tax (CAT) purposes Inheritance Tax will be payable.

Gift tax

A liability to gift tax arises when a person receives a benefit liable to CAT other than on a death.

Tax-free threshold for Capital Aquisitions Tax (CAT)

There are three tax free thresholds which apply for CAT purposes.

Group A Where the beneficiary is a child, including adopted child, step child and certain foster children, or minor grandchild of the benefactor, if the parent is dead. In some cases this threshold can also apply to a parent, niece or nephew who have worked in a family business for a period of time.

Group B Where the beneficiary is a parent, brother, sister, niece, nephew or linear ancestor/descendent of the disponer.

Group C All other cases not covered by Group A or Group B

The Group A Threshold applies to a gift/inheritance taken from a foster parent to a foster child provided the child was cared for, maintained and lived with the foster parent from a young age up to the age of 18 for a period of at least five years.

CAT thresholds for inheritance or gifts			
	Group A	Group B	Group C
On or after 09/10/2019	€335,000	€32,500	€16,250
On or after 10/10/2018	€320,000	€32,500	€16,250
12/10/2016 - 09/10/2018	€310,000	€32,500	€16,250
14/10/2015 -11/10/2016	€280,000	€30,150	€15,075
06/12/2012 - 13/10/2015	€225,000	€30,150	€15,075
07/12/2011 - 05/12/2012	€250,000	€33,500	€16,750

Inheritance/gift from a child to a parent

If a "child" gives a gift to a parent the Group B threshold applies. However, the Group A threshold applies if a parent receives an inheritance from "a child".

CAT rates

For benefits taken on / after 5 December 2012	
Amount	**Rate**
Below Threshold	Nil
Balance	33%

Exemptions

- Any inheritance or gifts made between spouses.

- The first €3,000 of all gifts received from a benefactor in any calendar year.

- Any inheritance received from a deceased child which had been given to that child as a gift by the parent.

- Irish Government stock given to a non-Irish domiciled beneficiary, so long as it had been held by the beneficiary for at least six years previously.

- Dwelling house relief

  There is an exemption from Capital Aquisitions Tax (CAT) where residential properties (dwelling house) are bequeathed by individuals who live there to successors who

  - Have lived there for a specified period of time before the inheritance,

  - Will continue to live there for a specified period of time after the inheritance, **and**

  - Who have no beneficial interest in any other residential property at the date of the inheritance.

  The exemption also applies to residential properties that are gifted to dependent relatives of a donor, i.e. individuals who are incapacitated to such extent that they are unable to maintain themselves by earning an income from working or who are aged 65 or over.

From 25 December 2016 the following conditions must be met for CAT dwelling house relief to apply;

- The inheritance must be of a 'relevant dwelling house' i.e. a house that was occupied by the disponer as their only or main residence at the date of their death, except in the case of a gift or inheritance taken by a dependent relative.

- The beneficiary cannot be beneficially entitled to an interest in any other dwelling at the date of inheritance.

- The beneficiary must have occupied the dwelling continuously as their only or main residence throughout the period of three years up to the date of the inheritance.

  If the dwelling has been replaced during this three-year period, then the beneficiary must have occupied the original dwelling, and the replacement property for at least three out of the four years up to the date of gift or inheritance.

- it is transfered by way of an inheritance except in the case of

  - A gift of a dwelling to a dependent relative

    or

  - A gift to a dependent relative that becomes an inheritance when a disponer dies within two years of making the gift.

Owning more than one dwelling

A beneficiary cannot have a beneficial interest in more than one dwelling house if they are to qualify for this relief. A residential property that is abroad (such as a foreign holiday home), or rented (such as an investment apartment) will prevent the relief applying. The beneficiary is not precluded from acquiring other dwellings after the benefit is received.

Clawback of relief

The beneficiary must generally continue to own and occupy the dwelling-house as their own or main residence throughout the relevant period of six years following the date of the benefit.

If the dwelling is sold within the six year period the exemption will be clawed back. However a beneficiary can replace the property during the six-year retention period without losing the exemption. The original and replacement properties must be occupied as the beneficiary's only or main residence for at least six out of seven years commencing on the date of gift or inheritance.

If all the sales proceeds are not reinvested there will be a clawback of part of the original relief granted, in proportion to the amount of the sales proceeds that is not re-invested.

The clawback condition does not apply if

● The beneficiary was over the age of 65 at the date of the gift or inheritance

● The sale or disposal, or non-occupation of the house occurs because the beneficiary needs long-term medical care in a hospital or nursing home.

● The house is not occupied because an employer requires them to live somewhere else or because they are working abroad.

Business relief

Relief from CAT is available where business property is acquired under a gift or inheritance. This relief works by reducing the value of the relevant business asset which pass under a gift or inheritance by 90%.

The following conditions apply to this relief:

● The relevant business assets must have been owned by the disponer for at least five years in the case of a gift or at least two years in the case of an inheritance.

● Relevant business assets are

● The business or an interest in the business in the case of a business carried on by a sole trader or by a partnership. "Business" is defined as one which is carried on for gain and it includes the exercise of a profession as well as a trade.

The relief will be clawed back if the assets are disposed of within six years of the gift/inheritance.

Agricultural relief

You can claim agricultural relief if you receive a gift or inheritance of agricultural property and you qualify as a farmer. Agricultural relief operates by reducing the market value of 'agricultural property' by 90% so that gift or inheritance tax is calculated on an amount - known as the 'agricultural value' - which is substantially less than the market value. To qualify as a "farmer" the value of your agricultural property must make up 80% of your total property value on the valuation date.

From 1 January 2015 agricultural relief is only available in respect of agricultural property gifted to or inherited by an individual who subsequently uses the property for agricultural purposes for a period of not less than six years or who leases out the agricultural property for not less than six years for agricultural use.

Also the beneficiary or lessee must have an agricultural qualification and spend at least 50 per cent of their normal working time farming agricultural property (including the agricultural property comprised in the gift or inheritance) on a commercial basis and with a view to the realisation of profits from that agricultural property.

CAT payments

You must pay and file your CAT liability on 31 October. All gifts and inheritances with a valuation date in the 12 month period ending on the previous 31 August should be included in the return to be filed by 31 October. That means that where the valuation date arises between 1 January and 31 August, the pay and file deadline would be 31 October in that year. Where the valuation date arises between 1 September and 31 December, the pay and file deadline would be 31 October in the following year.

Example

Valuation date

21 February 2019	File IT38 and pay taxes by 31 October 2019
6 November 2019	File IT38 and pay taxes by 31 October 2020

Section 72 & 73 insurance policy

Section 72 and 73 policies are special insurance policies taken out specifically to be used to discharge inheritance and gift tax.

The proceeds of these policies, in so far as they are used to discharge any gift or inheritance tax, are not themselves liable to tax. However, if there is any part of the proceeds remaining after the tax liability has been discharged, this excess is liable to gift/inheritance tax.

Foreign inheritance

If you receive an inheritance or gift from another jurisdiction there may be a tax liability to be met in that country and here. However, you may be entitled to a tax credit on the tax paid abroad to ensure you don't pay double tax. The tax credit will not exceed the Irish rate of tax payable.

If you are a surviving spouse / civil partner

This section gives an outline of the main tax exemption and reliefs specifically for surviving spouses / civil partners.

In summary these are covered under the following headings:

- Inheritance tax

- Income tax

Inheritance tax

If you take an inheritance from your late spouse /civil partner you do not have to pay inheritance tax. The exemption is unlimited - it doesn't matter how much you inherit, it is entirely exempt. It is not necessary to claim this exemption and you don't have to fill in any inheritance tax forms.

Widow(er)/surviving civil partner in year of bereavement

The tax treatment for individuals in the year of death depends on whether they were taxed under joint or separate assessment and whether it was the assessable spouse/civil partner who died.

Joint Assessment

- If your late spouse/civil partner was the assessable spouse/civil partner, i.e. the person responsible for making the joint tax return on behalf of both of you, you will receive the increased basic personal tax credit in respect of the post death period and you will be assessed on your own total income from the date of death of your spouse/civil partner until the end of the tax year. The Widowed persons / surviving civil partners standard rate band will apply for this period.

- If you were the assessable spouse/civil partner, you will continue to get the married person/civil partner's credit and rate bands for the remainder of the tax year. You will be taxable on your own income for the full tax year in which your spouse/civil partner died plus your late spouse/civil partner's income from 1 January to the date of death.

Separate assessment

- If you were assessed on the basis of separate assessment prior to the death of your spouse or civil partner the tax credits that apply in respect of the post-death period will depend on whether you are deemed to be the assessable spouse/civil partner or the non-assessable spouse/civil partner.

- If you are regarded as the non-assessable spouse/civil partner you will be entitled to the increased basic personal tax credit in respect of your income from the date of death to the end of the tax year.

- If you are regarded as the assessable spouse/civil partner you will continue to be taxed on the basis of separate assessment for the entire year and assessed on your spouse's/civil partner's income from 1 January to the date of death.

Single assessment

- If you were assessed on the basis of single treatment prior to the death of your spouse/civil partner you will be granted the increased widowed person/civil partner tax credit and income tax rate band for the year of bereavement.

Widow(er)/surviving civil partner in subsequent tax years

The tax position of a widow(er)/surviving civil partner in subsequent tax years is as follows:

- A widowed persons/surviving civil partners tax credit.

- A single person's tax band.

- A single person's PAYE tax credit.

- Reduced mortgage interest relief, if applicable.

- Widowed person/surviving civil partner with a dependent child(ren)'s tax credit.

- Widowed parent tax credit (for five years following bereavement).

Widowed persons/surviving civil partner tax credit

A widowed person/surviving civil partner whose spouse/civil partner has died in a given tax year is entitled to the widowed person's bereaved credit, for that year only. This credit is the same as the married person/civil partner's credit but is not available to a surviving spouse/civil partner who is the subject of a joint assessment for the same year. A widowed person/surviving civil partner with dependent children is also entitled to

- Widowed person/surviving civil partner with a dependent child(ren)'s tax credit. **and**

- Widowed/surviving civil partner parent credit.

Special credit for surviving spouse/civil partner with a dependent child

If you have any dependent children you may be entitled to a special Income tax credit (called "widowed parent's credit") for the five tax years after the year of your spouse/civil partner's death. You may also be entitled to the "single persons child carer tax credit" for as long as you have any dependent children.

Widowed/surviving civil partner parent tax credit

This credit is available for the five years following the year of death. For the 2019 and 2020 tax year the amount of the credit are as follows:

€3,600	in first tax year after death.
€3,150	in second tax year after death.
€2,700	in third tax year after death.
€2,250	in fourth tax year after death
€1,800	in fifth tax year after death.

Example

A married couple/widow(er) with one dependent child and a salary of €55,000 p.a. (only one spouse working). see page 344.

Widow(er) in subsequent year

	2020	
	Married €	**Widow(er)** €
Gross salary	€55,000	€55,000
Taxable @ 20%	€44,300 €8,860	€39,300 €7,860
@ 40%	€10,700 €4,280	€15,700 €6,280
Total tax payable	€13,140	€14,140
Less: Tax credits		
Married person	(€3,300)	(€1,650)
PAYE	(€1,650)	(€1,650)
Widowed person	(n/a)	(€1,650)
Single parent	(n/a)	
Net tax payable	**€8,190**	**€9,190**

Index